CAMP ALL-AMERICAN, HANOI JANE, AND THE HIGH-AND-TIGHT

CAMP ALL-AMERICAN, HANOI JANE, AND THE HIGH-AND-TIGHT

Gender, Folklore, and Changing Military Culture

CAROL BURKE

 Beacon Press, Boston

BEACON PRESS
25 Beacon Street, Boston, Massachusetts 02108-2892
www.beacon.org

Beacon Press books are published under the auspices of the
Unitarian Universalist Association of Congregations.

Printed in the United States of America

08 07 06 05 04   8 7 6 5 4 3 2 1

This book is printed on acid-free paper that meets the uncoated paper
ANSI/NISO specifications for permanence as revised in 1992.

Text design by Isaac Tobin
Composition by Wilsted & Taylor Publishing Services

LIBRARY OF CONGRESS CATALOGING-IN-PUBLICATION DATA

Burke, Carol.
    Camp all-American, Hanoi Jane, and the high and tight : gender, folklore,
    and changing military culture / Carol Burke. – 1st cloth ed.
        p. cm.
Includes bibliographical references and index.
    ISBN 0-8070-4660-4 (cloth : alk. paper)
    1. Women and the military. 2. Sociology, Military. 3. Sex role.
    4. Women soldiers. i. Title.

U21.75.B87 2004
306.2'7 – DC22
    2003022390

This book is dedicated to Jerry Christensen.

Contents

Preface

This book's title includes a term of military slang that may be unfamiliar to those who have not served in the military in recent years. A "high-and-tight" is a style of military haircut in which the hair is shaved close to the head on the sides and stands at attention on top. Rules govern the haircuts of members of the military, but once soldiers and sailors complete basic training, they select among a number of permissible styles. The typical gung-ho, squared-away soldier sports the distinctive high-and-tight, a favorite of members of the Marine Corps, who cherish the style as a corporate sign of warrior spirit. In military life there is no female counterpart to the high-and-tight. Consider an enthusiastic woman soldier willing to affirm a cardinal military virtue—that group loyalty trumps individuality—by wearing a high-and-tight. Only in Hollywood can the attractive Demi Moore shave her head in an effort to be just one of the group. In today's military, such a gesture would be met with certain ridicule. The devil of military culture, at least as it pertains to gender, lives in the details.

No detail of military life—even as minor as a haircut, the pitch of a sailor's white cap, or the chants sung out in basic training—is without significance, whether its meaning is imposed from above or smuggled into the barracks or onto the parade ground by the grunts and common sailors. Like any occupational folk group, members of the military distinguish themselves not only by the jobs they do but by the rituals they share, the anecdotes they exchange, even the slang that lards their everyday conversations. They pass on these traditions from one generation of recruits to another, inculcating attitudes toward the missions they train for, the rigid hierarchy they confirm or chafe against, and the values they espouse. Over generations of soldiers and sailors, tank drivers and flyboys, both secret rituals and the official traditions that constitute the culture of the four branches of the United States military have largely issued from an exclusively male society, one designed to produce efficient, disciplined soldiers and sailors with the transformation of boys into men.

In the past thirty years, women who have left the auxiliary ranks to integrate the previously all-male ranks have put pressure on military culture to change—not as a conscious or concerted political effort, in most cases, but simply by being present and by participating in the tasks and routines that make up military life. The old and almost always unofficial rites that cement ties among postadolescent males don't work their bonding magic with women in the same company or platoon. The old jokes and songs that celebrate the sexual exploits of predatory males whose warrior skills are visited not upon the enemy in the battlefield but upon the women in port don't voice a fantasy shared by gender-integrated troops. Rather, they function to separate and to exclude. Adherents of these exclusionary traditions risk perpetuating a gender apartheid, one that undermines professionalism and threatens cohesion by the social and cultural segregation of women.

I bring to this work on military culture my skills as a folklorist who has studied the military as an occupational folk group characterized by functional and dysfunctional traditions, integrative and exclusive initiation rites, and stated and unstated norms of dress, speech, and conduct. The job of any folklorist is to collect the lore of the folk group and to understand that lore in context. Despite the popular belief that folklore exists in a fixed state, it can and does change dramatically in response to changes in the folk group. A notorious example: minstrel shows, once performed among groups of shuffling white soldiers and sailors in blackface as a form of amateur entertainment, ceased as an accepted practice once African Americans were integrated in the military.

Much of the history of military culture stems from first-person accounts of their experiences by active-duty and retired soldiers and sailors. Although I have never been a member of the military, I served as a civilian faculty member of the Naval Academy in the late 1980s and early 1990s and there had the opportunity to observe the culture of one military institution intimately from the inside.

During my first couple of years, I was completing fieldwork for a book on the folklore of women in prison. While investigating the ways in which tradition functions in prison society to indoctrinate rookies, censure inappropriate behavior, explain the irrational, and inscribe a corporate identity, I discovered the relevance of the questions raised by my investigation of prison culture to another closed institution, the military academy. I was fascinated by the wealth of folk tradition I found when I started looking at the academy at Annapolis—both the general military lore passed on from service to service and war to war and the folklore and folk practices peculiar to the Naval Academy. I did not set out to write a book on military culture. I set out simply to make sense of the incredibly rich and sometimes eccentric culture I had entered.

As students and faculty became aware of my interest in collecting academy lore, they brought me jokes scribbled on sheets of lined paper; lyrics to bawdy marching chants; latrinalia; legends; accounts of pranks, rituals, and rites of passage; stories of academy antiheroes; and personal narratives of life among the Brigade of Midshipmen. I jotted down the lyrics to cadence calls chanted by recruits as they "chopped" across the yard during summer basic training. I was given copies of officially banned songs that nevertheless continued to be performed in small groups, songs like "The S&M Man," sung to the tune of "The Candy Man":

Who can take a chainsaw
Cut the bitch in two
Fuck the bottom half
and give the upper half to you . . .

[Chorus] The S&M Man, the S&M Man,
The S&M Man 'cause he mixes it with love
and makes the hurt feel good!

Who can take a bicycle
Then take off the seat
Set his girlfriend on it
ride her down a bumpy street . . .

[Chorus]

Who can take some jumper cables
Clamp them to her tits
Jump-start your car
and electrocute the bitch

[Chorus]

Who can take an icepick
Ram it through her ear
Ride her like a Harley
As you fuck her from the rear.

I attended official and unofficial academy ceremonies. Midshipmen invited me to their frantic and outrageously campy skits, performed at night outside their dorm, in part as a parody of the administration and in part, I imagine, as a carnivalesque release.

The more I saw and heard, the more I wondered how female students managed to adjust to such a culture. To mark the end of each academic year and the end of plebedom, all members of the outgoing freshman class run from their dorm across the yard at a signal. The heftier linebackers are the first to hurl themselves into the trench around Herndon Memorial, dug out each year for the event, while the others scramble to construct a human scaffold secure enough to raise a midshipman to the top of the larded obelisk more quickly than any preceding first-year class. The classmate who topples the cap resting on top of the monument will be named admiral before any of his colleagues—or so the tradition goes, even though no midshipman who has removed the Dixie cup has ever made admiral.

The noisy struggle typically takes over an hour, and every year female midshipmen join their male peers in the ritual that will measure their class against previous and succeeding classes. But a woman never gets far up the pyramid before her male counterparts toss her off, for no class wants to be the first to send a woman to the top of Herndon, a monument that in all its phallic splendor symbolizes for many an exclusive male rite of passage. Why do these women annually jump onto the mass of bodies scrambling to mount the greased Herndon Monument, when they know that they will be rebuffed if they get too close to the top?

After leaving the Naval Academy for Johns Hopkins University, I continued to collect military folklore as the director of a military folklore archive and through fieldwork. During that time I was invited to visit Camp All-American, a summer training program for Army ROTC cadets conducted at Fort Bragg, North Carolina. My book opens with a personal essay recounting that visit. Narrative seems the appropriate form in which to describe an event that was overpoweringly theatrical through and through. Camp All-American is a staging *by* the Army *of* the Army *for* the Army—a spectacle designed to pump up morale among a group of officers-in-training and polish the image of the new Army among the educators who decide whether to continue to house ROTC programs on their campuses. Such theatricality is not unique to this training program or to Fort Bragg, or even to the Army. Theater has been an important element of military culture across the services, in past and present, in peace and war. One finds it in the "crossing-the-line" ceremonies that take place on ships as they cross the equator, in the camp skits enacted by prisoners of war, even in the routine "hi-bye parties" staged at every military base at home and abroad.

This narrative introduces the topics that thread their way throughout this book. It asks how women who share the same high ideals of service and duty are perceived by males on and up the chain of command. If women can do the work traditionally thought to be the work of men and even distinguish themselves in the process, why does the culture hold fast to its cult of masculinity?

The military, of course, affirms a structural commitment to a masculine culture by continuing to designate certain jobs as "combat" positions, which are off-limits to women. But such set-asides are diminishing in response to a blurring of the line between combat and support, and in the face of the proven effectiveness of women in carrying out assignments that are virtually indistinguishable from those of their favored male counterparts. Although several areas within the military remain male-only enclaves (the Army's combat arms, the Navy's sub-marines, and elite forces like the Seals), women now perform many tasks previously reserved for men, and women have distinguished themselves in the process. They now fly attack aircraft. They serve as ship drivers. Yet the reach of organizational reform is limited. Official segregation may be on the wane, but a more insidious system of gender subordina-tion takes place as the military aggressively practices the unofficial rites handed down from man to man through the generations.

"Military culture" lays out those traditions and serves as the book's formal introduction, identifying the signs and practices of a shared cul-ture. Rich and enduring, the unofficial folklore and folk practices of mil-itary culture exist in an uneasy, often parodic relationship to official military procedures, routines, rewards, and punishments. To the extent that these aspects of culture allow all to participate in a corporate identity, they serve the mission of the military, which recognizes the importance of morale to combat readiness and to zeal in the diligent performance of the numerous tasks that support combat forces. To the extent that these practices create a cultural zone off-limits to women, they undermine the military values of teamwork and efficiency.

The chapters entitled "Transformation" and "A Few Good Men" look at how basic training takes recruits from all backgrounds and all regions of the country and through debasement, discipline, simulated chaos, and sleep deprivation suppresses individuality in order to forge a new, corporate identity. Traditional elements of that transformation, such as marching chants, which at one time might have abetted the functional incorporation of the individual into the group, now jeopar-dize unit cohesiveness by promoting hostility among men toward their female counterparts. Rather than preparing soldiers and sailors to face an enemy on the battlefield, they create a virtual enemy on the parade ground and in the barracks.

Members of the armed forces receive an identity that assigns them not only to a specific branch of the military (Air Force, Army, Navy, or Marine Corps) but also to specialized subgroups. Rituals of incorpora-tion often follow an introductory period, and "Sex, GIs, and Videotape" focuses narrowly on one such tradition: an initiation ritual performed by enlisted trainees. Male initiation rituals typically stage a second birth for the society that sponsors them. In this one, a group of slightly older and more seasoned soldiers established a set of rituals designed to birth soldier boys into the world of men. "Sex, GIs, and Videotape" describes the treatment members of a Canadian commando received before being acknowledged as members of the elite group. What makes this particular initiation ritual especially important is not its details—which are probably shared in numerous units in Canada and the United States— but its dissemination, which produced a scandal. A videotape that documented this ritual at the time later exposed bizarre practices that had always been secret and exclusively military and masculine to the civilian viewing public—that is, to women, some of them taxpayers, some of them mothers and sisters of brutalized soldiers, some of them aspirants to the same elite corps that was disgracing itself on the television screen. The second half of this chapter chronicles the author's firsthand account of the public exposure of this secret rite on a popular Canadian talk show.

If the processes by which aspirants are initiated into the exclusive unit are often secret, the uniform of the military person often becomes the canvas on which such membership is marked. The most conspicuous mark of incorporation is the uniform bestowed at induction into the armed services. "Clothes Make the Soldier" discusses how military clothing has historically differed from other clothing. Other than rank, military uniforms are designed to erase all signs of difference in order to cultivate a lateral affiliation among similar men with shared allegiance to the service—equality in the ranks. Such imposed homogeneity challenges the ingenuity of American youths accustomed to the costume of statement and flair. Historically, soldiers have managed to personalize their khakis and whites with cultic signs of potency and prestige. Such tribal markings have been tolerated, especially in wartime, as devices that promote esprit de corps. But distinction has often become invidious in the wake of the introduction of women into the service. The lore of mockery and contempt has become associated with the unflattering hybrid of feminine look and military function in which women must perform their duties. Despite the designers' success in erasing signs of social class and geographical and ethnic background, they have failed to produce a uniform that would be gender-neutral, save the Army's working BDUs.

"Military Speech" demonstrates that the transformation from civilian to soldier involves more than a change of clothes. It demands a new language, a folk speech that relieves anxiety, passes the time, adds levity, permits safe criticism of superiors, and, most important, distinguishes outsiders from insiders. To be full members of the corps, women must be capable of wielding this speech as fluently as men. This is not a matter of individual inclination. Too often they are faced with a pattern of coded speech that subjects them to gender-based slurs and individual mockery. I don't advocate a speech without fire and humor, just one that does not single out one group. Military discipline is based on a well-justified confidence in the effectiveness of meticulous training. All codes, official and unofficial, are learned. Just as the military has eliminated racist slurs as it has become increasingly racially integrated, it must deliberately work to eliminate patterns of informal speech that debase women.

Attainment of membership in the elite echelons of the service by rising through the enlisted ranks is extremely unusual. High-ranking officers have rarely emerged from the ranks of enlisted soldiers or sailors. No enlisted man or woman before Admiral Jeremy Boorda had ever achieved the Navy's highest uniformed rank: chief of naval operations (CNO). Boorda was exceptional in many respects. A Jew, a "mustang" (someone who had risen from the enlisted into the commissioned ranks), and a "tin can" (a member of the surface Navy rather than the more prestigious submarine and aviation branches), he not only gained admission to the group of elite overlords who run the military, he did so without ever forgetting his noncom roots. Indeed, his identification with the common sailor, conspicuous among the joint chiefs, had the effect of making him unusually reverent of the lofty ideal of the commissioned officer.

Boorda's rabid detractors within the larger Navy community consisted of active-duty and retired officers who denounced him for a politically motivated advocacy of the full integration of women into the

Navy. They believed that this advocacy prevented him from standing up for naval aviators in the face of the notorious Tailhook scandal in 1991, when female officers were subjected to verbal and physical abuse at a semiofficial convention. Admiral Boorda's decision to take his own life in response to concerted attacks on his record and his character in a senseless attempt to uphold the Navy's honor tragically illustrates the devastating consequences of the culture wars within the Navy in the 1990s.

Chapter VIII is the account of the way in which certain men have abused the military code to advance their own agendas and protect their friends. Chapter IX recounts the way in which that code has given vital strength to soldiers who have suffered the hardship and humiliation of being seized as prisoners of war. Prisoners of war have constructed communities and cemented comradeship in the face of barbarous cruelty. These men and women have overcome relentless physical and psychological repression to exercise their ingenuity, in the most deprived circumstances and on the most unpromising materials, to create the stuff that produces human solidarity in the face of horror: from humorous songs and jokes about their own predicaments to full-scale dramatic presentations that parody their captors, from makeshift garments to barter economies, from hidden diaries to elaborate codes that allow them to maintain communication when conversations would result in certain torture.

Most American wars have not been fought by professional soldiers. Most soldiers in those wars have not been prisoners. Most have rarely had their transformation into the identity of warrior tested in combat. Almost all of those who have survived warfare, however, have had to undergo a second transformation from soldier to civilian. The military invests much of its energy in transforming civilians into soldiers (whether through boot camp routines or initiation ceremonies intended to certify that transformation). It works hard to acculturate individuals used to thinking of themselves as free and independent so that they deny self-interest and work as a team within the chain of command. It consciously constructs a culture that trains nonviolent individuals to execute violence on command. Compared with the efforts to transform the civilian into the soldier, the military invests relatively little effort into reversing the process. Civil War soldiers suffering the psychological effects of combat were described as suffering from "sunstroke." The "shell-shock," "battle fatigue," and "post-traumatic stress disorder" of subsequent wars described interior wounds slow to heal. To a lesser extent, any veteran who has participated in the horrors of war or who has witnessed its horrific results has carried home his or her memory as a scar of military service. When the civilian population acknowledges the veteran's sacrifice and shares the moral responsibility for the war, the burden of its horrors is borne collectively. When it does not, the veteran must shoulder it alone or with fellow veterans, as was the case during and after the widely unpopular Vietnam War. "Jane Fonda, the Woman the Military Loves to Hate," investigates why some Vietnam vets nurture their resentment against this antiwar activist thirty years after she protested the war and why today's military finds it useful to inculcate in young recruits a resentment against a woman of whom many have never even heard.

Even if there were no women in the military, the masculine warrior code that informs military culture and military training would soon prove to be an anachronism owing to technological changes that have resulted from the pressure to make warfare more efficient and effective. The book's final chapter speculates about the future of warfare. As warfare becomes increasingly computerized, a culture that celebrates the hand-to-hand combatant of old will need to change dramatically in response to technological innovation. As new weapons fire with increased precision ever farther back from the battlefield, and as unmanned aerial vehicles and stealth robots survey enemy terrain, sparing small-unit recon squads, close combat with the enemy will become a specialized field in which only high-tech Special Forces and specially trained urban Marine units apply their expertise. As lighter and faster tank divisions replace the heavy armored army of the past, and as high-tech Jeeps, complete with sophisticated control panels, accompany any artillery division to the battlefield, the reasons for excluding women from combat will become increasingly difficult to sustain. The military will grow more dependent on minds than on bodies. A soldier's technical expertise will count for more than the circumference of his or her biceps. Even the grunt of 2010 will need to operate sophisticated individual computer equipment, which will reveal in an instant the location of every enemy and every friendly. While proponents and opponents of expanded roles for women in the military argue the merits of the issue from trenches dug deeply in the dirt, new warfare technology will soon render the issue of gender an anachronism.

CAMP ALL-AMERICAN, HANOI JANE, AND THE HIGH-AND-TIGHT

1. Camp All-American

Wearing shorts and combat boots, I clomped around the house in a state of mirror avoidance, preparing myself for an early morning departure the next day for Fort Bragg, North Carolina, where I hoped to get a closer look at ROTC training programs. The shorts made sense on a humid Baltimore afternoon, and the boots made a kind of sense too. "You need to break them in," the officer in charge of the ROTC program had instructed me, "if you don't want to head back to Baltimore with the civilian equivalent of combat wounds—blisters the size of distinguished service medals." And that's what I was doing, breaking them in before heading off to spend a few days in the field with ROTC cadets undergoing their summer field training at Fort Bragg, two hundred square miles of sand hills and pine trees in North Carolina.

Officer training programs on university campuses across the country produce far more of the commissioned officers in the military (70 percent of the Army officers, for example) than their counterparts, the service academies, do. I was to be one of many representatives from the fifteen eastern seaboard states that constitute the Army's First Region, the region with the largest number of ROTC cadets, more than 12,000. My counterparts from other colleges and universities were either faculty members who were serving as deans, as I was, or permanent administrators with no faculty affiliation (registrars, deans of admissions, and deans of students). We had all been invited to participate in Fort Bragg's "Camp All-American," and were offered the opportunity not only to observe some of the two thousand cadets at training but to participate in "outward bound" activities ourselves.

Along with my BDUs (battle dress uniform) I received a canary-yellow card picturing a squarely built, faceless soldier, clearly of male proportions but devoid of facial features so as to be taken as either a man or a women, dressed in the uniform I was about to try on and instructing me in the exact details of my outfit. I didn't want to make any mistakes, so I followed the card exactly: opened my top button, checked all pockets and waist flaps to be sure that they were flat and buttoned, and tucked my trousers and excess laces inside my boots. I noted that the overhanging shirt was kind to both middle-aged women and middle-aged men. The uniform was comfortable, the material of good quality and wrinkle-resistant.

I confess to standing before the mirror feeling pretty cool in my BDUs, a swirling camouflage of black, brown, green, and khaki, designed to replace what the species lost when it first stood up on the forest floor: invisibility in nature. The pants had all the pockets anyone could ever want. The bottom of the instruction card assured me that "YOU ARE NOW AN ALL-AMERICAN SOLDIER," but even though I'd followed the instructions to the letter, I still didn't look like an All-American soldier. No, I looked more like a forty-year-old woman duded up for a survivalist camp meeting.

Before heading off to Fort Bragg, I read the large public relations packet I had been given. It included *Cadet*, a newspaper that welcomed cadets to Camp All-American. In the commandant's column, Colonel Thomas D. MacIver spelled out his formula for cadet success in Camp All-American in a list of maxims:

> It will tax you both physically and mentally.
> Be an effective member of a winning team.
> Put mission first, people always. [from the "Cadet's Creed"]
> Do the right thing the first time without having to be told
>   to do it.
> Show us your best effort.
> An officer is both a leader and a follower.
> Good followers make winning teams; good leaders make good
>   followers.
> People make the difference.
> Be a person who helps make that difference for your team.
> Be a Warrior Leader!

The *Cadet* identified the theme of this year's Camp All-American as "Warrior Leaders" and warned that supervisors would place cadets "under a leadership microscope" to determine whether they were in fact on their way to becoming warrior leaders. The *Cadet* announced that "Advanced Camp must stress them both physically and mentally in order to evaluate their potential as leaders for the fast-paced and ever-changing global and military landscape." In any military training, *stress* typically implies lack of sleep, poor living conditions, and harsh commanders. Cadets were to be encouraged to tackle these challenges with "Warrior Spirit," aggression, and common sense. "You have the opportunity to be all you can be and more." The *Cadet* went to all ROTC participants, male and female, and seemed to be an example of the new Army's commitment to gender equity. But although everyone received the exhortation to embody the warrior spirit, only the men would qualify for combat. For women, embracing the warrior spirit would be a spiritual exercise rather than a professional one.

On our first morning we left our hotel in the intense humidity that Bragg is famous for and traveled by bus to the artillery range, where a group of cadets joined us on bleachers overlooking the enormous field. A pumped-up lieutenant led us all in a round of spirited, from-the-gut, affirmative "huahs," the Army's equivalent of "Praise the Lord," an enthusiastic retort appropriate for almost any circumstance. The enlisted guys, decked out in camouflage face paint, jogged onto the field in exact formation as rock music boomed from the megawatt PA system. They effortlessly fell into a stiff, formal line, shouted "Airborne" as if on some invisible command, and one by one stepped out to give name, rank, and hometown and to explain some aspect of the tasks they performed.

At Camp All-American, each branch of the Army did its best to recruit these officers-in-training into its particular corner of the Army world. Fort Bragg is the home of the 82nd Airborne Division, the largest parachute force in the world and a sort of mini-army in its own domain, complete with pilots, infantry, artillery, and armor soldiers as well as parachute-trained cooks, mechanics, radiomen, electricians, photojournalists, and computer operators. Touted for its swift deployability, the 82nd Airborne boasts that all its personnel can parachute in to bivouac or battlefront. The 82nd Airborne's introduction was followed by a dramatic presentation by the Artillery. It had the big guns that make big noises, and it showed marketing savvy by fully exploiting that firepower in a thrilling battlefield ballet. Busby Berkeley would have been impressed.

As rock music thundered, several trucks, also in formation, drove onto the field in front of our bleachers and unloaded their enormous guns. Overhead, helicopters swept in from all directions and hovered as soldiers dropped out and shimmied swiftly down "fast lines" to the ground below, like circus performers choreographed to awe and dismay. Larger helicopters lumbered into place and lowered large guns and tanks to their assigned places. Two even bigger troop transport helicopters veered in from nowhere with enormous guns dangling from cables. Each of those copters, I later learned, could carry eight tons of guns and soldiers. As the arrayed guns were fired, their concussive force drowned out the pounding bass of "We will, We will rock you" and ignited the horizon with a flash. Then, as a gorgeous cloud of violet smoke momentarily eclipsed the Carolina sun, the music stopped and the announcer triumphantly pronounced, "Target destroyed!" "Cadets," he added, "that's fire support working for you. As you can see, the distinctive power of artillery is *awesome.*" He then introduced gunners, cannoneers, and chiefs in groups and officers singly. Finally, as the cadets rose to leave the bleachers, the PA once again blared "We will rock you" as a fitting recessional.

Special Forces' presentation was as understated as Artillery's was showy. The "Ballad of the Green Berets" whined from a boom box as three enlisted soldiers lined up before us. The first sergeant, who had apparently conquered any public reticence though not his lisp, hollered his military bio with impressive confidence. He had been deployed thirty times to Latin America, fourteen times to El Salvador and the others to Venezuela and Chile. He announced that he spoke fluent Spanish and that his job was to assist foreign forces on their missions. The weapons sergeant told us that he was proficient in eighty-nine weapons systems. The engineer built bridges. After that group marched off, a new quartet toed the same line in the sand. Each of the soldiers sported a different outfit. The first described himself as a "free-fall parachutist" and came equipped with parachute harness, rappeling gear, and what looked like a fighter pilot's helmet with an oxygen mask and an intimidating assortment of dials. The second guy had hard duty. Oversized and fully stuffed packs hung from his shoulders, and sweat poured from his face as the heat locked in the high nineties. A combat diver, he explained that the kind of parachute he wore depended on whether he was falling from a high or low altitude and whether or not he needed to open at the last minute. His companion, equally drenched in Carolina dew, modeled the rough-terrain number: a padded suit, a visored helmet, and heavy leather gloves. The final Special Forces soldier was a diver who described his combat ensemble: one suit for waters above 32 degrees Fahrenheit and another for waters below freezing. Although the presenters entertained questions, they spoke little about their missions except to say that they were trained to land behind enemy lines. No one disclosed who the enemy in Venezuela was.

Over to the side, Special Forces' high-tech Signal Corps soldiers proudly displayed their latest equipment, including a snazzy portable satellite dish complete with transmitters and receivers that folded up for travel. I asked the sergeant how he could transport all of his equipment, for even though it was compact, it still required several large metal boxes. He replied that on some missions he and his equipment were airlifted in; for example, he deployed to the American embassy in Kuwait in the Gulf War and managed to broadcast from inside the embassy while the Iraqis were closing in. More often, however, in order to be as inconspicuous as possible, he and two fellow soldiers dressed in civilian clothes and traveled to foreign countries on commercial flights. If they were trying to enter the country without being recognized, I asked, what happened when they showed their military passports? Not a problem: they traveled on diplomatic passports, and if necessary they told airport officials that they were reporters for CNN. I pressed him: "What would happen if airport security called CNN and found out you were not on the payroll?" "That's no problem either; the Army has made arrangements with CNN so that they will verify that we are their employees." Whether the sergeant was ad-libbing or really knew about such collusion, I was never able to confirm.[1]

Although none of the university administrators was required to

5

parachute in, we did more than just sit in the stands. Besides attending the shows designed to impress ROTC cadets, we rappelled down wooden towers, squeezed into tanks, fired a howitzer, and went along with a squad of cadets ordered to take a bunker. We were urged to shimmy out on a cable slung thirty feet above a stream and drop into the water below. We each finished as much as we could of the obstacle course, but only the heartiest slithered through the mud under the barbed wire.

Our visit was not entirely conducted in the hot sun. On the last evening, the commanding general hosted a formal dinner, complete with reception line, drinks, and entertainment. We stood for toasts: first to country and president, then to the Army, to our various colleges and universities, and, last and most peculiar, to women. For this final toast, Brigadier General Thomas Konitzer, who looked tall, slim, and boyish (even at fifty-one), asked all the women to sit down and the men to toast the women. "There is a Chinese proverb," he said, "that it takes a thousand men to make a camp, but it takes only one woman to make a home." A young woman seated at my table said softly, "Well, we now know where women belong in this man's army!" I thought of all those ROTC women struggling in their field exercises to prove themselves combat-worthy and wondered how they would react if they heard their commander at that moment. My guess was that they would be clever enough to suggest that' the Army would be more efficient if women, not men, were assigned the task of setting up field camps.

The evening concluded with a performance by the 82nd Airborne Singers. Wearing fatigues with spiffy neck scarves and red Airborne berets all tilted at the same angle, they marched into the dining room and along the rows of tables, calling a cadence about rappelling out of helicopters down the fast ropes to their DZ (drop zone) below. The singers' steps were more intricately choreographed than those of the usual drill team. Near the conclusion of their number, each man stood with his toes touching the heels of the soldier in front of him, and the first in line bent over at the waist while the soldier behind him put his right arm on the other's shoulder, moved it down his back, over his rear, and down his right thigh, imitating the Ranger safety check to insure that ropes are secure. Each dancer in turn concluded his sweep of the body with the "seal of approval," the slap on the rear of the buddy before him. As the last one was slapped, the soldiers formed a tight line, each soldier with his torso leaning on the back of the man in front of him.

Amazed by the contrast between the salute to women that began the dinner and the finale—a chorus line of gaily scarved Airborne soldiers intimately linked groin to rear—I welcomed the request for questions from Konitzer the next day. I said, "Yesterday we went out into the field with a small combat group. We listened as the squad leader explained the objective—to take a bunker—issued instructions to each team, gave coordinates, and double-checked to see that each team understood the mission. We followed through the woods as the cadets approached and then took the bunker. Then we listened in on the "after-action review." During this critique session, one of the two women in the unit was praised. I'm sure that you, General Konitzer, have seen numerous women come through your program and have known some who have really excelled. In fact, one of your staff members told me that women are generally more motivated and try harder than men. Would you welcome one of those women in a combat unit you might be commanding?"

Konitzer evasively contended that women really didn't want to be in combat specialties. If they were assigned to such positions, he claimed, they'd have problems with the eighty-pound pack. Now, even Konitzer knows that if such an argument holds, it should apply only to those branches of the infantry where a soldier might need to carry an eighty-pound pack, and then the rule should be applied to both women and men. The Army is willing to apply simple merit tests to fit soldiers to tasks regardless of gender, because behind the eighty-pound pack hides the centuries-old bogeyman: the fear that in a military where technology has provided lighter, quicker, more remote, and more lethal weapons of destruction, there is no refuge for the tradition of the masculine warrior except in arbitrary and irrational gender discrimination. None of the arguments against using women in combat addresses the *military = masculinity?*

great unspoken reason for keeping them out: the presence of women threatens a concept of masculinity to which the military adheres and by which many of its members define themselves. If military women can do what military men do, then what makes the soldiers' patriotic acts "manly"?

Women continue to be classified as noncombatants despite the fact that they have wielded deadly weapons against the enemy since the invasion of Panama. In the fight against terrorists in Afghanistan, they demonstrated their expertise at firing from the turrets of armored Humvees, flying attack helicopters and fighter planes, and maintaining security at detainee centers.

For years women have demonstrated their expertise on the rifle range. In her days in the Naval Security Administration in the 1970s, a young officer named Donna Dean organized a group of women to compete in the annual air pistol competition, which had never included a female team and had long featured the shooting skills of the Marine Guards. At first piqued by these upstart women, the Marines resorted to devious means when they feared that they might actually lose to a group of women. Dean explained:

> As the matches progressed, it became obvious that we were winning a disproportionate number, and there was every possibility that we would prevail, winning the entire competition, including the nifty jackets proclaiming the wearers to be Champions of the NSA Air Pistol League. Try as they might, the Marines could not best us. Finally, desperate, they resorted to trickery and guile, never a good idea for Marines, as they lack subtlety and finesse. In the Finals Elimination Matches they began to use a type of ammunition called "wad-cutter," which made a much larger hole in the paper targets than the standard lead pellets utilized exclusively heretofore. The larger holes, of course, made the chances of their scores being higher, albeit artificially, substantially better, and a Marine team ultimately "won" by this scurrilous means by one point. I, outraged, appealed the decision, charging the use of wad-cutter ammo was il-

legal, and if not illegal, dishonorable, and the battle went all the way to the admiral. Honor and the rules of engagement prevailed, and we women were awarded the decision. We wore the jackets with great pride.[2]

The ability to become a good marksman knows no gender. Women have long demonstrated themselves to be good hunters. During World War II, Russia trained 100,000 female snipers at special sniper schools, and they are credited with 10,000 kills of enemy personnel.[3] Female police officers have certainly demonstrated their ability to use firearms effectively. The United States has recently begun training female snipers through its National Guard sniper training school, but the Army and the Marine Corps hold fast to combat exclusion as a way of keeping certain territories exclusively male. In this way, gender exclusion looks a lot like cultic interdiction.

If the subject of gender makes officers such as Konitzer resort to proverbs or contradictions, the subject of homosexuals in the military makes them sound even more confused. Asked his views on the introduction of homosexuals into the military, Konitzer began with the rhetorical question, "Why is someone willing to risk his life for god and country?" He went on to explain that 10 percent of the willingness to put your life on the line might be attributed to motivation and another 10 percent to loyalty to the Army as an organization; the remaining 80 percent comes from the willingness of soldiers to risk their lives for each other. To illustrate—not to answer to the question, but to evade an answer—Konitzer told the story of an Airborne officer who saw a fireball headed in his direction. Immediately he grabbed the female officer next to him, threw her to the tarmac, and covered her body with his own. The fireball rolled over them, and then he whispered to her to go get herself a medic. When the medic came to check on him, the Airborne lieutenant was dead, having demonstrated the highest act of heroism, a quality, Konitzer emphasized, that the Army looks for. It was a stirring story, if less than transparent in its application. I could not decide whether we were to presume that the Airborne officer who sacrificed

Konitzer rejected the question of homosexuality in the military.

himself would not have done this for a gay male officer or whether a gay officer would not have thrown himself in harm's way to protect another, especially a woman.

No amount of evasiveness by the brass can dispel the simple truth that women play a vital and increasingly critical role in today's military. Yet the anecdotes that commanders tell, the lore that they propagate, have the pernicious effect of distorting that role and repressing the talent and energy of young women who want to serve their country and succeed in that service. The way commanders portray female personnel in stories powerfully communicates to their peers and subordinates whether women are to be respected as fellow soldiers capable of heroism and sacrifice or whether they are to be tolerated as defenseless civilians dressed in khaki.

The average final score of women participating in the rigorous summer ROTC program, a compilation of scores on several different events, has often exceeded that of men. What version of cost-benefit analysis could justify a system that trains women to perform in combat, charts their superior performance, yet prohibits their entry into ground-combat specialties? The female cadets who struggled when I was at Fort Bragg would certainly have read *Cadet* and thought of themselves as warrior leaders with warrior spirit. They thought of themselves as warriors and performed as warriors, but how many of their male peers and supervisors were willing to imagine them as the Army's future warrior leaders?

The anecdotes of a commanding officer and the toasts that cordially put women in their domestic place are not to be dismissed. Officers carry these with them, and they are truer in some respects than the public relations platitudes about warrior spirit. The unofficial traditions— the stories, songs, rituals, and jokes—and the attitudes they impart have been handed down from previous generations of officers. Military folklore will always be with us. But the uncritical propagation of such folklore threatens both the official recruitment and acceptance of women, which have become absolutely crucial to the maintenance of the armed forces' strength, and the good order and discipline upon which the military must stake its readiness to exercise that strength in defense of the nation's security. Full integration of women into the armed services will not be accomplished by tailoring a few darts into the uniform, by designing odd little hats, or by insisting that women practice a lower, more male sounding "command" voice. It will require fresh, thorough, and critical examination of training principles and methods to insure that from the bottom up and from the first day forward, the military fosters a new professionalism and creates an esprit de corps open to all, regardless of gender, ethnicity, and sexual preference. Rational justification rather than reactionary sanctification of traditions will force biases out of the shadows where they acquire magical power and into the light of argument, to be vindicated or to die.

The pragmatic approach is obviously much easier to accomplish in ROTC programs, which are by design more open, than in the service academies. Although ROTC cadets receive professional training on military bases, they go through most of their preparation on the campuses of America's public and private universities. Their counterparts at service academies live in walled institutions closed to nonmembers except during public parades, tours, and hours when the public is invited to enjoy the grounds. The degree to which the service academies have already welcomed women and minorities and the degree to which they will continue that process depend on enlightened leaders. Because leaders of the service academies come and go on an average of every three years, asking them to be agents of change, especially when they harbor an understandable reverence for the institutional system that produced them, is expecting a great deal. If those leaders are to reform the academies to meet the challenge of the twenty-first century rather than merely reproduce the nineteenth-century charms that still abide, they must effectively respond to the forces of radical demographic and technological change, not in the name of political correctness but for the sake of maintaining American military might and in the spirit of the United States Constitution.

2. Military Culture

Culture is simply a way of life informed by those who came before us, by how we grow up, and by the beliefs we hold; it is manifest in the rituals we observe, the jokes we tell, the slang we use, the clothes we wear, the food we eat, the work we do, and the ways we interact with those who share our workplace. Members of the military, whether on duty or off, combatants or noncombatants, active-duty or retired, share an identity fashioned by an always distinctive, frequently compelling, and occasionally bizarre military culture. Military culture embraces not only the official traditions of military life (formal dress parades, heroes' welcomes, Blue Angel flyovers, military dress, deference to rank) but also their unofficial, ostensibly transgressive counterparts: parodies, pranks, fake commendations, the hazing of new recruits, the drinking games that inevitably follow a formal "dining in" (that is, a dinner for visiting officers and other dignitaries). The relationship between official culture and its parody is intimate, a secret sharing. At the end of Airborne training, for example, a soldier chooses a military mentor or relative to fasten his wings, a small metal pin, onto his uniform. Back in the barracks, another ceremony follows the official one. Here fellow soldiers award the same wings a second time: one by one the soldier's buddies step up and punch the wings, its pins exposed, directly into the proud pincushion's flesh. Only then, when pricked by his peers, has the soldier earned his "blood wings."

On the rare occasions that the military brass has admitted to such rituals, it has either dismissed them as adolescent high jinks or selectively defended them as essential to the formation of unit cohesion. Yet what might have been tolerated as a harmless prank or promoted as a useful way to maintain morale in the armed forces of a former day takes on a sinister cast in a professional military committed by statute and policy to the inclusion of women. I say sinister, not immoral or criminal, because I do not claim that women are more moral or more civilized than men. On the contrary, the folklore of the military, the prospect of absorbing the traditions and living the life of a disciplined and close-knit unit, is what attracts most women to the armed services. Indeed, many of them have been raised in military families. It is because women share the aspirations of men for full membership in the corps but are excluded from the initiatory warrior rituals for no reason other than their gender that the unavowed collaboration between official and unofficial practices is sinister—or, to put it more academically, that the American military culture is fundamentally and dangerously cultic. Although unofficial military traditions have a rich history in the all-male military institution, which has been convinced that it cannot make soldiers and officers without first making men, the same traditions have now become potent antagonists of the reforms necessary to create a gender-blind professional military in a digital era. Today, muscle-bound macho nostalgia is more likely to thwart than to impel the successful execution of the military's mission.

To grasp how military culture is transmitted from one generation of recruits to the next, we need only to look at boot camp. Boot camp transforms recruits from jocks and nerds, boys from the 'hood and women from the suburbs, into knockoffs of model soldiers by stripping them of their clothes, shaving off their hair, forbidding them their accustomed freedoms, and instilling military discipline in them as second nature. Drill instructors, the engineers of their transformation, control every minute of the recruits' days: they deprive them of sleep, tax them physically, infantilize them, and, if the recruits are male, feminize them through the kind of humiliation designed to impress on them that to be degraded is to be female ("Come on, ladies").

Under this perversely scripted scenario there can be no parity between the experiences of men and women in basic training. We can corroborate that claim by reconstructing the subterranean history of the marching chant: the "jodie" in the Army and the Marine Corps, the "cadence call" in the Navy. Such chants celebrate the need to repudiate the pleasures associated with a recruit's civilian past and to embrace a martial future (or, more literally, to leave your girl and love your rifle).

Cindy, Cindy, Cindy Lou
Love my rifle more than you.

You used to be my beauty queen,
Now I love my M-16.

Used to go to the county fair,
Now I don't take you anywhere.

Send me off to Vietnam
Goin' to get me some Viet Cong.

With my knife or with my gun
Either way it's just as fun.

The history of such marching chants snakes through military culture from its elusive roots in American popular song during World War II, to the incorporation of the African American work-song tradition after the Korean War, when more and more African Americans filled the ranks of drill instructors, to the macabre turn of the outlawed genre in the Vietnam and post-Vietnam years with choruses of "Napalm sticks to kids; napalm sticks to ribs."

If the marching chant keeps the beat of boot camp days, the climactic rite of passage celebrates its culmination. As in primitive societies the world over, the rite of passage dramatically enacts the transformation from boyhood to manhood, the induction of the initiate into full membership in the cult. Veteran sailors ("shellbacks") crossing the equator summon King Neptune from his royal depths to initiate the "polliwogs"—those making their maiden crossing of the equator (especially fresh officers)—through a series of humiliating rituals. Such "crossing-the-line ceremonies," performed on board ships since the 1600s, ritualistically subvert military hierarchy by installing a new command for at least a day: the costumed sailor as King Neptune, his cross-dressing buddy as his queen, and their royal baby (generally the fattest sailor on board, dressed in a diaper). The scantily clad initiate must run through a gauntlet of wet towels and paddles, worm his way through the "whale's asshole," a long tube filled with the leavings of the previous day's meals, consume foul-tasting libations, and endure total-

immersion baptism in a vat of putrid-smelling liquid. In some ceremonies the polliwog is required to lick lard from the belly of the royal
baby, in others to simulate oral sex by sucking on a section of rubber
hose extending from the groin of King Neptune. The equator is not the
only line that is crossed.

Stories of less elaborate yet thematically similar rituals that celebrate the ways in which a crusty chief petty officer teaches arrogant,
inexperienced officers a lesson circulate widely among enlisted troops.
The fool's errand is a typical one. The young ensign is sent to deliver a
flask of "primary water" from one part of a submarine to another. Routinely, anyone transporting any substance that might be radioactive
must be scanned immediately after he completes the task to insure that
he is not contaminated. When the ensign reports, the sailor passes a
wand over his body while concealing in the palm of his hand a small
amount of the substance that will activate the alarm. First the sailor
passes the wand over the front of the ensign. He proceeds down the
back of his neck and his back. When the wand gets near his anus, the
alarm sounds.

Before their elective summer cruise aboard a submarine, midshipmen at the Naval Academy frighten and amuse each other with such
stories. They tell of experienced sailors eager to put green midshipmen
in their places, humiliating them by taping two of them in a 69 position. Such pranks and rituals and the legends they spawn articulate in
erotic overtones the struggle between rank and experience.

To suggest that military ritual resides only in discrete ceremonies to
mark what Victor Turner identifies as "threshold experiences" (Turner,
1969) offers only a partial picture. Ritual orders soldiers' lives. From the
cut of their hair to the crease in their shirts to the edge dressing on their
shoes, soldiers prepare themselves for work. Simple acts are freighted
with significance; done well, they identify the individual as one who
successfully conforms to the norm, an idealized version of the anonymous disciplined soldier who grasps and is held by his place in the chain
of command. Such precisely regulated behavior prescribes conformity
for the service member's family as well. Reports of misbehavior at the
base school often make their way back to a superior; "If an officer can't

15

control his family," the adage goes, "how can he control his men?" The higher the rank of a male officer is, the more extensive the social obligations demanded of his wife are; yet the husbands of female officers rarely fill an analogous supporting role.

The ritual life extends to the battlefield as well. Before going into battle, warriors of all cultures perform rituals (maybe only as simple as a prayer or a cheer). In Vietnam, one unit filled a porcelain toilet bowl with beer, or liquor when they had it, and one by one the soldiers dipped out a libation before heading out of camp. Troops decorated helmets with political, religious, and personal slogans, carried tokens as good luck charms, fashioned in-country patches, and painted planes and helicopters as ferocious animals or friendly mascots, or, like their World War II predecessors, adorned them with long-legged, large-breasted women.

In wartime, the soldier or sailor whose service is drawing to a close is a subject of envy and uneasiness. To mark this transitional status, members of all branches of the military exchange short-timer calendars, either a patriotic or a bawdy image intricately divided into 365 shapes which the short-timer progressively colors, one each day until he returns home and the calendar is completely filled in. Short-timer sayings ("He's so short he could jump off a dime"; "He's so short he could wipe an ant's ass") and superstitions about the inadvisability of fighting alongside someone who has less than a month to serve proliferate during times of war.

An even more pervasive aspect of military culture is the demotic idiom of soldiers and sailors. Military folk speech is replete with acronyms: *snafu* may be the best known, but perhaps more useful in the end is *fng*, "fuckin' new guy." Military speech is seasoned with terms of praise and blame that sanction certain kinds of behavior; for instance, *to bilge* is to tell on a fellow midshipman. Its enormous lexicon of slang is both reliably conventional and unstintingly prolific. Like other groups of workers, military units invent their own language. The richly metaphorical speech that colors military life permits soldiers and sailors to converse on two levels at once, to affect compliance with authority while safely ridiculing a superior, complaining about a dreaded task, and distinguishing themselves as insiders who have mastered a lingo impenetrable to outsiders.

Whether they are from the same branch of the service, the same subspecialty, or the same company, members of the armed services recycle the repertoire of their immediate predecessors and invent new slang to fit their circumstances. In the same way, they pass along legends glorious and inglorious from soldier to soldier, unit to unit, and war to war: stories of bullets deflected by Bibles, dog tags, and amulets and tales of battlefield ghosts and crazed combat soldiers. These legends deal in the marvelous and the uncanny. The tellers claim authenticity for the events they narrate and demand credence from their audience. Stories of preternatural visitations, undeserved luck, and unforeseen misfortune are located in historical (as opposed to mythic) time and involve strange events that occurred to someone just like them, just over the horizon of this hill, this battle, this war.

Every war produces its share of angel helper stories. In the typical tale, an older soldier helps a struggling younger soldier, one too tired or too wounded to keep up with his retreating buddies. When he wakes the next morning, eager to thank his rescuer, the young soldier finds that the one who helped him back to friendly lines never existed or died in combat months or years before. Phantom soldiers fight in every war. The spirits of downed pilots repeat their distress calls on the anniversary of their death. In one Vietnam account, a soldier fights valorously until the day when he sees himself in VC clothing, stalking through the bushes. Such radical ambivalence marks the end of his tour of duty.

Some legends actually make their way into civilian discourse. The Vietnam War, more than any other, produced a constellation of lore associated with the return home. An account often told to sum up what happened to the returning vet, whose sacrifices went unacknowledged and whose heroism was unhailed by an American population fed up with the war, is the spat-upon story.[1] The war-weary soldier walks across the tarmac from his plane, but instead of hearing the cheers and bands that welcomed his predecessors, he walks through a jeering crowd, one of whom spits on him. Although the account defies reality—how many troop transport planes flew into commercial airports?—it is always told seriously. This story epitomized for many the terrible irony of the war. But such a story predates Vietnam. It was told about Korean War vets, whose pain and hardship seemed to many in the States to have been for naught. The story penetrated popular culture as well. In the fifties film *Shock Corridor,* a journalist going undercover in an insane asylum tells a first-person version of this story in order to bolster his disguise as a shell-shocked Korean vet.

Stories of unappreciative civilians spitting on veterans, of soldiers returning home from Vietnam early only to be shot by their fathers, who suspect they are intruders, of extraordinary draft evasion attempts that failed, even of crazed combat soldiers fashioning necklaces from the ears of the enemy: these stories and many more constitute the legendary repertoire of Vietnam.

Just as the telling of legends serves both a psychological and a social purpose within the folk group, so the makeshift rituals devised by military personnel to cope with extraordinary circumstances of deprivation have similar purposes. The experiences of female prisoners who endured harrowing internment in Japanese prison camps in the Philippines during World War II are a case in point. Sixty-eight nurses imprisoned on Bataan and Corregidor fashioned greeting cards on scraps of paper to commemorate significant occasions in their lives. They made dolls from bits of discarded fabric. They outfitted one doll in a perfect nurse's uniform, down to the details of kit and toothbrush; the doll was the only nurse who maintained regulation uniform during the women's long internment. These nurses and their male counterparts demonstrated astonishing resourcefulness in preserving an identity—a visible, distinctively military identity—apart from the one prescribed by their harsh captors. They buried jokes about their overseers in camp plays. They drew humorous caricatures depicting obese Japanese soldiers and emaciated GIs. They kept diaries in tiny script on scraps of paper and secreted them, despite the risk of certain beating or even death if they were discovered. Faced with virtual extinction at the hands of real enemies, the men and women who lived in prison camps were able to rely on their military training and culture not just to survive but to create viable communities.

One sector of the military that comes with its own set of traditions is the service academy. Anxious that more and more members of the middle class would invade its officer corps, French noblemen invented the service academy in the eighteenth century. To reserve the top positions in the military for their sons, they constructed an institution designed not only to provide a general education in academic subjects but to train its members in new military techniques. England was not long in following the French example. Contemporary service academies in democratic countries like America, Canada, and Australia were modeled on the British public school.

In every military academy from Sandhurst to West Point, from Annapolis to Kingston in Canada, the first year (or a portion of it) marks a period of transition from childhood to manhood, from civilian status to membership in the corps. Upperclassmen debase their juniors in painful but traditional ways. Rarely do upperclassmen invent new forms of humiliation; the most brutal merely increase the frequency of their aggression. Both through "plebe indoctrination" at the U.S. Naval Academy and through ritual abuse (called "bastardization") at the Australian Defense Force Academy, three fourths of the student body assumes the role of master and one fourth reluctantly plays the part of slave. Ceremonies confirm the end of this period and mark the exchange of probationary status for membership.

The history of service academies is punctuated by thorough reviews of such indoctrination systems, usually initiated after charges of hazing have made their way into the press. In Australia, official inquiries have addressed scandal about every seven years. Recent scandals in the United States have afflicted more than service academies; they have exposed misogynistic practices that were previously excused as military culture ("high jinks" or "letting off steam"). At its annual gathering of pilots, the now infamous Tailhook Convention, partygoers sported "He-Man Woman Hater Club" T-shirts and "rhino headgear" in honor of the rhino wall "trophy," equipped with protruding penis, from which women were urged to "suck down the booze." Pilots went "ballwalking" and "mooning" through the hospitality suites of the Las Vegas Hilton. Some women—compliant participants and prostitutes—exposed their breasts to aviators, who zapped them with squadron logos; even un-willing female officers and civilians could not escape the assaults of drunken officers, who propelled them down a two-hundred-man gauntlet (Zimmerman, 1995).

Since the Tailhook investigation, which produced few culprits and no convictions, two Marines and a sailor have been convicted of bru-tally raping a twelve-year-old schoolgirl in Okinawa, and midshipmen at the Naval Academy have been accused of rape and pedophilia. These scandals, coupled with harsh criticisms of proposed reforms that were said to threaten "emasculation" of the nation's warriors by conservatives like James Webb, a former secretary of the Navy, roiled the waters of Admiral Jeremy Boorda's command. Boorda's subsequent suicide played in the press as another sensational episode in the Navy's alarming fall from its former prestige as the "gentleman's service."

If Tailhook exposed the excesses of officer culture by a group of drunken, cocksure aviators and the leadership's inability to discipline its own, Aberdeen raised questions about the sober and sinister application of discipline against women. At the Tailhook Convention, male officers assaulted female officers and civilian women in the urine- and beer-soaked hallways. At Aberdeen Proving Ground, drill instructors co-erced or sexually assaulted women under their command. Whereas the naval scandal laid bare the arrogance of naval command, Aberdeen raised questions about the absolute nature of the privileged relationship between the all-powerful drill instructor and the powerless recruit. The potential for abuse by drill instructors has always existed; the zeal to erase a civilian identity and to inscribe a military one has resulted in in-jury and even death in training. With more women in training, with the great differential in power between trainers and trainees, and with the lack of mediation or effective oversight, abuse can assume a sexist form. Conventionally, male initiation in warrior cultures begins with infan-tilization and feminization and proceeds to practices designed to rid the adolescent of all traces of the female. To the extent that the military brass have permitted training to operate as a male rite of passage, they have furthered a culture hostile to women.

The Aberdeen scandal has not only invited
claim that the Army has not gone far enough in i
fair and professional treatment; it has also firec
who blame neither the system nor the perpetr
themselves. Calling for separate but equal training
ple maintain that it is "natural" or "inevitable" for
cur when men and women are placed in close qu ....
experience as intense as basic training. This rationale fails to take into
account that the problem is not the amorous relations of peers but sexual relations that, because of the extraordinary difference in power, can
never be purely consensual.

Very few critics and commentators would argue that there is not or
should be no military culture. It is important, however, to understand
the extent to which the military's culture has come to be at odds with
its mission. Why should women and homosexuals take the place of
the vanquished enemy? Why are rampant misogyny and homophobia
countenanced throughout the armed services? Why does the military
respond to the accident of gender or sexual preference with more in-
tensity than it responds to the accident of skin color or social class?

The answer cannot be that the military is a reflection of society: it
is not and never has been. In some cases the institution has been more
socially progressive than the civilian world. Whatever the quarrels that
members of both political parties have had with the military since the
McCarthy era, they have generally agreed that the armed services
should be an arena where merit will rule. With his decision to racially
integrate the military, so the story goes, Harry Truman opened the
doors of the nation's greatest meritocracy to a large group of disenfran-
chised African Americans, who found in the military the opportunity
for advancement that was closed to them in society at large. Progress
has not been continuous, and its effects have not been uniform. Some
African Americans, most notably General Colin Powell, have moved
into the military's highest offices, yet integration of the military is still
far from complete. Although African Americans account for 22 percent
of enlisted forces, they constitute only 8.5 percent of officers (U.S.

, DEOMI, 1998). Such residual effects of racism have not, how-
er, been justified as necessary to the preservation of the military's cultural identity.

If culture is the defense, then an investigation of culture may hold
the answer to the systematic prejudice toward women and gays, who are
treated as if they are a race or a class in an organization where the markers of race and class are otherwise rigorously suppressed. Although the
answer is complex, a suggestion of its major coordinates may be in order here. First, the treatment of women and homosexuals is not sym-
metrical (women who are homosexual lose their status as women). A
professional military is no longer a civilian army. I suspect that the rise
of the militia movement is an aftereffect of the abolition of the draft,
with fantasy taking the place of experience; militiamen are antiprofes-
sionals with guns. Professional military culture defines itself against
nonprofessionals. It is not the failure of women to meet standards that
excludes them from certain places and positions in the military, but
the failure of the military to *apply* standards, as if the definition of the
specific skills and abilities needed for each specialty would open the way
for women to qualify for billets in the infantry and the cavalry and to
serve aboard submarines.

In considering the cultural aspects of the military, we must distinguish them from cultic aspects as they have been practiced in the last
half-century. Military culture is made, not born; it has a history; its future should be directed toward serving democratically approved ends.
Insofar as the armed services promote personal integrity, discipline, respect, and sacrifice in their members, regardless of background or gender, they further the values of today's democratic society, although they
may not themselves be democratic. Insofar as they are inward-looking,
exclusionary, destructive, and inefficient, they threaten to undermine
those values and establish in their place a cult of masculinity, one that
harbors the gay male as its secret sharer.

The shift to the volunteer army has accelerated the shift in the racial
and ethnic composition of the armed forces that began during the Vietnam War, with its broad extension of the draft to feed a burgeoning
combat force. The recruitment of more African Americans, Hispanic

Americans, Asian Americans, and women and their appearance throughout the chain of command complicate traditional values in an institution that prizes uniformity over difference and that sees itself, and is seen by many outside the military, as conferring "manhood" on its members. Traditions that may not be officially sanctioned but that resist extinction persist—traditions that may have little to do with efficiency, skill, and readiness (qualities essential to any fighting force) but that have everything to do with the inscription of manhood.

Such an investigation of culture rests on two assumptions: 1) that claims to a culture or a distinctive way of life are and must be public—that a culture is visible and can describe itself in terms of an ethics, an imitable path by which its values can be put into practice in order to achieve prescribed ends; and 2) that culture is not the same as nature, although the language of culturalism would seem to make it so.

Organizations large and small have cultures, but insofar as they are organized to achieve socially legitimate ends, such cultures inform and support an ethics that is the avowed rationale for the purposive activity of members of the organization. Although the relation between culture and ethics may be complicated by changing circumstances, there is no inherent secrecy or mystery to such a relation. A culture is not a cult. Moreover, involvement in a culture cannot trump the rights and obligations of a citizen in a republic, as democratically defined.

Cultures are not determined, nor do they determine. On the contrary, a culture is a made thing or a set of practices subject to change in the face of imperious circumstances or as a consequence of the orderly expression of the popular will. For example, the culture of the sharecroppers of the Midwest did not survive the dust bowl and migration to California; women's colleges that have integrated male undergraduates have witnessed cultural transformation in recent years.[2] Military culture is made and made for a purpose. Any cultural practices that cannot be justified as serving directly or indirectly the mission of service and protection cannot be tolerated. It may be argued that barracks games that increase vigilance and therefore combat readiness have an indirect benefit. Rites that can be said to enhance the sense of manhood among aviators, such as the sexual assaults of the Tailhook convention, cannot be tolerated—not only because they violate the law and aggressively exclude fellow officers, but because they cannot be shown to have an indirect benefit, and because there is no detectable link between something called manhood and the capacity to carry out one's duty efficiently. Let me say this clearly. There is no detectable, reasoned link between the warrior and the professional soldier. In a republic, the military is an institution, not a caste or a gender or a race as those are commonly conceived. It can make no claims that cannot be subjected to constitutional debate and democratic decision.

3. Transformation

Everyone has seen the movies about basic training. Some celebrate it;
some mock it, but each typically depicts a tight-lipped, square-jawed
dynamo of a drill instructor barking commands at a group of hapless
recruits whose every act subjects them to merciless criticism seasoned
by colorful profanities. Although today's real drill instructors may not
be as square-jawed or as tall as their cinematic equivalents, they do bark
out commands to each new cohort of recruits to arrive at basic training. For their part, recruits soon figure out which answers are acceptable
and which will be ridiculed. They learn to walk or run in step, to endure
petty humiliations, and to internalize the will of their drill instructor as
their own. The smart-aleck trades in his smirk for a "squared-away" attitude. The out-of-shape recruit either develops the stamina required
or packs up for home. Basic training aims to transform individuals into
standard "government-issue" soldiers by erasing civilian identities that
have been formed over many years on tough city streets or in tree-lined
suburbs, in safe schools with competent teachers or in remedial classes
for slow students, in families whose attitudes toward work, honesty, and
trust have made their way from one generation to the next. Basic training prohibits contact with the civilian world, the anchor to recruits'
former selves. No previous accomplishments matter in basic training.
Personal intelligence, charm, and humor count for little. Above all, basic training demands a suppression of individual difference and exacts
conformity in all outward actions and dress.

In the social encounters of civilians, people typically exchange personal information, but basic training subverts the typical social encounter at every point. The military regards the exchange of personal
information among recruits as irrelevant to the overriding task of making soldiers and actively discourages such disclosures. No individual
alone can hope to define or shape the situation; the system designates
who the individual is in terms of unit and rank. The system shears and
strips recruits, confiscates T-shirts, Nikes, khakis, corduroys, and jeans,
and doles out the featureless uniforms. Drill instructors deliberately

treat the recruits as children, scolding these babes in arms because in the eyes of the institution they do not speak properly, walk properly, or even eat properly. They cannot accomplish even the simplest of tasks— making the bed or cleaning the floor—to the satisfaction of their over- seers. Recruits cannot keep time; therefore they are allowed no control over their time. The noncoms determine when they wake, when they go to the bathroom, and when they sleep. Basic training withdraws re- cruits from society and consigns them to a liminal, deindividualized state where it comes to seem natural to refer to themselves in the third person, to get little, then less sleep, to swallow complaints when the body rebels at the relentless demands that it leap, crawl, squat, swing, carry, march and march and march.

Most new recruits experience a profound disorientation. Drill in- structors talk to them in ways they have never been addressed before. Forced to suppress their anger and frustration, they must endure emo- tional bullying and the cognitive confusion that results from incessant and often contradictory commands: ordered to march one way on the parade ground, then suddenly reversed, only to be reversed again. On the face of it, you would think that an institution that so prizes order (every minute planned, every recruit under constant surveillance) would have no use for confusion; yet confusion is a state that drill instructors intentionally induce in their recruits. Planned confusion increases the dependence of recruits on their harsh taskmaster. Only the drill in- structor, the god of their universe and the architect of their transfor- mation, can erase their confusion. According to Lieutenant Colonel Michael Becker, commander at Parris Island, "The reason we do this [simulate confusion] the way we do is to create uncertainty. . . . From the recruit's perspective, it appears to be chaos. War is chaos. And then they see this drill instructor—this magnificent creature who brings order to chaos. They learn that if they follow orders, their life will be calmer. . . . The recruits aren't the enemy—don't get me wrong. The enemy is their values—their un-Marinelike values" (Ricks, 57).

In boot camp, the civilian life is regarded as a fallen world from which military discipline and training promise redemption. To the struggling recruit, error feels a lot like sin, evidence of unfitness to join the world of the corps. In the intensely ordered little cosmos of basic training, the all-powerful drill instructor represents the perfect military specimen, one who commands respect from every trainee in camp. If recruits are the military's raw material, drill instructors, not Annapolis or West Point grads, are its polished product. They articulate the new military virtues that must replace older, wrong-headed civilian ones. Blind obedience to authority replaces willful self-interest, and fraternity replaces attachments from the civilian world.

Without uniformity, the highly choreographed dance of the military parade would dissolve into chaos. Drill effectively teaches recruits that each must keep every step, every line of the body, even every gaze in sync with the group. Close-order drill is important figuratively— to train individual soldiers under the orchestration of their leaders to configure an army collectively.

Drill has played an important part in military training since the seventeenth century, when Dutch forces demonstrated the power of rigorous drill to transform the rank and file into a cohesive unit that would be efficient in battle and obedient in the garrison (McNeill, 1982: 254). The carefully choreographed movements of drill (walking in step, loading, and firing) were rehearsals for the greater drama of the battlefield. But today's drill, considered essential to any training program, has no direct parallel to movements in war. A vestige of a time when men fought standing up, not on their stomachs and certainly not behind technologically complex control panels, drill today teaches obedience, erases individuality, and inscribes a corporate identity in which the movements of individuals are indistinguishable from the whole.

Marching chants accompany drill in all branches of today's military. Practical in their purpose, they build morale, insure group cohesion, and ease strain by diverting attention from monotonous and often strenuous labor or training. As military traditions, these verses pass from company to company, division to division, service to service, even war to war, graphically conveying indelible attitudes toward the military life the soldier has adopted and the civilian life he or she has left behind. Although some chants celebrate the bravado of combat, most complain of the daily discomforts suffered away from home ("Ain't no use in going to chow/They never feed you anyhow").

Through marching chants, humor lightens the tedium and pain of training, providing opportunities for even the lowliest to mock a superior and for the group to express its disdain for a rival. Sometimes wit and originality are applied to amend the most familiar chants and express a group's sentiments, thus particularizing a form of verse sung over and over by thousands experiencing the rigors of training. The improvised additions to standard chants are evidence that even within the rigid practice of discipline there is room for collective innovation.

Offensiveness drives marching chants. It can take the form of insult to a superior:

The cabin boy, the cabin boy,
That naughty little nipper:
He lined his ass with shards of glass
And circumcised the skipper.[1]

It can also be a ghoulish celebration of the slaughter of innocents:

See the family by the stream,
Watch the parents run and scream.

Viet Cong will never learn.
Push a button and watch'em burn.

or the playful objectification of women:

I wish all the girls were bricks in a pile,
And I was a mason; I'd lay'em all in style.

I wish all the girls were pies on a shelf,
And I was a baker; I'd eat'em all myself.[2]

Through such chants, the group asserts itself as the tough "bad boy," equally ready to slaughter or to screw. For the trainee, these chants transform the horrifying prospect of combat into a humorous, macabre sport.

Typically, marching chants oppose the longing for loved ones with the celebration of a new life as a member of the group:

Suzie said to me one day long ago
"Honey, please don't join the corps [pronounced *co*]
All they do is fuss'n fight
and they look kinda weird with those 'high-and-tights.' "[3]

I said, "Suzie, let me tell you what I'll do
I'll join the corps for a year or two."
So I packed up my trash and headed for the plane
and I went to the place where they make Marines.

Quantico was the name of the place.
The first thing I saw was a drill instructor's face.
He had razor creases and a Smokey Bear,[4]
Mountain-climbin' privates everywhere.

Now Suzie said, "It's me or the corps,
I can't take this life no more."
So I looked at her with a big ole grin.
I haven't seen Suzie since I don't know when.[5]

Presented with Suzie's ultimatum, the recruit exchanges his girl for the corps—or rather, the stern drill instructor shouts the lines and his trainees repeat it in unison. These chants celebrate the displacement of sexual energy from the female left behind to the enemy waiting on the battlefield. Women are as infinitely replaceable as the enemy, and combat, according to marching chants, is as exhilarating as sex. They devalue all nonprofessional affiliations and mark a soldier's passage from civilian life to combat by encouraging masturbatory compensation: "I don't want no teenage queen./ I just want my M-16."

Such compensation was illustrated first in James Jones's novel *From Here to Eternity* and later in Stanley Kubrick's Vietnam film, *Full Metal Jacket*. In the latter, a drill instructor leads his trainees, clad only in underwear, one hand on their rifles, the other grasping their genitals, in a truly universal marching chant, one that has crossed all service lines:

full metal jacket

> This is my rifle; this is my gun.
> This is for fighting; this is for fun.

In step, the barefoot, scantily clad trainees stroke their genitals in perfect beat to the command of the uniformed drill instructor. In another context, a group of males stroking their penises in unison could be considered autoeroticism, but in this context and for these trainees it is a form of collective humiliation. In practice, this chant appears early in training, usually as punishment when someone drops his rifle or mistakenly calls it his "gun." Such a punishment chant reinforces the new professional vocabulary.

no more individuality. they become a group identity

The education of all military trainees exchanges guns for lovers, harsh drill sergeants for fathers, and group survival for the needs of the individual. The freshly forged identity of the young trainee distinguishes him from other military professionals and celebrates group identity. Every branch of the service chants a call addressed to mothers, a sort of letter home complaining about the painful transition to military life. While the young soldier trains, he sings of the loss of his past—of his possessions, of his leisure time, even of his lover—a loss made permanent by the legendary "Jody" or "Joe de Grinder" of black oral tradition.

In an African American work song, Joe de Grinder is the devilish ladies' man who makes time with the workingman's lover, mother, and sister and makes off with his possessions while the cuckold goes out to earn an honest living (Jackson, 1967: 387). During the Korean war, many African American sergeants joined the ranks of effective drill sergeants, taking with them their work-song tradition, one that spread through every training unit, black or white, and that transformed the marching chant. Joe de Grinder became the character Jody, and the word *jody* itself became synonymous with marching chants. Even today in the Marine Corps or the Army, one calls a jody, not a marching chant. For the trainee, Jody is the clever civilian who brutally divorces the recruit from the civilian world by appropriating all his possessions and loved ones:

Ain't no use in callin' home.
Jody's on your telephone.

Ain't no use in lookin' back.
Jody's got your Cadillac.

Ain't no use in goin' home.
Jody's got your girl and gone.

Ain't no use in feelin' blue.
Jody's got your sister too.[6]

Echoing the drill instructor, each trainee complains of the eternally potent Jody, who doubles for the soldier in his absence, filling his vacated civilian role. Jody's behavior at home will be used to justify similar predatory behavior by the soldier in the theater of battle. Only through war will the soldier get a chance to get back at Jody. During Vietnam, "Charlie" (short for Viet Cong, VC, or Victory Charlie), the ambiguous military/civilian enemy, stepped in for the insidious Jody:

Mama, Mama, can't ya see
what the Navy's done to me.

Shaved my head and broke my back.
Now Charlie drives my Cadillac.

Wo, wo, wo, wo.
Wo wo, wo, wo.

Tried to write my Susie Q.
Seems Charlie's got my girlfriend too.[7]

Well into the 1990s, both the Charlie and the Jody version flour-
ished in basic training programs.

In training, the recruit is never alone, but chants from previous wars
rarely speak of war's loneliness. The exception, Vietnam chants contain
several references to the isolation of the single combat soldier. Take, for
example, the following:

Vietnam, Vietnam,
late at night,
while you're sleeping,
Charlie company comes creeping.

You're sitting in your foxhole.
You think you got it made.
But there lies your buddy
with a bullet in his head.

You're sitting in your foxhole,
You're thinking about your wife.
Charlie's on the move.
He's out to take your life.

They take you up in choppers
to the battle zone.
You think they're all around you.
Then you find you're all alone.[8]

Here the bitter voice of experience speaks as one who has known
the darkness, a darkness through which Charlie invisibly creeps, firing

silent bullets. Without his buddy, without his wife, even without the "they" who take him to the battle zone, the soldier is alone with Charlie. In a way, thinking of the past and of home presents a distraction that leaves the soldier vulnerable to the "backdoor man" who comes at him from behind in the dark.

But out of the darkness legends are also born. One such demonic figure is Slippery Sam, a recon Marine who creeps back after Charlie, driving him mad:

Up from the jungle of Vietnam
Came a recon Marine they called Slippery Sam.

Wore a string of ears right across his chest
Just show the Charlie he was the best.

Ten, twenty, thirty, forty, fifty, or more,
Sam kept shootin"em and addin' up the score.

Many VC died tryin' to kill this Marine,
But Slippery Sam was too damn mean.

One day, while crawlin' through the jungle trees,
Sam shot a gook right in the knees.

He pulled out his K-bar before he died
And stuck it right between his eyes.

One day on a hill they called Khe Sanh
Sam decided to have some fun.

He put fifty claymores in a line
And then watched ole Charlie blow his mind.[9]

Such brutality was certainly not unique to Vietnam. Each war carries its own brand of dark, twisted humor that laughs at what is too horrible to take seriously. The chilling irony of battlefield humor removes the speaker from the terror close at hand and imposes a momentary control that softens the shriek into uneasy laughter. In response to a *New Yorker* article by Jonathan Schell in 1967, General William Westmoreland, the commander of all allied forces in Vietnam, rationalized the need for gallows humor: "Soldiers have employed gallows humor through the ages. What paratrooper, for example, singing the drinking song 'Blood on the Risers,' really revels in the gory death of the man he is singing about? Gallows humor is, after all, merely a defense mechanism for men engaged in perilous and distasteful duties" (Westmoreland, 1980: 377). To explain the bitter humor of Vietnam, Westmoreland universalized it in the illustration of "Blood on the Risers" (sung to the tune of "The Battle Hymn of the Republic"), which was popular during World War II and Korea. Relaxed and away from the horrors of combat, Airborne soldiers released their tensions by singing of violence that accidentally befalls one of their own, a paratrooper whose chute fails to open:

He hits the ground, the sound was *splat*.
The blood, it spurted high.
His comrades, they were heard to say,
"What a pretty way to die."

He lay there rolling 'round
in the welter of his gore.
And he ain't gonna jump no more.

There was blood upon the risers,
There were brains upon the chute.
Intestines were a-danglin'
from his paratrooper suit.

They picked him up still in his chute
And poured him from his boots.
And he ain't gonna jump no more.[10]

To laugh at the chance accident, to minimize the fear that every jumper faces, is a way of keeping that fear under control, or at least within the ordered rhythm of a patriotic hymn. "He was just a rookie trooper and he surely shook with fright," the song opens, and each stanza is followed by the chorus:

Gory, gory, what a helluva way to die!
Gory, gory, what a helluva way to die!
Gory, gory, what a helluva way to die!
And he ain't gonna jump no more.

Westmoreland could certainly have found more appropriate examples of battlefield humor, Vietnam style. To shrug off in song a real danger that confronts each paratrooper is very different from chanting of one's pleasure at inflicting pain on civilians, as in the following Vietnam chant:

See the family beside the stream,
flyin' high and feelin' mean.
Pick one out and watch'em scream.
Yo, oh! Napalm, it sticks to kids.

See the hippies upon the hills
Smokin' grass and poppin' pills.
Don't they know that drugs can kill?
Yo, oh! Napalm, it sticks to kids.

See the women beside the river,
Washin' clothes and cookin' dinner.
Pick one out and watch her quiver.
Yo, oh! Napalm, it sticks to kids.

See the baby in its mother's arms,
Ain't never done no one no harm.
Barbecue baby ain't got no charm.
Yo, oh! Napalm, it sticks to kids.

See the orphans in the school,
Don't they know that they're all fools.
Burnin' flesh, it smells so cool.
Yo, oh! Napalm, it sticks to kids.

See the kiddies in the street,
Cryin' and lookin' for som' to eat.
Drop trick toys that look real neat,
Blow up in their face and make 'em all meat.

See the choppers come and go,
Oh they're flyin' much too low.
Rotor blades are not too slow.
Heads go flyin' to and fro.[11]

From his remote and mighty perspective, the demonic pilot delights in repeated demonstrations of his own power, or rather the power of American technology to unleash napalm. The napalm in these chants rarely lands on enemy troops and does little to insure victory, but falls from the skies like blazing rain, searing the civilian population below. The speaker fiendishly narrates in the first person one brutal scene after another—barbecued babies, burned orphans, and decapitated peasants—in an almost cartoonish litany.

If "to see" for the narrator is equivalent to "to kill," then why would he shift his gaze from Vietnam to America and hippies "smokin' grass and poppin' pills"? And why pose the question, "Don't they know that drugs can kill?" The answer seems obvious: to suggest that the two forms of killing are somehow to be equated. I would venture that the intended victims of this chant include the hippies, those civilians (roughly the same age as the trainee) who smoke dope, drop acid, and protest the very war in which this narrator cynically participates. The napalm chant can, in fact be read as an angry response to protesters who recited their own chants outside the White House: "Hey, hey, LBJ/ How many kids did you kill today?" This song transforms the protesters' image of the American slaughterer, the "baby killer," into the haunting voice of someone who has seen the slaughter and enjoyed it—a protest against a protest. The warrior turned baby killer gleefully details stereotypical scenes of gratuitous violence as if to scandalize a critical public.

Each stanza of this formally interesting ballad begins with the command to adopt the godly perspective of the narrator, to sit with him flying above the civilian world and "see the family," "see the hippies," "see the women," "see the baby," "see the orphans," "see the choppers." Only when the pilot descends to smell the results of his work, the "cool" smell of burning flesh, does he violate his ironic distance. And each stanza concludes with the unrhymed line, "Yo, oh! Napalm, it sticks to kids," as if such a statement were a fact that cannot be matched or balanced with a companion line in rhyme. The refrain itself, half playful exclamation ("Yo, oh!") and half cruel fact, sticks in the mind on first hearing, shocking and dissonant. But according to many who have sung or who continue to recite this call, successive performances empty the line of its horror, transforming the dark acknowledgment of collective cynicism and guilt into a grim advertising jingle. Napalm, the sign of American extravagance, luxuriously annihilates even the harmless. The narrator who wields such a weapon does not speak as the brave warrior of the previously quoted paratrooper chant, who defends himself against assault on all sides, but sounds instead like a crazed adolescent who delights in his own power, the puny guy inside the big machine.

Such sadistic pleasure rings through calls sung during and after Vietnam that have no explicit Vietnam theme. Consider the following:

A little bird with a yellow bill
Landed on my windowsill.
I coaxed him in with a piece of pie
And then I poked out his little eye.

A little bird with a yellow bill
Landed on my windowsill.
I coaxed him in with a crust of bread
And then I crushed his little head.[12]

The giving hand is the hand of destruction in this call, as it is in another napalm chant:

Shell the town and kill the people.
Drop the napalm in the square.
Do it on a Sunday morning
While they're on their way to prayer.

Aim your missiles at the schoolhouse.
See the teacher ring the bell.
See the children's smiling faces
As their schoolhouse burns to hell.

Throw some candy to the children.
Wait till they all gather round.
Then you take your M-16 now
and mow the little fuckers down.

See the Cobras in formation.
Watch them flying way down low.
See them fly into the children,
Heads are tossed to and fro.[13]

The motif of the helping hand becoming the hand of destruction grasps the irony at the center of American ambivalence toward its role in Vietnam. American soldiers sent to defend South Vietnam against outside aggressors found themselves performing aggressive acts against the people and the land they were ostensibly attempting to defend. Vietnam lore inverts an American stereotype: the friendly GI surrounded by foreign children, familiar in accounts of World War II veterans. The GI's gesture of generosity becomes the act of destruction.

That discordant mixture of affection and hatred characterizes this poignant scene legendary in the accounts of Vietnam veterans. Ser-

geant Jack Smith narrates one such account: "The GIs, when they originally get in the country, they feel friendly toward the Vietnamese and
they toss candy at the kids, but as they become hardened to it and kind
of embittered against the war, as you drive through the village you take
cans of C-rats [combat rations] . . . and you peg 'em at the kids! . . . You
try to belt them over the head. And one of the fun games was that you
dropped C-rat cans or candy off the back of your truck just so kids will
have time to dash out, grab the candy, and get run over by the next truck"
(Vietnam Veterans Against the War, 1972: 36). Stories of this sinister
game of gift-giving circulated widely. One account even appears in a
poem by Vietnam veteran Bruce Weigl, "The Last Lie":

Some guy in the miserable convoy
raised up in the back of our open truck
and threw a can of C-rations at a child
who called into the rumble for food.
He didn't toss the can, he wound up and hung it
on the child's forehead and she was stunned
backwards into the dust of our trucks.

Across the sudden angle of the road's curving
I could still see her when she rose,
waving one hand across her swollen, bleeding head,
wildly swinging her other hand
at the children who mobbed her,
who tried to take her food.

I grit my teeth to myself to remember that girl
smiling as she fought off her brothers and sisters.
She laughed as if she thought it were a joke
and the guy with me laughed
and fingered the edge of another can
like it was the seam of a baseball
until his rage ripped

again into the faces of children
who called to us for food (Weigl, 1988: 18–19).

More complicated than the simple verse of marching chants,
Weigl's poem balances the two contradictory gestures of the soldier
(offering food and inflicting pain) with the two hands of the girl (one
securing food, the other fending off brothers and sisters who threaten
to steal it from her). Trapped between these contradictory alternatives,
both the girl and the poem's speaker share the same joke: the awful ambiguity of the war.

Unlike the contemplative narrator, the "guy in the miserable convoy" perceives no ambiguity. He laughs as his pitches rip into the faces
of children. He, and not the reflective speaker of Weigl's poem, is the
narrator of napalm marching chants, his rage erupting in hideous delight at the game of war. Such dismal delight infects all battlefield humor, from legends of grunts gone crazy in combat to macabre jokes,
from accounts of ear necklaces to stories of photo albums of VC corpses
(with their grim mockery of photojournalism). Like these, napalm calls
articulate the anger and enthusiasm of the soldier in combat: two emo-
tions, many would argue, that enable the soldier to fight. In preparing
thousands to fight and kill, training programs that employ such marching chants seek to regulate the fears of young recruits through the perfectly measured recitation of sadistic verse.

Drilling also prepares units for the showy spectacle of the formal
parade, but beyond those ceremonial occasions and basic training,
marching is rare. When demanded of troops near the front, it can seem
to be a bizarre anomaly. Arthur Schrader, a World War II veteran, recounts his passage in early 1944 from Buffalo, New York, across the
Atlantic to Morocco, Algeria, and Naples. At Pozzuoli, just north of
Naples, Schrader's auxiliary unit joined three divisions to train for an
amphibious landing in southern France that was to take place in a
month. Between the purposeful practice of invasion maneuvers, troops
were put through the old basic training drill. Through the dust and heat
they drilled, first in platoons, then in companies, and ultimately in a battalion of approximately a thousand men. They grumbled to themselves,

speculating that their leaders were either sadistic or insane, but they nevertheless did as ordered. A few days before the scheduled invasion of France, the battalions gathered into three large divisions for the formal review before their commanders. As the thousands amassed into their respective battalion squares, the generals filled the reviewing stand. Schrader recalls that the battalion before his yelled

"48!"—"49!"—"50!"[14]—followed by a gloriously raucous "SOM-M-M-E SHIT!" as the battalion passed the reviewing stand. Our own officers began frantically yelling at us to keep our mouths shut, but we really didn't need to say anything. The imprecation had been yelled out for all of us, and somehow it made the miserable march back to our camp a little easier (Schrader, 1989: 157–158).

Schrader's story illustrates the contrast between parade ground and battlefield, between simulated war and the real one, between showy parades before generals and the hedgerow combat in France. Like other stories of humorous disturbances in formal parades, this one is about irreverence, not rebellion. There are many accounts among soldiers of perfectly disciplined troops who momentarily violate the solemnity of the formal parade. In all of these stories, the prank subverts the serious event with humor: A company marches out of its shoes. A company leaves its swords sticking out of the ground. When the command is given to "pass in review" one company responds, "Piss in your shoe" or "No sex for you." At the end of a formal graduation-week parade of some 2,500 midshipmen at the Naval Academy, the two midshipmen on either side of the line bringing up the rear dangled lanterns from their bayonets, and the six midshipmen framed by their lantern-clad colleagues wore letters on the backs of their uniforms spelling out "THE END." Marchers often wear "improper" uniforms (nothing under their overcoats in a winter parade, no socks, brightly colored T-shirts). The girlfriend or father of a soldier dresses in uniform and marches with the troops. The band marches the wrong way. A sword scabbard is filled with catsup; swords are cut in half; blades are removed from their handles. One group of inductees at Officer Candidate School removed their covers (caps) and used their swords as canes and did a soft-shoe before the reviewing stand. In some cases, those in command overlook these improprieties; in others they punish the group. On a couple of occasions officers have even been relieved of their commands because their companies chanted obscene calls during a formal parade.

Why are such breaches of decorum so widespread? Disdain for the brass as out of touch, as redundant, as blinded by the reflection of their own stars and bars pervades military folklore. The troops in Schrader's story question the sanity of officers who order them to drill in a way usually reserved for basic training camps, but they finally accept their orders as further evidence of routine military sadism. In protest, those gathered in formal parades symbolically assert their collective defiance of those in power. The one truly rebellious act on the parade field would be a refusal to move. That never happens. Pranks rather than mutinous acts, the acts I've cited, all occur within the unbroken stride of the orchestrated parade.

Through lore the powerless celebrate their imaginary independence of those in authority. Such accounts of defiance serve the conservative will of the institution by constraining the eruption of resistance within the bounds of a humorous narrative. Authority can tolerate a humorous story of defiance more easily than a defiant act, just as it can endure mock mutiny on the parade ground more easily than rebellion on the battlefield.

4. A Few Good Men

In training, even mock mutiny can invite rebuke, for all communication in basic training flows down the chain of command. Recruits learn quickly that to question a command invites punishment in the form of humiliation or extra PT (physical training). Veterans often psychologically recuperate from the debasement of training by explaining it as the sacrificial moment necessary to forge a new identity and demonstrate their fitness for membership. James Webb, the former secretary of the Navy, recollects the abuse and humiliation he suffered at the hands of an upperclassman during his plebe (freshman) year at the Naval Academy, an extended period of basic training. Determined to break him, the upperclassman called him to his room and ordered him to "rig three M-1 rifles" by standing at attention and propping up the rifles with his outstretched arms. As his arms began to weaken, his tormentor removed one of the rifles, then another, and finally the third. After that, he ordered Webb to do the same thing with several books, reducing the number by one each time Webb nearly collapsed. In traditional fashion, the abuser worked his way down to pencils and finally toothpicks. The next day this upperclassman paddled the freshman with a cricket bat. He offered to relent when the plebe hollered "uncle," but Webb never asked for mercy. Finally the paddle broke, and Webb ran off to the privacy of his closet where he put a laundry bag over his head and cried. The debasement becomes a moment of transformation for Webb: "I had reached a place deep inside myself, and when I got up at 5:30 the next morning and began preparing to enter that man's room yet another time, I knew something about myself that I could never have learned in any other way" (*Washingtonian*, 272–273).

Webb's insight is as vague as the details of the story itself. Nearly ten years after telling the story in print, Webb recounted it for the journalist Robert Timberg, only this time it was not a lone midshipman who paddled him but four upperclassmen, and Webb did not simply resist calling for mercy but boldly shouted between each painful blow, "Beat

Army, sir" or "Harder, sir" (Timberg, 1995: 71). Whether or not he was actually abused by one or several upperclassmen, Webb did tell the elemental truth of training in his narrative of ritual abuse: its aim is infantilization, during which an older male plays the role of spanking parent, and its atmosphere is homoerotic, during which the institutionally induced sexual desire for the younger plebe is exorcised by paddling in the zone of the forbidden attraction. In his embrace of manly abuse, Webb identified himself as a Marine's Marine.

In his psychoanalytic study of surrender and transfiguration in the Marine Corps, Chaim Shatan characterizes the recruit's submission to abuse in this way: "Far from promoting self-reliance, this aspect of basic combat training means giving up responsibility for one's own well-being and for the consequences of one's own actions. It means becoming dependent upon a higher power—becoming a boy again. The recruit has become a tool, a blind instrument to enforce another's aims and purposes" (Shatan, 1977: 605). Accounts like Webb's elevate ritual abuse to the status of defining moment. The recruit sacrifices himself and in return is rewarded by a sense of belonging. He suppresses individuality in exchange for collective potency. The telling confers a social logic on the events—an eighteen-year-old with outstretched arms straining to hold up three rifles, a youth being paddled with a cricket bat—that might elude a civilian observer.

The hazing that Webb credits for his transformation was never officially condoned at the Naval Academy. Unofficially it persisted as one of the tools of discipline employed by the few upperclass bullies who took pleasure in debasing their juniors. By the mid 1990s, military training facilities forcefully condemned such brutal physical debasement. The military has sought to eliminate the abuse while maintaining a high level of physical and psychological rigor at the hands of a harsh and exacting overseer. Training not only strives to discipline the body and the mind to automatic response; it also aims to reintegrate the trainee's personality into a rigid system of superiors and subordinates and, in turn, to win him membership in something larger than himself.

Basic training culminates in the formal acknowledgment of recruits' new identity and their integration as members of a platoon or company into the greater Air Force, Navy, Army, or Marine Corps—especially the Marine Corps, which, implacably committed to making men in the mold of the warrior ethos, has set the standard for basic training.

To work, according to this model, basic training must capitalize on notions of manhood propagated by popular culture but anachronistic in practically any institution but the military. It is a technical problem facing the drill instructors to produce blind obedience and mechanical discipline and yet convince recruits that the perfect subordination they have learned has made them men.[1] But there can be little doubt that the armed services have developed the social technology to solve that problem. The real question is why, having achieved that extraordinary success, they are so eager to disavow it. Despite the official policy that men must be made and the proof that drill sergeants can make them, propagandists for a manly tradition numbly insist that recruits must be men to begin with.

For much of our history, basic training was a categorically male realm. Women were kept out or relegated to their own training units, and men who failed to meet the standards were cast as females, branded by the drill instructor as "girls," "ladies," "faggots," "fairies," or "pussies."[2] Those scapegoats symbolically absorbed the group's weaknesses and when punished or driven out ritualistically sanctified the group's manhood. According to one young Army recruit who was cast as a scapegoat by his drill instructor and experienced weeks of taunting, the abuse reached its climax when the drill instructor singled him out to play the part of the enemy while the instructor demonstrated how to disable an opponent by tearing his cartilage. Unfortunately for the five-foot two-inch, slightly built recruit, the sergeant's administration of force resulted in severe injury and release from the Army with medical disability.[3] A classic account of the function of the scapegoat is offered by Eisenhart in his article "You Can't Hack It, Little Girl," published in the *Journal of Social Issues*. He relates a story about a fellow recruit who, while lacking the aggressive tendencies of others, was not particularly effeminate in appearance, although the drill instructor continually called him "girl" or "faggot." Each time the recruit failed to keep up with the group on a strenuous run, his fellow recruits were ordered to run circles around him. Angry that he couldn't keep up, four men from the formation tried to spur him on with kicks. Finally, platoon members had to carry him back to the base. Once back, the drill instructor ordered those who had completed the seven-mile run to perform calisthenics and the one who had failed to laugh at his suffering counterparts. Before leaving, the drill instructor exhorted his platoon: "As long as there are faggots in this outfit who can't hack it, you're all going to suffer." As he turned to go into the duty hut he sneered, "Unless you women get with the program, straighten out the queers, and grow some balls of your own, you best give your soul to God, because your ass is mine and so is your mother's on visiting day." With a roar sixty to seventy enraged men engulfed Green, knocking him to the ground and kicking and beating him.

Training is designed to teach discipline, but where is discipline when the group gangs up on a weak member? Obviously, the drill instructor is complicitous in this extreme example of boot camp violence; he sets the scene by singling out someone who can stand for everything weak, inferior, and unmanly and on whom the others can express their rage. The DI arbitrarily commands the recruits to make the grueling run followed by strenuous exercises despite their condition. He goads them into venting their anger and frustration on the scapegoat. He simply sets up the situation to insure that someone will fail. Since his recruits cannot retaliate against their tormentor, they go for the scapegoat. They have found "something deep within" themselves by finding its absence in someone else—a compensation that is purely structural and, of course, thoroughly nihilistic.

What happens in basic training to transform the tightly controlled unit into a vengeful mob? Recruits undergo a process of "deindividuation," the suspension of the self and the uncritical investment in a group identity.[4] With that group identity comes a sense of anonymity, a loss of self and of the inhibitions that allow a person to perform acts that a self-conscious individual ordinarily would not. By erasing self-awareness, military training dissolves the inclination toward self-regulation and crystallizes the willingness to be regulated by others. In wartime missions, soldiers may risk their lives for other group members and perform acts of violence toward others more willingly than they would in civilian life. Under the command of unscrupulous leaders, such as those who condoned the massacre perpetrated at My Lai in Vietnam, they may also willingly participate in atrocities. The dynamics of groupthink in basic training situations like the one elaborated above, an obvious infraction rather than normal drilling, come perilously close to the commission of violence in the name of cults (for example, lynchings). Group members undergo a dissociation that erases the prohibitions that normally exist against such violence; they perceive the victims of their rage as less than human and as deserving what they get—as scapegoats.

No one would defend such obvious atrocities. Yet some ardently maintain that deindividuation is both inevitable and desirable in soldiers preparing for the hardships, the stress, and the unexampled gruesomeness of war. The problem is that deindividuation goes hand in hand with anarchic spontaneity, a lack of planning, and sporadic bursts of energy—traits more befitting a rogue outfit than one operating in concert with other units under a shared command structure. Deindividuation stands in stark opposition to the military recognition inherent in the practice of awarding medals and commendations, distinctions that recognize individual deeds and that affirm the military as a meritocracy.

Basic training aims to produce soldiers willing to play by new rules, rules that sanction violence even if the intention is not simply assertion of might but death to the enemy. Milgram's famous study demonstrates the willingness of ordinary people to inflict extraordinary pain on others simply in deference to authority: when told by a lab-coated scientist to increase the severity of the electric shocks they believed they were administering, subjects complied, even in the face of screams from the recipients. Other studies have shown that subjects in this position experience a moral disengagement that facilitates increased tolerance for inflicting pain. The perpetrator adjusts to performing abhorrent acts by splitting into separate selves (the torturer at work, the loving father and husband at home), by dehumanizing his victims, or by blaming them:

they brought upon themselves the pain he inflicts, and his acts are merely the punishment necessary to restore order. Moral justification, palliative comparison, euphemistic labeling, displacement of responsibility, and diffusion of responsibility offer ways in which repugnant conduct is transformed into sanctioned behavior.[5] The soldier executes violence not as the aggressor but simply as the justified moral agent.

Sometimes, as in Vietnam, the process does not work; brutality is not transformed; acts of violence are not justified. In an unpopular war like the Vietnam conflict, soldiers are often unable to see their brutal acts as heroic deeds. Without having developed the conviction that the war serves some noble or at least legitimate cause, soldiers—particularly citizen soldiers—have no way to diminish the fear of battle or discount the absurdity of army life in an alien world: "The predominant emotional tone is one of all-encompassing absurdity and moral inversion. The absurdity has to do with a sense of being alien and profoundly lost, yet at the same time locked into a situation as meaningless and unreal as it is deadly . . . The men were adrift in an environment not only strange and hostile, but offering no honorable encounter, no warrior grandeur" (Lifton, 1973: 282).

In the years since Vietnam whimpered to its close, the likelihood of troops enduring long and grisly wars has drastically diminished. Without that threat, the services have had to invent even more precious causes to explain the brutalities of basic training. Macho methods are more suited to some wars than others; they generally succeed best with enlistees who have chosen to be born again as soldiers and who embrace military professionalism, not with draftees, who are characteristically reluctant to divest themselves of their civilian identities. These methods force trainees to abandon the distractions of the larger civilian world and focus attention on the smooth coordination of the unit. Yet engineering unit cohesiveness does not entail promoting intimacy among its members. Reflecting on his own boot camp experiences during the Vietnam War, Wayne Eisenhart recalled the two forces at work on young draftees: "a constant proving of adequacy and a prohibition of intimacy." Unfortunately, according to Eisenhart, "the means to prove adequacy (dominance and aggression) were not to be found in Vietnam."

The Marine Corps enthusiast and journalist Thomas Ricks followed an all-male platoon of recruits through basic training to write his book *Making the Corps*. For Ricks, the Marine Corps is "the most well-adjusted of the U.S. military services today" and "one of the few parts of the federal government that retains the deep trust of most of the American people" (Ricks, 1997: 20). Ricks only treats in passing the significant damage done to the corps' image of honesty by Oliver North and his role in the Iran-contra scandal. North's outlawry epitomizes the condition against which Ricks warns in the last section of his book: the disconnection of segments of the all-volunteer force from civil society. But Ricks himself shows symptoms of that disconnection when, parroting the Marine Corps line, he justifies the corps' growing disdain for all that is not military with the sophomoric sociological observation that "over the last thirty years ... American culture has grown more fragmented, individualistic, and consumerist." He goes on to say, "The Marines are rebels with a cause ... articulately rejecting the vague nihilism that pervades American popular culture" (22–23). Joining the Marine Corps, then, becomes an opportunity not to protect and defend the American citizenry but to repudiate it "articulately" by adopting a self-serving perspective that mistakes vanity for criticism, and by indulging the dangerous belief that all that is not gung-ho jingoism is effete nihilism. The Marine Corps offers, according to Ricks, "the straightforward and simple definition of manhood" and a training program in which "cultural indoctrination" has replaced the sadism of old (44 and 86). He is pleased to affirm that the Marine Corps has so reformed its drill instructors that these newly articulate pedagogues no longer use obscenities.

In the 1960s the folklorist George Carey decided that he would document the salty basic training marching chants he recalled from his days as a recruit a few years earlier. When he asked the public affairs officer for permission to record the chants, the officer informed him that the colorful jodies were no longer performed. Disappointed, Carey drove away. But when he pulled over to listen to a unit marching outside the gates, he heard the very chants he was told no longer existed (52). In 1989, drill instructors in the Army's military police training camp at Fort Meade told me much the same: they no longer used any sexist or off-color chants. Subsequently, however, the same soldiers admitted that although they did not perform them on short marches or runs on base, they often sang them to pass the time on longer runs that went well out of earshot. Journalists like Ricks serve the institutionally useful purpose of bringing the corps within earshot of opinion-makers and legislators. In his book on Marine Corps training, Ricks fails to acknowledge the extent to which he, a writer for the *Wall Street Journal,* influences the very thing he observes. He naively assumes that because drill instructors don't curse while a journalist is present, they don't curse at all.

Ricks's account of basic training mentions in passing that the Marine Corps trains women as well as men on Parris Island, where he followed the platoon, but theirs is not the story he wishes to tell. To admit women into *Making the Corps* would require the author to chronicle their identity transformation and laud their membership in the corps, a step that neither Ricks nor the Marine Corps is ready to take. What straightforward and simple definition does the Marine Corps communicate to women? Would Ricks take the reactionaries' articulate but misguided position that the mere presence of women, even if they are segregated, imperils the boys' acquisition of manhood? Is manhood so precarious that segregation must be supplemented by repression? If manhood is what the Marine Corps fosters, why are women there? Does becoming a Marine require that a recruit be or aspire to be a man? Given the official silence on these matters, the conclusion is inescapable. Training that sets its sights not only on instilling discipline, teamwork, and the knowledge of military skills but also on sculpting ineffable "manhood" must set itself in opposition to all that is not "manly." What boys are trained to cast away as despised is called female. The feminine names traits to be loathed, ridiculed, and exorcised.

Basic training, the first place where military values are formulated and implanted, has historically fixed on the borderline between the old life of family and friends and the new professional life, between individual concerns and institutional demands, between boyhood and manhood. When boys make mistakes they are referred to as "girls."

Although officials denounce sadistic physical abuse like the painting of caustic chemicals onto the genitals of male initiates during hell night festivities (see Chapter 5, "Sex, GIs, and Videotape"), advocates of the old system still sing its praises and initiation still reenact such primitive phallic rituals as man-affirming vestiges of a bygone era of purity and pride.

What happens when women enter this environment? Today the Air Force maintains integrated training units, each with a large group of men and a small group of women. The Navy integrates only a portion of its basic training units, but at a ratio of fifty-fifty. In its efforts to integrate women into training units, the Army constitutes integrated units with no fewer than 25 percent women. That leaves many all-male units in all branches of the service. Only the Marine Corps continues to insist on the rigid segregation of females at the battalion level. As we have noted, in the aftermath of the 1996 scandal at the Army's training base in Aberdeen, Maryland, conservatives called for the military to reinstitute segregated training, arguing that if women were not trained alongside men, such abuses would not happen. They praised the Marine Corps and conveniently ignored the fact that the women at Aberdeen were not sexually abused by male trainees but were singled out for discriminatory treatment by those charged to inculcate "responsibility."

Sexual assaults at the Air Force Academy, which invited little concern on the part of the institution's oversight board for years, became public in 2003, and they too have been met with calls for gender segregation from conservatives, many of whom hold that women shouldn't be at the academy in the first place. One of the conservative leaders is Anita Blair, the vice president and general counsel of the Independent Women's Forum, an organization founded in part to defend Clarence Thomas against charges of sexual harassment. In a friend-of-the-court brief, Blair and her colleagues defended the Virginia Military Institute's right to maintain its "code of a gentleman" by excluding women. Blair argued that VMI "may hold the key for helping us socialize and civilize young males, many of whom grow up without fathers. With its ancient honor system and old-fashioned ways of discipline, VMI's methods may help us learn again how to inculcate morality in our children."[6] Blair assumes that the American male (or rather, those males raised by a single, female parent) exists in a bestial state and must be civilized by the rigors of an all-male institution that inculcates a clearly defined concept of morality—a notion certainly less far-fetched than Blair's take on the institution of marriage. Concerned over the prospect of homosexual marriage, Blair affirms: "I wouldn't object to a law that said we're not going to give you the benefits of marriage unless you're intending to have children."[7]

Blair's reactionary views are well known. She was appointed by the Bush administration to the position of deputy assistant secretary of the Navy in July 2001 and was named executive director of the committee investigating the sexual assaults at the Air Force Academy in 2003 by Secretary of Defense Donald Rumsfeld. Owing no doubt to pressure from women's groups, the committee's chair, Tillie Fowler, a retired Republican congressional representative from Florida, replaced Blair soon after her appointment.

The military does have a problem perfecting a formula for the fair and efficient inclusion of women, but to suggest that the solution is total segregation is about as reasonable as to suggest that because some drill instructors have exhibited racism in their treatment of minority recruits under their charge, all minority recruits should be trained in segregated units, or that because some soldiers have beaten their spouses, all married soldiers should be forced to billet apart from their spouses. Critics of gender-integrated training and of the Kassebaum Committee, a committee charged in 1997 with assessing the integration of women into the armed services, have cited the informal "no talk, no touch" policy, which supposedly evolved in reaction to the fear of fraternization and sexual harassment, as evidence that the military should return to gender-segregated training. They produce anecdotal evidence that some military men have simply pretended that women do not exist and refuse not only to correct a salute (because that would mean

touching) but even to talk to women in uniform. Such an extre[...]
tion in gender-integrated units sounds more like an angry backlash [...]
a fear of unfair charges. If all males, peers and superiors alike, are in[...]
structed not to talk to females, female soldiers will undoubtedly be
hard-pressed to do their jobs, which depend on communication and
team effort. The "no talk, no touch" policy, a hyperbolic version of the
tried-and-true boys' school punishment of the misfit by "sending him
to Coventry," is not a defense against being charged with sexual discrimination but sexual discrimination itself.

Critics deplore any and all efforts by the military to integrate training as "social experiments" brought about by pressure from feminists—
pressure, these critics believe, that threatens military readiness. In their
yearning for the old days, these critics fail to acknowledge the many
gender-integrated training programs that have proven highly successful. Those officers and enlisted men who have regularly worked with
women tend to see beyond the inflammatory issue of gender. The dedication, hard work, and skills of each recruit count far more than
whether the individual is male or female. A study published in 1997 concluded that both men and women in newly integrated units perceived
gender integration as having little effect on readiness, morale, and cohesion (Harrell and Miller, 1997: 87).

Formal approval of women's entrance into combat units will signal
real integration. Chief among the arguments marshaled against the full
participation of females is the biological or evolutionary one:

Throughout all of recorded history, war has been a male occupation,
a fact that seems to be firmly rooted in the biology of our species.
Human beings, like the other primates, are products of an evolutionary process that has taken place within the context of biological and social systems that define divisions of labor and function.
Until the Neolithic period and the rise of specialized division of
function within communities, male evolution was controlled to a
great degree by fighting ability. Women, as bearers and rearers of
young and as gatherers of foodstuffs, evolved within what some
have called a more domestic and less antagonistic framework.

ı identical, selective pressures have operated
:n. In response to these pressures, the evolu-
ıefined biologically ordered gender differences
those of simple primary and secondary sexual
ı differences do indeed interact with culture to
ɡe of behavioral possibilities, competencies, and
ınge of possibilities remains constrained, however, ʋy ... ɡical substrate that characterizes each gender
(Marlow, 1983: 189).

If biology predominates so heavily, however, why would males need basic training at all? Physical training presupposes that not just some men but all men need to and can get stronger and fitter. Why not women?

The biological/evolutionary argument stigmatizes women as physically unfit for combat and relegates them to supportive roles on the home front. Because of their physiological differences, because they can become pregnant rather than impregnate, be raped rather than rape, women supposedly threaten the readiness of troops. Those who sought to maintain the policy of mandatory discharge for pregnancy in the 1970s argued that women would have greater absenteeism because of pregnancy and child care. In fact, a major Department of Defense study of lost time revealed when all causes of lost time were taken into account (including absence without leave, desertion, and substance abuse), the average man lost more time than the average woman (Holm, 1992: 303). But that strongly—one might say aggressively—held belief persists despite considerable evidence to the contrary. In a recent study conducted for the secretary of defense by the National Defense Research Institute, the presence of women shows no negative impact on readiness. In fact, in some units men reported that a more positive and professional atmosphere resulted from the incorporation of women (Harrell, and Miller, 1997: 34). Pregnancy may indeed affect whether or not a female soldier can be deployed. In sheer numbers, however, the military has more male single parents in the ranks than female ones.

The most important measure of fitness for combat, according to proponents of this line of argument, is upper-body strength. Because women on average tend to weigh less and have less muscle mass than men, they should therefore be excluded as a class from combat jobs. Assuming that nature has endowed all males with superior upper-body strength, which it has not, and deprived all women of it, which it also has not, wouldn't the fact that weaponry has been miniaturized argue that women may in fact be as skilled at combat today as men were in other wars? The fact that some women are strong and some men weak argues against a uniform standard based simply on gender. A strong, athletic, six-foot-tall woman will outperform a slim, five-foot-tall man who lacks substantially developed muscle mass. In some areas of combat, the smaller size and greater agility of women would be an advantage. Inside a tank or a submarine, for example, a small, quick female soldier might be more effective than a thickly muscled linebacker.

To advance such counterarguments against the misogynists is not to try to impose women on hostile men to prove an ideological point. Despite the fact that the "average" woman's upper-body strength will make it more difficult for her to haul heavy loads than for the "average" male, an impressive majority of Army, Navy, and Marine Corps men in newly integrated units favor the admission of women into their career field.[8] In situations that require upper-body strength (hauling heavy equipment and supplies), superiors usually assign heavy work to teams, and women have had no problem. Women have advocated specific physical requirements for specific occupations rather than the crude application of a mythical average to all. Such standards would provide a more effective measure of both women and men by replacing the outmoded hand-to-hand model of combat cherished by many rearguarders and institutionalized by current physical standards.

Even though the Marine Corps has officially made "the crucible" the last major qualifying event of basic training for both men and women, General Charles Krulak, the head of the Marine Corps until 1999, insisted on referring to women as "combat extenders" in a interview soon after his retirement.[9] He admitted that some women (the example he used was the U.S. world champion women's soccer team) could certainly meet the physical requirements for combat. Yet because the military requires all males, even the weak ones, potentially to serve in combat, he objected to women being selected on the basis of their performance: "If you allow certain women who can [meet the physical requirements], how do you justify that to the male who might not be as strong?" For Krulak, the prospect of how a man would feel to know that a woman was stronger justifies the exclusion of women. Why not take the few good women along with the few good men and leave those less qualified to the civilian jobs? The only answer Krulak offered is that preventing hurt feelings in men is more important than assembling the fittest and most effective combat force.

Krulak's concern for men's feelings is the flip side of anxiety over men's libido. Women, it seems, are a dangerous distraction. Critics argue that men fight better without women around and that when the fighting stops, the sexualization of women so dominates male thinking that men can never develop professional relationships with them. Having sentimentalized over the competency question, Krulak adapted the defense to another angle: women's parents, he claimed, wouldn't want to see them go off to combat. Few parents relish the sight of their daughter or their son going off to combat; most approach the moment with a combination of pride and dread.

All the arguments of this sort add up to one thing: women are not men. "While undoubtedly a number of women possess physical skills and abilities that do overlap into the normal male distribution, physical competence alone does not demarcate the successful combat soldier or combat group. The combat soldier has historically defined himself in terms of masculinity" (Marlow, 1983: 191).

Even when women demonstrate their strength, their stamina, and their battlefield expertise, as they do in field training exercises, detractors, pressed to the point where they confess their religious dread, have recourse to an argument drawn from Leviticus: women are unfit to serve in combat because they menstruate. Women in premodern societies were and are separated from the community during menstruation because of the superstitious fear that their potent, magical blood might poison those around them or damage crops and wildlife. Because they are polluted, the argument goes, women need more sanitary conditions than men. If not kept safely in the world of noncombatants, they risk "infecting" the close quarters they share with men.

Why is the thought of the natural flow of menstrual blood on the battlefield so disturbing? Perhaps because it suggests the mixing of masculine blood with the prenatal blood of the mother. If soldiers can only attest to their manhood in battle, according to the myth propagated by the Marine Corps and its admirers, then mixing masculine blood spent in proving one's manhood with feminine blood has the force of breaking a taboo. No wonder the word *infection* is invoked to explain why women aren't fit for combat: according to former Speaker of the House Newt Gingrich, who discussed this subject in a lecture as part of his broadly disseminated course, women are unfit for combat because every thirty days they get "infections." In a recent posting on the Internet much the same sentiment was ventured: "Having infected male-created institutions—always by government compulsion, which is the only way otherwise rationally segregated institutions can be desegregated—the standards of male-created institutions must be eviscerated to accommodate the smaller, slower, and weaker females." The notion of women as polluted enjoys a rich history in soldier lore. Sailors in World War II told stories of tossing WACs' and WAVEs' Kotex and Tampax overboard as pranks. A few women in gender-integrated field exercises have flouted the taboo by using sanitary pads as padding for the shoulder straps of their packs and by proudly carrying tampons in the bands of their helmets.

As inconsistent as they are, the array of objections to women's full participation in the military can be distilled to the implicit claim that the armed services ought to be permitted to discriminate in order to maintain its special culture. Because military personnel may risk their lives to perform their tasks, the military must be granted exemption from the legally mandated equal rights that apply to all aspects of civilian life, even in other lines of work that call for members to risk their lives in the line of duty, such as policing and firefighting. Proponents of this argument set the military apart, exempt from social demands for transformation, free to operate with a different set of rules.

But the culture is changing. No reactionary force can hold back the technological tide that has swept away so many conceptions of war and so many traditional ways of soldiering. As more and more women fill the ranks at all levels and in all branches, they increase the pressure on the military to train them alongside men. Currently the military either integrates the training of women with the training of men or runs mirror training programs for women. In the Marine Corps' new field training program, women and men are segregated into separate platoons, yet they endure the same rugged training together, a grueling seventeen-day program required of all non-infantry Marines going through boot camp, including demanding exercises in which trainees spend their days and nights bivouacking in the field. Early reviews indicate that women have performed as well as men, that they have learned what it is to be a grunt. But there's the crux of the problem: training allows women to learn what it feels like to be a grunt but never allows them to be one. Can't we just put feelings aside and arrange training so that every recruit can be the best that he or she can be?

The proof of any system of training is its success rate. One third of those enlisted by the military fail to make it through their first tour of duty, wasting one taxpayer dollar in three spent on basic training. Either recruiters are to be faulted, or the system of basic training is deeply flawed. Reforming training requires upgrading the professionalism of the instructors. The Kassebaum Committee concluded that the military needs to screen those they select to serve as trainers more thoroughly, through psychological testing, checks of family stability, and a review of prior records, including law enforcement and security checks. The committee also recommended that tight controls be put in place to insure that these background checks are done in a professional manner and are not merely an exercise in checking off boxes by superiors. They advised that background checks for disciplinary action include the entire service record of the candidate and that all trainers receive more extensive training. Except in the Marine Corps, noncommissioned officers have typically not viewed serving as a drill instructor as a career-enhancing position. In an all-volunteer force, skillful noncommissioned officers serve as role models for those under their charge and determine in part how long a recruit will stay in the military. The performance of recruiters must be evaluated not simply by the number of recruits they enlist but by the success rate of those they bring in the door.

To insure an efficient and effective fighting force, all branches of the military must subject basic training programs, their chief instruments of transformation, to needed changes. Practices must be assessed according to how well they prepare gender-integrated and racially mixed troops to work as effective, dedicated teams. To insist stubbornly on tradition for tradition's sake will guarantee a military that grows increasingly out of touch with the populace it exists to protect.

5. Sex, GIs, and Videotape

Twenty-three Canadian Airborne soldiers were lined up in a row, made to drink beer until they were drunk and to chew soft bread rolled up with chewing tobacco. The first to vomit was required to urinate on the masticated wad and put it back in his mouth before he passed it on to the next soldier. One soldier struggled to perform pushups in excrement while another urinated on him. A couple of soldiers smeared feces on the face of the one black soldier in the unit, a practice known within the Canadian military as "bearding." He was also led around by a leash while he crawled on all fours. On his back in camouflage paint was inscribed "I love the KKK." An onlooker shouted, "We're not racist—we just don't want niggers in the Airborne." Soldiers urinated and defecated on one another, simulated sodomy and masturbation, all in broad daylight, all under the watchful eyes of officers and in front of the lens of a video recorder.

This initiation ritual took place in August 1992 at Canadian Forces Base Petawawa, Ontario, home to the elite forces of the Canadian Airborne Regiment, a unit later tainted by the scandal surrounding the death of a sixteen-year-old Somali youth in the unit's custody while the regiment served as United Nations peacekeepers in Somalia in 1993. For that crime, eight soldiers were tried, and a ninth, who attempted suicide, was judged unfit to stand trial. Some were cleared of charges, others rebuked with a conviction of negligence. Only one was found guilty of manslaughter and torture; he was given a five-year sentence. The commanding officer was cleared of all charges. In March 1995, this regiment, despite its distinguished twenty-seven-year history and its reputation as a crack parachute unit, was officially disbanded and its seven hundred soldiers dispersed to other units. Given the international attention paid to the atrocity in Somalia, it is something of a curiosity that what finally precipitated the dramatic dissolution of the regiment by the minister of defense was not a war crime committed in the name of nation-building but an amateur videotape of barracks high jinks. That tape, which graphically recorded the studied outrage of the Airborne initiation ritual, was turned over to a Canadian TV station in January 1995 by a repentant former member of the unit. It scandalized the nation, galvanized the news media, and attracted the hungry eyes of topic scouts for television talk shows. Eventually the publicity forced the government to act.

How is it that publicizing an initiation rite, which twenty years earlier would never have interested reporters, let alone concerned a prime minister, could in the 1990s ruin a regiment? Was it the shame of Airborne soldiers pictured in degraded poses? Was it the obvious racism of singling out the one black initiate for a different form of humiliation (hardly likely, given the evident racism of the Somali incident)? Or was it the seemingly unignorable evidence that a military unit whose barracks antics included having recruits urinate on one another had willfully abandoned all semblance of military discipline?

Since the establishment of the British Commandos and the first U.S. Army Special Forces in World War II, military commanders have questioned the governability of such a corps-within-the-corps, but they have never doubted the appeal of elite forces to highly motivated soldiers. Even during periods of universal conscription, volunteers have filled the ranks of these elite units. Officers and enlisted men have regularly opted to leave the ranks to join units of select Army Rangers, Marine Green Berets, and Navy Seals and have submitted themselves to a training regimen generally more rugged and demanding than anything they endured in basic training. Trainers deprive them of sleep, push them to the point of extreme exhaustion, and simulate as closely as possible the psychological and physical stress of combat. On occasion, the theater of training too closely approximates reality, as it did in a U.S. field exercise in which trainees died of hypothermia when forced to spend long periods trekking through cold swampwater. This catastrophe occurred despite intensive preparation to prevent overexposure and despite the application of strict guidelines. It dramatizes a fundamental and perhaps inevitable incompatibility between the requirement to instill a level of esprit de corps immune to self-doubt or outside challenge and the need for disciplined adherence to established norms and tactical flexibility in the face of changing circumstances.

To survive the rigorous training that these units undergo and to be distinguished by the Airborne beret is not only to be recognized as singularly tough and formidably lethal; it is to be prepared for a certain kind of warfare: the kind of fighting we've witnessed in Somalia and Afghanistan rather than that carried out by infantry massed for frontal assault on fixed positions or ships and planes strategically deployed in battle array. In the regular army, soldiers learn conventional methods of combat designed to destroy a uniformed enemy; in special forces training camps, soldiers learn unconventional methods that they may someday employ in small groups behind enemy lines, with limited contact with headquarters. If the success of the regular infantry is judged by territory taken or enemy subdued, the operative model for branches of special forces such as the Seals is covert movement and unforeseen and undetected fatal action. The modern infantryman may never see the face of the enemy, because he kills at great distance. Elite forces train to get closer. Because modern militaries have prepared elite forces to fight wars of intimate violence and schooled their regulars to wage wars of blinking computer screens and mechanical calibrations, they face the continual challenge of keeping the special forces under the command of the regular army. Special forces units can be counted on to execute the riskiest endeavors, yet the risk is that their unique élan will render them a renegade force. A special unit out of control—the rogue soldier, platoon, or regiment—is a frightening prospect either on the battlefield or in the barracks.

Rarely is the opposition quite so clear-cut, however. With U.S. Special Forces and the Canadian commando units, it is the considerable complications of their missions that produce a dangerous tension. The Canadian commando units are trained to wage aggressive behind-the-lines assaults on the enemy but were sent to Somalia to participate in urban pacification. They had been introduced to some cultural nuances and trained in basic communication skills which were expected to enable them to survive in enemy territory: to converse with civilians and interrogate prisoners. But in Somalia there were no lines, either of the enemy or of the friendly forces. And the training in guerrilla warfare was to be applied to the emergent but still vaguely defined post–cold war goal of nation-building—a goal abandoned by George W. Bush's administration as soon as it took office. In Somalia, the good intentions of policymakers had nothing to do with the capability of the men on the ground to transform themselves into a Peace Corps in khaki and fulfill those intentions. The Canadian commando units lacked adequate training to perform as an effective military welfare agency or even to maintain the civil peace—a job that more appropriately demanded the skills of military police. Frustration mounted; on the night the soldiers beat the Somali youth to death, discipline dissolved. When there was the clear need to impose restraint, no authority emerged to do so.

Given Bush's abandonment of a commitment to nation-building early in his term and his about-face in Afghanistan and Iraq, it is challenging to imagine how elite units could be trained to prevent the occurrence of such breakdowns in the future. The atrocity in Somalia raises the question of how to instill, maintain, and effectively apply an understanding of other cultures. But as I have said, the more urgent question raised by the controversy surrounding initiation rites is how to understand "our" (and I definitely want to extract the full measure of tentativeness from those quotation marks) own culture—the way it is continually instilled, maintained, and applied.

The Canadian Airborne could survive an egregious failure of command in Somalia but couldn't survive the other scandal, which involved only men's excrement and semen, not a man's lifeblood. If the former was a consequence of imprecise policy and orders, the latter was the consequence of extreme, indeed ritualized, exactness. During the initiation, officers clearly condoned an event that occurred in front of them on the base in broad daylight. None of the detailed practices of the initiation were novel; such practices were traditional to the regiment and had deep roots in other masculine initiation ceremonies, about which the individuals involved had no direct knowledge. It was certainly a passing incident, but unlike after-the-fact reports on the murder in the camp in Somalia, the scenes of the Airborne initiation played and replayed on news reports broadcast into Canadian homes. The camera seems to have been introduced as a way to prove that the unit had gotten the rite right. In the process, the indifferent camera eye transformed a ritual into a semipublic event. The instrument of ritual certification became the tool for removing authority from the ritual by breaking down the crucial partitions between an exoteric civilian order and an esoteric military order. To put it another way, the Airborne's excrement was smeared onto the nightly news in the only way it could be, not as initiation but as *news*. As that occurred, the videotape permanently preserved the pollution that the initiation ritual was designed symbolically to expunge. We might say that the fact the ritual was filmed was itself the physical evidence of its misfire as a symbolic action. That physical evidence reproduced and propagated, before a mass audience, the manifest distinctions and abject differences that the initiation had invoked in order to heal them and channel the individuals' disparate energies into the service of the group. The videotape transformed invisible rite into visible behavior and revealed to excluded women—the vast, undifferentiated, feminized public—the secret acts of intimacy between men, acts that can lose their potency only in the process of indiscriminate revelation.

Modern initiation rites like the one enacted by the Canadian Special Forces unit resemble the male puberty rites of tribal cultures.[1] Pubescent boys are separated from the women and children of their community. After separation from their families, youths enter what Arnold Van Gennep in his classic work, *The Rites of Passage*, refers to as a "liminal" or threshold period. They are stripped of their former possessions (sometimes even of the hair on their bodies), infantilized, and reduced to an egalitarian servitude in which obedience and submission facilitate the formation of their new identity. They are deprived of sleep and subjected to physical pain and humiliation—an ordeal that delivers them into manhood. Supplementing their birth from the bodies of women, the initiation enacts a second birth, which takes place in exclusive male quarters under the total control of men who have passed this way before. According to Victor Turner, author of *The Ritual Process*,

> The neophyte in liminality must be a tabula rasa, a blank slate, on which is inscribed the knowledge and wisdom of the group, in those respects that pertain to the new status. The ordeals and humilia-

tions, often of a grossly physiological character, to which neophytes are submitted represent partly a destruction of the previous status and partly a tempering of their essence in order to prepare them to cope with their new responsibilities and restrain them in advance from abusing their new privileges. They have to be shown that in themselves they are clay or dust, mere matter, whose form is impressed upon them by society (Turner, 1969: 103).

Or as the former head of drill instructors at Parris Island put it:

Training was designed at Parris Island to break the umbilical cord between military and civilian life, designed to break him down to his fundamental self, take away all that he possesses and get him started out in the way that you want him to be. Issue him all new clothes, cut his hair, send his possessions home and tell him he doesn't know a damn thing, that he's the sorriest thing you've ever seen, but with my help you're going to be worthwhile again.[2]

It could be argued that all indoctrination into unquestioning group loyalty or institutional fealty incorporates such disciplinary techniques. Certainly military training programmatically recapitulates the transformation that Turner analyzes. The single difference between the contemporary military and, say, the Spanish Jesuits is that in practice, when a noncom or an officer sets about breaking the recruit down to his "fundamental self," he often strips him of his clothes to expose not just his abject selfhood but also his flaccid manhood. For example, in the 1970s, upperclassmen at the Royal Military College in Kingston, Ontario, ordered first-year students to stand naked at attention outside of their rooms while a record player down the hall played love songs.[3] The first cadet to achieve an erection on the sweet promise of Donna Summer (or Lionel Ritchie) was awarded a prize and the rest of the company was permitted to return to their beds and their own discretion about whether or not to continue the drill.[4]

Perhaps discipline crosses over into initiation with the emergence of rites of incorporation or ingestion. Like their tribal counterparts, modern male initiations into an elite group characteristically involve ingestion of substances that symbolize taking on a masculine spirit. Initiates often consume ample quantities of alcohol. But substitutes are permitted. In recent military initiations, U.S. soldiers have been forced to drink Tabasco sauce and, in an especially piquant variation, to eat an apple protruding from another soldier's buttocks. In the paramilitary world of Canadian ice hockey, initiates used to pass around a doughnut, which each young blade was expected to masturbate into and on. The last person to ejaculate was required to eat the doughnut. That sacrament of group solidarity recalls the requirement set by a hockey team that each new member ejaculate into a shared glass, the feckless last comer being required to spread a cracker with the mixed semen and chow down on what is referred to as the "ookie cookie."

Some perspective on such eroticization of the relations between aspirants to inclusion in the group is provided by Gilbert Herdt, who in his work on Melanesian culture investigates the ways in which Sambia warriors initiate each generation of boys by ritual and by homosexual "insemination." Boys ingest, through fellatio, the semen of unmarried men so that they might be nourished and mature into warriors. The milk from their mothers' breasts provided the nourishment they needed to grow from babies into boys. The semen from mature men provides the nourishment they need to develop into virile and ultimately heterosexual warriors. The Sambia boy who enters initiation rids himself of the contamination he carries with him from his mother. His body hair is removed, and the top layer of his skin is exfoliated in an effort to discard external female pollution. He is bled and purged through vomiting and defecation, to eradicate traces of his mother's blood, which is believed to slow his growth. The boy is painted with a yellow pigment mixed with cassowary feces and taken to a place that the men call a "birth house"(Herdt, 1994: 33).

At Australia's West Point, Duntroon, it was a tradition that one night during the year upperclassmen would rouse first-year students from their sleep, order them to strip, and herd them into bathrooms, from which they would be taken out one by one to run a gauntlet. The second- and third-year students would slap freshmen with towels, belts, and suspenders and force them to climb a ladder while fire hoses sprayed their genitals. They would demand that initiates perform songs and dances and attempt to answer impossible questions. In some years each victim would be seated in turn on a block of ice at the top of a slide. After repeating a loyalty oath, he would be dubbed a member of the corps with a sword, which in later years was electrified to deliver a shock to the shivering rookie astride the block of ice. After the administration of the shock, the ice block and the cadet were shoved down the slide into a vat of foul-smelling liquids. In some years, broken bottles were added to the vat, necessitating treatment for minor—in some years major—lacerations. With only small variations from year to year, this ritual continued until 1986, when Duntroon merged into a triservice academy incorporating Navy and Air Force cadets.[5]

Like the adolescent male rites of passage documented by Emile Durkheim (1965), Mircea Eliade (1965), and Bruno Bettelheim (1955), this tradition ran the initiate through a series of ordeals, in which he often suffered some pain to the genitals, symbolically died, and was born again into the world of men. In a 1969 article in his alma mater's quarterly magazine, the *R.M.C. Journal,* a former graduate made his experience by setting it in the context (both literally and figuratively) of another, more ancient rite:

> The end of the week came. The great event arrived, the initiation. We welcomed this as a aboriginal boy would welcome the "man" ritual. It was in the evening. . . . We were required to disrobe. We were led blindfolded to the sacred corroboree grounds. Females were forbidden to the area, although rumour had it that female eyes sparkled on the slopes of [Mt.] Pleasant.
>
> Questions were asked but answers were gagged. Songs had to be sung, but oiled waste plugged the notes. Finally, one had to slide down the symbolic slippery dip. A . . . bath at the bottom consummated our declining status. And all punctuated with wet and knotted towels on our naked torsos.
>
> Then it was over. How wonderful, we were now gentlemen cadets of the Royal Military College "de facto" and "de jure."

Around us were the exalted ones, shaking hands, telling us that we were now of the order (JHT, 1969: 50).

Although the Duntroon initiation did not survive the merger, new rituals evolved to replace it. In 1992, articles in the Australian press on the abuse of first-year cadets prompted an inquiry into allegations that freshmen had been made to lick cream off a senior cadet's underpants, to simulate sex, and to suffer a "woofering," in which a cadet was hand-cuffed and had his head covered, his pants pulled down, and a vacuum cleaner applied to his genitals.[34] The freshmen who endured these abuses were typically accused by upperclassmen of some trumped-up charge and convicted in a kangaroo court (in a "morals trial," if the victim had been friendly with a female cadet, or in an "atrocity trial" if he had associated with a girl others regarded as unattractive). The young male cadets received their punishment before an excited audience of upperclassmen. In some instances they were ordered to perform "RVOs" (reverse Vienna oysters), in which one freshman would lie on his back while the other, atop him in missionary position, performed pushups to the cheers of an aroused crowd.

Ceremonies that mix the homoerotic and the humiliating enjoy a long history in male groups and, despite official interdictions, have persisted long past the official integration of women into the military. They facilitate the assertion of collective masculinity and at once celebrate and restrain homoerotic enthusiasm. Because much of the point is to cast out the female or to recast it in male terms, there is no part for mere women to play. When women do attempt to participate in military initiation rituals, they are often pushed aside.

On February 22, 1995, I arrived at the Toronto airport as a guest of *The Shirley Show*, a daytime television talk show on which I had agreed to appear and discuss my research on military ritual. The show's limo driver, a stocky, fortyish man with a thick accent, picked me up and, with no coaxing, volunteered his opinion of the upcoming show on the ride to the hotel. "These soldiers think it's all television. They go to Somalia; they go to Serbia; they don't know what they're doing. How could they? People in those countries are fighting for their land, for their little piece of it. These Canadian soldiers are acting like they're in some TV show about a war." He wondered how these soldiers would act as peacekeepers in his homeland, Yugoslavia. According to him, no course of discipline or training could compensate for the fact that war is a crazy, chaotic spectacle to all who are not fighting desperately to save their country. This taxi driver's wisdom seemed worth considering as I approached my own equivalent of a baptism by fire.

In the hotel lobby that evening I met three other guests of *The Shirley Show*, also waiting to be taxied to the studio: Justin Chenier; his mother, Elise Chenier; and Lyne Sylvestre, all French Canadians. Justin Chenier had suffered hazing at Wainwright, an infantry base in Alberta, a few months earlier and had appeared on other television shows, where he had testified about the mistreatment he suffered. His mother, a small, permed blonde in her forties, had taken time off her work at a male prison in Ontario to come to Toronto in support of her son. While waiting in the lobby of the Royal York Hotel, she commiserated with Lyne Sylvestre, the wife of a member of the Canadian Mounted Police and a potter who taught ceramics classes. Sylvestre blamed the military for condoning beatings and abuse in the name of training. Her son, Jonathan, had not been suicidal when he joined the infantry, she insisted, but something in his training radically changed him, and he was found one morning hanging in the doorway at the entrance to his barracks. She was persistent in petitioning the army for answers and airing her suspicions on television. The mothers fell into immediate sympathy, holding in check their anger and their sadness at what military training had done to their sons.

What struck me about our group was that one man had been invited to recount his victimization and three women, myself included, had been called to comment on such victimization in all-male units within closed institutions. Like the clips from the Airborne initiation which introduced the show, Chenier's humiliation at the hands of other men had become the sensational subject for a show whose audience was largely female—a ritual in its own right to be consumed, if not ingested, by the television viewers.

If our waiting room at the studio was commissioned to relate the feminine view of this subject, the room next door held those gathered to represent the male view: Scott Taylor, a former infantry soldier and editor of *Esprit de Corps;* Mike (the station never disclosed his last name), who had been invited to defend hazing in the military; and two Airborne wives who had organized a group to oppose the disbanding of their husbands' regiment. In exchange for writing a letter of protest to the prime minister, the Airborne wives sent supporters maroon ribbons (the color of the berets worn by Airborne soldiers) to wear in solidarity with the dishonored unit, as if its members were also to be seen as victims. The wives had won extensive media coverage to promote their cause, but they found it much more difficult to rally demonstrators. On the day they gathered supporters to protest outside Parliament, only twenty people raised their voices in faint opposition. And they had even run out of maroon ribbon; having bought all that Petawawa had to sell, they purchased every available yard of maroon ribbon in Ottawa. They had ordered new stock from a ribbon supplier, but there wasn't enough maroon ribbon in Canada to save the doomed Airborne.

When we waited our turns with the makeup lady and the hairdresser, one of the wives came to our waiting room and introduced herself. She and I had talked on the phone, so I was eager to meet this young, dedicated army wife who had suddenly become a leader in her community. She was there to speak nationally for all seven hundred members of the Airborne, whose commanders had ordered their silence. She and her companion were speaking up on behalf of their husbands because they felt it was unjust for these men to be stripped of their identity as Canadian Airborne soldiers because of the actions of a few. Although they did not explicitly condone the activities captured on the videotape, they maintained that the military had the right to set its own standard of acceptable conduct in training, which could not be judged according to civilian standards. Although their husbands had participated in initiation ceremonies of their own, these soldiers, according to their wives, had not crossed the line of acceptable behavior.

In a previous conversation I had talked with one of the politically active wives about her campaign and its results. "I trust that the Airborne soldiers are pretty pleased with all the effort you've expended on their cause," I said. "Yes," she replied. "Maybe they'll make me an honorary member before this is over." "As long as they don't put you through an initiation," I joked. "I wouldn't mind if that initiation was the one my husband had. I would do what he had to do," she told me.

Her husband's initiation involved a ritual known to Canadian and British soldiers as the "Zulu Warrior." Naked from the waist down, a soldier stands on an overturned trashcan or on a table while the end of a four-foot strip of toilet paper is tucked into his anus. When the initiate lifts a pitcher of beer to his lips, a soldier lights the other end of the toilet paper. The trick is to down the beer before the flaming paper singes your buttocks. Sometimes two initiates, joined anus to anus by a strip of toilet paper, compete to see who can keep the flame from licking his rear by quickly downing their pitchers.

The night of the show the wife had little time to expound on military rituals. We had only chatted for a few minutes when the producer asked her to leave. When she had, he slipped back in to apologize, saying that she shouldn't have come into our room. No one but the management objected to her presence. Motivated by the desire to prevent any differences from arising until they could explode before the camera, or by the fear that we would discover something that might unite rather than polarize us, or by the realization that past prefilming antagonisms had erupted into chaos, the crew insisted on segregating us from taxi ride to taping.

But this seemed to most of us an artificial decision clearly meant to heighten tension and invent antagonisms. Justin Chenier, for example, admired Scott Taylor, whom the show had grouped among the apologists for the military, with boyish enthusiasm. Taylor, a ruggedly handsome soldier's soldier, had appealed to enlisted servicemen with his magazine's crusade to expose the misdeeds of those in positions of power within the military and with his healthy disdain for officers and politicians motivated more by concerns for reelection and promotion than by the welfare of those who served under them. Taylor was also no stranger to Lyne Sylvestre, having offered her useful advice in her investigation of the circumstances of her son's death. Although grouped with the apologists, Taylor was actually critical of the initiation rite, because officers never intervened. And he did not agree with the rationalization of the Airborne wives, who insisted that if their husbands spoke up for themselves and their unit, they would be court-martialed and imprisoned. "If they cared about their unit, they wouldn't let a woman do all their fighting for them," insisted Taylor after the show.

As show time neared, the producer paid a visit. "I'm here to pump you up," he said. "For this show to work, we need to have quick exchange. Exchange is the key. Start talking early and keep talking. Don't wait to be asked, just interrupt and jump in. As soon as you start talking you'll relax." Soon after he left, the tall, slender, blond Shirley arrived. Unlike the coy Geraldo, the confessional Oprah, and the provocative Rickie, Shirley conveyed the friendly suburban look of a regular at the country club. For each of us she had a piece of advice. Chenier was to have the floor first and to tell of the abuses he had suffered at Wainwright. "You can't just tell what happened—you've got to communicate it with emotion," she said. "There are people next door who will defend this hazing as necessary. You have to answer them." At that point Chenier's mother broke in: "That makes me mad! Where were they when my son called me and told me he had a rope and was going to hang himself? Where were they?" "I want you to say that on the program *just as you said it to me*," Shirley replied, beaming approvingly. She saved her last directive for me. "I know you do research on this topic, but you need to understand that I have to go up against Oprah and Geraldo, and you can't use any big words—my audience will not stay with you. You can't say *homoerotic*, for example—they won't understand."

We could hear the shouts of Shirley's studio audience as we entered the stage from behind the pink backdrop. A white-haired man with a ponytail was leading the audience in cheers, having them practice yells of enthusiasm and shouts of disapproval, priming them for the gladiatorial contest the crew clearly hoped to encourage. The crew had grouped military supporters in the lower half of the audience with Airborne wives in their maroon sweatshirts, blue jeans, and teased hair. College-aged civilians filled the upper half.

As Shirley promised, Justin Chenier was allowed a few uninterrupted minutes to tell of his trials at Wainwright and the humiliations he had endured. He described the nighttime assaults by fellow recruits, who take out their frustrations on those they view as weak by punching and kicking them as they attempt to sleep in their bunks. Defenders of these "blanket parties" claim that such harassment serves to weed out those they regard as unfit for their unit. In such a way, those on the bottom rung of the hierarchy create an even lower rung, one they reserve for those they judge unfit for their corps, for their Airborne, or for their navy. If a recruit cannot take the punishment from his peers, defenders of the practice argue, how will he be able to withstand the rigors of war? According to Chenier, an officer gathered the new recruits together when they arrived and encouraged them to take such forms of clandestine punishment upon themselves. In such a way the company selects one member it deems weak and invests its collective weakness in him, until he is eventually expelled, an act that confirms the group's strength and tenacity.

In addition to the blanket parties, Chenier suffered the indignity of having an officer order him to pull his pants down to his ankles and smile as he stood at attention, while the officer photographed him and made derisive comments about the size of his penis. But the most disturbing incident took place while Chenier was sleeping. Fellow recruits poured a mysterious concoction over his head, a liquid they later identified as a mixture of urine, saliva, and semen. When he learned this, Chenier collapsed and spent the next three weeks in a psychiatric care unit. When he asked for help from the military, superiors simply advised him to "soldier on and be a man." *"be a man" a solution to all problems.*

During a pause, the producer ran over and coached us to jump in when the filming began again. And most did; aggressively and passionately, they interrupted each other, either condemning the brutality of the initiation clips broadcast at the beginning of the show or defending the men of the Canadian Airborne. The heated argument soon escalated to a shouting match. But the free-for-all was not restricted to the invited guests; audience members interrupted with cheers of support and jeers of disapproval, as if they wanted to jump into the angry exchange. They called Chenier a "wimp," and he referred to them as "an-

73

imals." When Elise Chenier discussed the humiliation her son had suffered, she criticized the military's hypocritical rhetoric of characterizing itself as a family. "If you were a father, would you sexually assault your child?" she asked. "Some do!" yelled one of the Airborne wives in the audience.

A large woman shouted, and Shirley invited her to the microphone. "If I'm going to be in the trenches with somebody," she said, "I would not want their urine and their crap swiped all over me. I would not want to be belittled to bond." The audience laughed, and soldier Mike responded, "You've got to eat, sleep, shit in this little hole for three weeks. You're going to be rolling around in it anyway; you got to get used to it." A pale young man stood up at the back of the audience; with an inflamed and contorted face, he shouted at one of the Airborne wives onstage, "I haven't heard anything about your husband and those other scumbags weeding those twenty-five bastards out. I would be willing to pick up a gun and kill any son of a bitch who would do that to another human being. That is inhuman. Why didn't the other seven hundred weed out these twenty-five?" His condemnation of Airborne brutality was matched only by his own brutishness. Whether he was genuinely outraged or staging his anger, his outburst contributed to the carnival atmosphere. The audience shouted insults at the guests, and the guests responded in kind.

An angry Airborne wife yelled with a fierce look, "If ya can't handle someone throwing semen on your face, how can you handle someone shooting at you?" Trying to paraphrase Chenier's position, Shirley explained, "Justin left the armed forces. He believed . . . He believed he got no support. He believed that he was treated as an outsider after that, as if *he* had done something wrong. And he believed that *he* was victimized and then that the victim was further victimized, because basically in the army they said, 'Be a man, shut up about this and we don't want to hear about it.'"

The host's attempt to construct a coherent narrative of Chenier's experiences centered on the word *victim*, the term on which all talk shows turn and on which they cash in. Chenier's story was chosen to lead because it was a story of victimization in a medium that merchandises victims. Why did *The Shirley Show* feature the unit's initiation rather than its murder? I suppose it was because the tape embraces sensational episodes involving strange, quasi-sexual practices and racism as the ingredients of a good talk show.

Like religious revival meetings, talk shows ignite the fire of personal testimony, but unlike revival meetings, they offer no catharsis. They trade on the exposure and humiliation of victims, as do initiations, yet they offer no incorporation of the Other that would symbolically ratify the existence of the group with a single identity and purpose. Instead, they fuel an insatiable desire for more and more revelation and bank on a viewing audience keen to be entertained by the misfortunes and private scandals of others. To me, it became perfectly clear that *The Shirley Show* provided a confirmation rather than a critique of the military ethos that was under attack by being subject to such public exposure. If the military could claim that its hazing weeded out the weak and its initiations welded together the strong, it was difficult to see what claims could be made for the talk show, which similarly required victims but aroused its audience by inducing identification with the victims in a kind of imaginary bonding. Although inherently antagonistic to the claims of military authority to police its own professional practice, *The Shirley Show* clearly adhered to the ethos of ritual initiation to animate its scenario of mass participation. Whereas the disputes onstage appeared at times to teeter on the brink of anarchy, the chaos was choreographed, subject to its own kind of mystified discipline. If in the heat of exchange guests appeared to soften their position, the crew lifted quotes from a transcript of a previous interview to get them back on track. When veteran Mike equivocated about the necessity of hazing and initiations, the crew produced quotations from an earlier telephone interview that armed Shirley's cross-examination once the cameras began to roll. The show's hostility to the military was not waged on behalf of a social analysis of the place of separate spheres of power and authority in a democratic society; instead, it was manufactured on behalf of a competing sphere of power and authority that was in the

75

process of laying claim to its right to represent democratic society as an aggregate of victimized consumers, whose victimization is what they consume.

But the show's confirmation of the military's anthropological intuitions went deeper, for it fully confirmed the analysis of those in the unit who had launched and sustained the hazing of Chenier. The charge had been that Chenier could not tolerate the rigors of military life—and the fact that he left the army for civilian life was prima facie evidence of the truth of that claim. The deeper charge was that his feminization was *deserved*, that in some way he *was* feminine—that he was available to be positioned as the victim of masculine assault. His appearance on *The Shirley Show* could allow him to complain of such characterization but not to contradict it. Accompanied by his mother, who vented her outrage in his defense, and surrounded by women, Chenier seemed to embrace the feminization of which he had been accused, and to embrace it in the army's own degraded terms, as physically weak, emotionally hysterical, and psychologically dependent, thus vindicating the intuition, if not the specific techniques, by which he had been singled out for scapegoating. The army's refusal to allow the participation of enlisted men in the talk show affirmed an absent masculinity and an indissoluble authority, an authority that Shirley confirmed even as she attempted to condemn it.

I tried to avoid being an accomplice in the spectacle by refusing to obey the producer's instructions to jump into the debate. When the cue cards flashed, Shirley asked me a question, and I spoke midway through the taping and again at the conclusion to discuss initiation rites in general and research on unit cohesion in particular. I pointed out that the atavistic persistence of degrading initiation rituals in all-male units in the American, Canadian, and Australian militaries does not attest to the usefulness of those rituals in insuring military effectiveness, but it does attest to the absence of any plausible standard of effectiveness. They can be justified only by insisting on a separate sphere for the military, one that holds fast to the traditions of the past regardless of their utility.

I was very relieved that I hadn't been pulled into the vortex of the show and that no one had shouted insults at me. On the contrary, when I spoke, everyone was uncharacteristically silent and graciously let me finish whole lines of thought. But my satisfaction at having survived an event that I found excessively manipulative and exploitive came, I felt, at the expense of refusing to participate as we had been coached by the producer. As I left for drinks with Scott Taylor, the Cheniers, and Lyne Sylvestre, the assistant producer congratulated me on my performance. I replied, "I'm afraid you didn't get your money's worth from me—I didn't actually get in the thick of it." "No, that was great!" he replied. "Things got out of control, and then you spoke, and they calmed down a little. They got out of control again, and you brought them under control at the end." My illusion of having participated on my own terms, of having refused to play the game of sensation and exploitation, dissolved. I had played my part as it had been scripted for me by the producers and predicted by the taxi driver. I had been, in my own way, initiated into the new world order.

6. Clothes Make the Soldier

Every day we make impromptu interpretations of the clothes people wear as indicators of their occupational, class, and community affiliations, as expressions of their moods, as habits, statements, and suggestions. According to cultural critics, we read the language of clothes by deciphering a code that communicates tastes, attitudes, orientations, and beliefs. It may be the ensemble—Goth or Fifth Avenue, the Gap or Eddie Bauer—that makes us look and in looking acknowledge who someone is or wants to be. Or it may be the impertinent accessory that tells: the lavishly tooled leather cowboy boots, white shoes in March, the expensive watch and sunglasses or their cheap imitations, gold chains on men or on women, or the carefully folded silk handkerchief in the vest pocket (that small patch of color redeeming pinstriped tedium). Style is an occasion for interpretation but also for judgment. Some people wear what's right. Some people wear what they must. Some people wear what's wrong when they ought to know better. We discriminate between the worn, ripped jeans of the homeless person and the stylish, fringed jeans of chic poverty, and we view quite differently the sixteen-year-old mall rat in a miniskirt and the fifty-year-old barfly clothed in little more than her embarrassment.

Uniforms are a special kind of clothing. The uniform exempts the wearer from responsibility for his or her look (what else could a janitor, a baseball player, or a Supreme Court justice wear?) and redirects our interpretative energies and judgment toward the institution the man or woman in uniform represents: "No matter what sort of uniform it is—military, civil, or religious; the outfit of a general, a postman, a nun, a butler, a football player, or a waitress—to put on such livery is to give up one's right to act as an individual—in terms of speech, to be partially or wholly censored" (Lurie, 1981: 18). Livery may sound invidious—"Thank God, I am free to dress as I please, speak as I please, and be a full-fledged individual!"—but it does capture the sense of service that institutional uniforms are designed to impart—service not as the Good

Samaritan might choose to render it, from the goodness of his heart, but service that must be performed, that is hierarchically enjoined.

Uniforms separate the group from the rest of society, but the degree of that separation varies with the style of the uniform. The more "civilianized" the uniform, the less separate the group of wearers. The bank teller's navy blue jacket, standard bow tie or gray skirt, when rhymed all the way down the counter, is clearly a uniform; but the single teller catching the bus home may not appear to be wearing a uniform. In their zeal to be more in touch with the laity to whom they ministered, orders of Roman Catholic nuns in the 1970s traded in their classic habits for mufti: conservative below-the-knee skirts, sensible shoes, and blue oxford shirts. Some orders retained a simple headscarf, the vestige of a habit, but it soon disappeared. The nuns still represented an order and, as Lurie might say, were still ordered in appearance and speech, but once out of their habits, they melded more with the civilian social workers and teachers they toiled among.

Military uniforms stand out. There is no chance of mistaking a soldier for a civilian. Trained to maintain a ceaselessly formal bearing and tonsured to order, the uniformed soldier is easily recognized both on and off duty, in and out of context, whether training in the field or catching a plane at the airport. So thoroughly perfected and indelibly impressed is the military carriage that it speaks clearly to all who view it. Even the soldier who hangs up his uniform and puts on civvies for a night on the town looks like a soldier. Without his livery, his style of walk, his spoken address, and his distinct hairstyle betray a member of the armed services dressed down, disguised as a civilian. The military's reach extends to civilian attire. The guidebooks caution against any exaggerated style and counsel a conservative look while out of uniform.

Even that uniform hanging back in the closet is not an inert husk. It lives almost as a person lives. The institution, not the individual, speaks through military dress. Trainees are taught that a uniform can be disgraced even when they are not wearing it. To commit acts that dishonor the corps off duty and off base is to disgrace the uniform and the service, imperiling the miscreant's right to resume his livery. New recruits are warned, "Never bring dishonor on the uniform," as if they were merely the temporary occupants of clothes magically invested with the collective honor of all who have similarly served.

> Because of its association with a group, the uniform assumes the properties of a totemic emblem and embodies the attributes of that group. In a peculiar sense, the uniform becomes the group, and the uniform rather than the group can become the focus of thought and affect. Thus, an individual's behavior may reflect favorably or unfavorably upon his uniform rather than his group and, in extreme instances, one may disgrace the uniform. Reciprocally, the uniform may enhance or diminish the honor of the wearer . . . The uniform is not only an emblem but also a reminder of the behavior appropriate toward this emblem; it becomes a third factor in the interaction between wearer and other. It is an impersonal objectification of the group (Joseph, 1986: 66).

In war, troops exploit the magic by seizing a piece of the uniform of a dead enemy soldier as a souvenir, proof of the kill, death followed by dishonor.

The honor of the uniform can be credited and still be a burden. Although trainees at the service academies welcome the conferral of the official dress uniform as a mark of their accomplishment in completing a challenging regimen, seasoned cadets and midshipmen take advantage of every opportunity they can to dress like other twenty-year-olds. When taking a group of midshipmen on a trip to West Point once, I witnessed a vivid example of this. Required to leave the Naval Academy grounds in dress uniform and to report five hours later at West Point in the same uniform, the students insisted on stopping before leaving the city limits of Annapolis to switch from dress blues to jeans and shirts. They got back in the van, relaxed for the drive, and then reversed the transformation just before we reached our destination. Taking off their jackets and ties for the van ride might have increased their physical comfort, but only a complete metamorphosis could eliminate the class

*After returning home from North Africa in 1943, field service driver serving with
the British 8th Army David Briggs presents his sister, Captain Ruth H. Briggs of the
WAAC, with a souvenir. This photograph is reprinted with the permission of the
Military History Institute, Carlisle, Pennsylvania.*

and office hierarchies the uniforms registered and thus loosen lips in conversation freed of the imperative.

Regulations stipulate not only which uniform is to be worn on what occasion but also when one is forbidden to wear one's uniform: when military fabric might be profaned by contact with civilian cloth, when one is engaged in civilian employment, participating in political activities, or attending any meeting of an extremist organization. (For security reasons, official regulations do not always define the negotiations between military and civilian attire that occur under exceptional circumstances.)

Wearing military clothing in civilian settings entails its own set of protocols. Removing a sword from its scabbard in a mess hall, ward room, or officers' club requires the officer to repudiate a bellicose intent by purchasing a round of drinks for all present. The sword is ritually displayed and wielded at military weddings. After the newlyweds leave the church under a canopy of raised swords, the last naval officer in line ceremoniously slaps the bride on her bottom with his sword. Not every bride regards this as a fitting end to a nuptial ceremony, but most put up with it. A handful have ruefully reminisced about an especially forceful blow by an aggressive junior officer. Less provocative is the use of the sword for cutting the wedding cake. Although to an outsider the symbolism seems transparent, the explanation offered by participants is that the act will bring good luck to the newlyweds.

Naval officers in training sometimes find themselves making the decision whether to elect the Navy or the Marine Corps based not on the look but on the comparative expense of the services' uniforms. Generally regarded as the most splendid and decidedly the costliest, Marine Corps uniforms vividly advertise the smallest branch of the armed forces, which must be continually vigilant in order to assure its survival. For the Marines, identity is sometimes defined by the uniform. Their very nickname, Leatherneck, refers to the stiff leather neckpiece originally intended, according to legend, to defend against the lethal sword blow to the neck.[1] Marines still sport a stand-up collar on their formal red jacket and carry swords, glittering grace notes that hang ornamentally at their sides. They take fierce pride in their glamorous uniforms, which successfully flatter the male form.

Driven by a clothing industry whose modifications of style entice the consumer to purchase a new set of clothes with wider lapels, a lower hem, or a slinkier fabric (it's platform shoes one year, workboots the next, and spike heels the following), civilian fashion thrives on change. Though more stable, military clothing occasionally borrows from civilian style, specifically the fashion of the well-turned-out gentleman, idle or occupied. In eighteenth-century Britain, when military service was one of the few professions open to the younger sons of the nobility, rank was synonymous with social class. High-ranking officers sported a good deal of braid and lace, like their counterparts among the landowning classes. A vestige of that gold lace, today's "scrambled eggs," decorates the visors of high-ranking officers, and braid still lines the jacket cuffs of officers.[2]

Currently (always with the exception of the Marines) the dominant influence on American uniforms is the businessman's suit. Today's officer, particularly in the noncombat branches, is in truth not a warrior whose sword must be ever at the ready but a manager responsible for coordinating the resources and services requisite for modern warfare, propelling ammunition, food, and fuel along intricate and extended supply lines, arranging for the right air support at the right time in the right force, even orchestrating the entertainment at the R&R outposts scattered across the globe.

Like the officer's braid and the vestigial officer's sword, elements of military style have a half-life considerably longer than that of civilian fashions. Odd accessories that have long outlived their function still ornament the military dress uniform. There are many pockets that never pocket anything lest a lump spoil the trim. Lapels that once crossed over to keep the chest warm are now stationed neatly in place. The chin strap is never lowered. Some ornamentation is justified by legendary attribution. The fourragère and the aiguillette, braided cords worn on the left and right shoulder, respectively, have a significance that comes from conflicting legends.[3] According to one, a commander, discouraged by the performance of his troops, threatened to hang the whole lot if they did not improve in the next battle. Outfacing the threat, each soldier went into the next battle with a noose around his shoulder. In another legend, Cromwell boasted that he would hang any soldier he captured from a specific Irish regiment. In turn, the soldiers in that regiment defiantly slung ropes over their shoulders. Short of troops during the Franco-Prussian War in 1870, the French army gathered together a unit of prisoners who wore hangman's knots over their shoulders into battle. They proved themselves valorous and were permitted to remain in the army after the war, maintaining their fourragères as a unit citation. The term *fourragère,* from the French word describing a plant one forages for, may actually refer to the ropes carried to tie up bundles of forage. *Aiguillette,* from the French word for needle, may refer to the metal-tipped thongs carried by squires to lace up knights' armor. Soldiers in the cavalry believe that the decorative rope hearkens back to the general's horse harness, carried by his aide.

Cadets at West Point believe that the cross at the top of their swords is descended from the time of the Crusades. More likely it imitates the pattern of the U.S. Finance Department logo (Todd, 1955: 40). A sailor who had survived the loss of his ship was allowed to wear an earring, according to one legend. Another traces the tradition of sailors wearing earrings to the piercing of sailors' ears at initiations. Members of the "Brown Water Navy," who saw significant combat while patrolling the inland waters of Vietnam, cut through the small ribbon loop on the back of their berets when they made their first kill, modifying their uniform with an unofficial mark of valor.

A commonplace today, uniform clothing for all ranks and all branches of the military is a relatively recent phenomenon in military history. Medieval sailors worked nude; later sailors, although clothed, often shivered in garments that offered no protection from the water. To foot soldiers, only a part of a uniform (a jacket, hat, or badge) might be issued by the government. The soldier was required to provide the remainder as best he could (Joseph, 1986: 115). Foot soldiers marching in the Crusades wore colored crosses, each identifying its wearer's country of origin (Tomes, 1924: 361). From the American Revolution through the nineteenth century, U.S. naval ships enlisted their crews at ports known to be populated with ample skilled labor to serve both merchant and naval vessels. On one voyage, a sailor might sign up with a merchant ship; on the next, he might ship out with a military vessel. As the government's fleet grew during the last half of the nineteenth century and technological changes required more specialized training, the government created a permanent enlisted force, one clothed in standard dress (Joseph, 1986: 36).

The design of the American military uniform marks the dawn of the garment industry and mass production. Mass-produced uniforms were proof that this young nation could turn soldiers out like clothing. If not the instrument of democracy and nationhood, the uniform was at least their manifestation; it managed to erase outward signs of personal wealth and to obscure regional background. It transformed the dapper dandy, the farm boy, and the hooligan into efficient soldiers whose uniform reflected the ideal proportions of masculinity.

Although civilian fashion fluctuates greatly over time, alterations in military uniform adhere to the canonical: each new uniform retains elements of the one it replaces. Military style remains fairly stable, making affiliation (whether a member of the engineers, the cavalry, the infantry, or a submarine group) and status (whether lieutenant, chief petty officer, or staff sergeant) immediately apparent to current and former members. As one changes station, one's uniform reflects that change; the uniform records the history of a career soldier's tenure in service. Not only do military uniforms mark professional advancement, they signal two systems of rank, enlisted and commissioned. While yesterday's aristocrats typically wore more flamboyant uniforms than common soldiers did, today's commissioned officers don a more subdued uniform than enlisted officers do. Uniforms instantly place the individual in the chain of command, and they stipulate behavior and dictate protocol. The small twin bars on a collar, for example, command deference on the part of all subordinates who approach. Uniformed privates who fail to salute uniformed lieutenants when they walk past on base will face certain reprimand.

When military uniforms have undergone change, troops have not

always reacted with enthusiasm. British seamen greeted the modi-
fication of their trousers from flap-front to zipper-front with general
disdain, viewing the innovation to be more feminine and less British,
more like the uniform of other navies (Joseph, 1986: 15). A similar
resentment met the American Navy's switch from bell-bottom to
straight-leg pants. Traditionalists defended the earlier style as a sign of
distinction that marked an essential naval identity and criticized the
new version as mere janitorial garb. They claimed the flared-legged
pants were easier to take off in an emergency and provided an ampler
flotation device for a sailor who found himself overboard. The designers of the bell-bottom pant, however, never imagined such virtues; they
simply modeled the sailor pants on the civilian pantaloon popular
at the time (Joseph, 1986: 113). Similarly, to protest the shipboard ban
on facial hair, sailors enclosed their shaved whiskers in letters to commanders. An aide to one commander reported to me that the protest
was so widespread that he routinely opened the correspondence of
shipmates with a letter opener, and before removing the letter turned
each envelope upside down over a trashcan to discard any enclosed
whiskers.

The uniform of the professional soldier cloaks its wearer in the
spirit of the corps, investing her or him in a solemn succession of generations. The West Point cadets' "long gray line" forms not just on the
parade ground but backward and forward in time, uniting the young
officers of today with all those who have endured the training on the
bluffs above the Hudson in years past and with all who will do so in
the future. That does not mean that even so revered a uniform cannot
be the subject of humor. A cartoon published in *The Pointer*, a West
Point cadet humor magazine, compares the academy's dress uniform to
corseted women's dresses.

The military dress uniform provides the field on which soldiers and
sailors display their honors and awards in all the splendor of gold and
bronze, medals and braid. On the work uniform or battle dress, the
marks of rank are austerely utilitarian. Officers must lead their men, not
overawe them. The Army's camouflage gear and the Navy's khaki shipboard uniform keep difference to a minimum. The British introduced

"Mine's Saks, Fifth Avenue, what's yours?"

Drawn by cadet William Kimble Vaughan and published in the West Point humor magazine The Pointer, *21 January 1944.*

the first camouflage uniform in the nineteenth century, when they replaced the haughty glare of summer whites with the simple khaki uniform (the word *khaki* is Urdu for dust-colored) for troops stationed in India (Fowler, 1993: 8). European and American uniform designers subsequently devised camouflage fabric suitable for warfare in jungles, in deserts, and in areas of heavy rain. Enthusiastically adopted today as the garb of paramilitary groups, the camouflage outfit, theoretically undetectable, has come to symbolize both official and unofficial combatants. Camouflage no longer camouflages. The point is not to blend into the landscape but to stand out as a guerrilla-in-waiting. For white supremacists, store-bought BDUs lend a spurious authenticity to ragtag renegade activities and permit them to see themselves as a vigilant militia organized in defense of fundamental American values.

Civilian dress typically allows for individual variation; even the most standard work attire, the dark business suit, can be supplemented by cufflinks, a monogrammed shirt, and an expensive silk tie indicating the wealth of the wearer. One military uniform is distinguished from another only by institutionally conferred signs of professional achievement. Variations register as idiosyncrasies of grooming: the overstated neatness of a tuck, the perfectly calibrated fall of a cuff, or the extravagant luster of an officer's gold braid.

Despite efforts to control all aspects of military dress, a standard decoration can mean different things in different branches of the service (see Chapter VIII, "Culture and Controversy"). And uniforms are not always uniform: soldiers and sailors have inventively, often covertly, personalized their uniforms. World War II sailors sewed hidden patches under the sleeve cuffs of their dress blue jumpers. Once on leave, they unbuttoned their "liberty cuffs" and turned them over to display colorful dragons, mermaids, dolphins (for submariners), and birds (for the "airedales" who worked on Navy aircraft). The practice of liberty cuffs continued into the early 1980s, except for a short period in the early 1970s, when the Navy attempted to do away with the blue-and-white jumpers and replace them with jackets similar to those worn by officers. One might expect that the Navy's democratic gesture—a single jacket for everyone from seaman to admiral—would have won widespread support; instead, it was denounced by sailors, who complained that the jackets did not fit well and were made of poor-quality material.[4] That uniform change cost the Navy dearly, not only because of the expense of making the unpopular jackets but also because the new, bulkier jackets did not fold up and stow in a sea bag as the jumpers had. The Navy had to rehabilitate its ships to provide hanging space for the crew's dress blue jackets.

The new jacket came with a new hat—the conventional stiff white dark-brimmed officer's hat—to replace the traditional sailor's "Dixie cup." Unlike the Dixie cup, the new hat was not foldable, washable, comfortable, or cheap (it cost ten times as much). Sailors also preferred the simpler cloth cap because they could personalize it in ways the hard hat inflexibly resisted. "Surface sailors," those tasked to operate a ship, tended to bend the brim down a little in the front. Those assigned to aviation pulled the sides out to look like wings.

After a few years and great investment, the Navy revived the jumpers. The dress blue jumper, also known as the "cracker jack," was a favorite among sailors because it showed their physique to advantage. This was particularly the case in special, slightly nonregulation dress blues that seamen occasionally had fashioned by local tailors. Instead of having a wide opening so the jumper would slide over the head and upper body, these customized jumpers had a side zipper running from the waist to the armpit and carefully concealed under one arm. Such a zipper allowed the sailor to slide the jumper over the head and chest easily but insured a snug fit that accentuated his slim waist. Likewise, the trousers of these "liberty blues," of lighter fabric and with a much tighter fit, displayed a sailor's other physical endowments.

In the Vietnam War, soldiers personalized their uniforms in more dramatic ways, not for liberty but for combat, by decorating their jungle jackets and helmets with nicknames, the names of their hometown, and slogans like "Born to Kill" and "Born to Raise Hell." These grunts turned themselves into cartoons and supplied their own captions, such as "Eat the apple, fuck the corps," which advertised their low morale and the emergence of a frontline adversarial culture. By donning love beads and peace symbols in imitation of stateside antiwar protestors, they editorialized against the war they were waging. As the war in Vietnam dragged on, the livery of the serviceman became not a tool of censorship but a canvas for flagrant speech.

GI self-fashioning was not officially condoned, but it was widely tolerated. The military authorized the wearing of unit patches on battle fatigues (the patch of the unit the soldier was serving with on the left shoulder and the patch of the unit he had previously seen combat with on the right), but many units and individuals deviated from the official design, improvising images of their own—poignant or profane—which they stitched to the shoulders and pockets of their battle uniforms. As the war progressed and troop strength grew, new units formed, and with them came new unit insignia. Army headquarters, suffering from its own battle fatigue, often did not bother to issue these new units with patches, so a couple of soldiers might improvise with marking pens; the unit would approve the design and contract with the local seamstress to make them for the whole crew. Or one squad might produce a variant of the official patch. The standard patch worn by the Military Assistance Command (MACV) features a raised sword. The parody substitutes a raised middle finger for the sword. The impulse to be colorful was not suppressed by any punctilious West Pointer; it was extinguished by VC gunfire. Just as the grunts learned to dye their towels and underclothes jungle-friendly green, so they dyed their patches. It's one thing to sport a logo, quite another to wear a target. Soon local entrepreneurs offered an entire line of subdued insignia (patches and shoulder tabs, both smaller arcs and larger scrolls), which replaced the more colorful decorations sewn on collars, shoulders, and pockets. Toward the end of the war, those subdued insignia became the official standard for battle dress adopted by the Army. We might call this evolutionary adaptation "situational insignification." At any rate, the officialization of the demotic is a rare case in the military.

What members of the military do with their uniforms after service comments poignantly on their experience. In his 1947 book *Back Home*, a moody sequel to his wildly successful collection of wartime drawings, *Upfront*, Bill Mauldin affiliated himself with those combat veterans who, eager to return to civilian life and embarrassed by the posturing of stateside "warriors," quickly mothballed their uniforms and stowed their decorations. Adjustment was difficult in part because the war in Europe was a conflict that almost everyone on the home front supported but few could understand. Vietnam was a war that everyone at home thought they understood and that a majority came to question. That it could plausibly be argued that the government and the military establishment had disgraced the uniform, not the GI with his patches and slogans, was no reliable defense against the painful conviction that the uniform and the combat decorations had been shamed past redemption. Stowing away the uniform was a way of hanging on to that shame. Whether they felt betrayed by the government or by an ungrateful populace, many Vietnam veterans protested the wrongness of the war by returning or trashing the medals bestowed on them. As one young vet exclaimed, "They gave me a Bronze Star and they put me up for a Silver Star. But I said you can shove it up your ass. I threw all of the others away. The only thing I kept was the Purple Heart, because I still think I was wounded" (Lifton, 1973: 178). To some the only decorations that counted were the ones that the GIs gave themselves or that commemorated an indubitable trauma of the body. No medals were given for trauma of the mind.

American combat soldiers in Vietnam were unique in that significant numbers branded their individuality on their uniforms. But American soldiers and sailors through several wars also emblazoned insignia on their bodies. On leave, often emboldened by liquor, soldiers and sailors crowd the tattoo parlors that dot the servicemen's strips near base. Whether tokens to mothers and lovers left behind or to the new fellowship or political beliefs, even those frowned on by military officials (for instance, the Nazi insignia of white supremacists), soldiers and sailors generally acquire their tattoos with the encouragement of buddies. Tattooing as a fraternal rite is not a uniquely American phenomenon. While a Samoan youth is being tattooed, his friends comfort him with a song that has the telling refrain, "When it comes to pain, women must bear the children, and men must be tattooed" (Cordwell, 1979: 56). Tattooing exploits bodies as billboards for affiliative logos, for daring slogans, for bawdy images, or for dreamy arabesques. Although the military tolerates tattoos on the bodies of enlisted soldiers, it frowns on officers who acquire them, reinforcing the stereotype of tattoos as lower-class adornment. A commissioned officer would tarnish his prestige if he were seen with tattoos in a short-sleeved summer uniform. Evasive actions are often taken. For example, members of the Naval

Academy crew team, after drinking alcohol, traditionally emblazon their signature anchor tattoo on an inconspicuous cheek tucked away in boxers.

Even the most ingenious efforts to hide forbidden tattoos sometimes fail. There is only so much body, and a tattoo is not a tattoo unless it is visible somewhere. In a 1997 official memo on the subject of tattoos addressed to all midshipmen at the Naval Academy, Captain Gerard Farrell, the deputy commandant, began by reassuring midshipmen that despite rumors to the contrary, none would be kicked out ("separated" is the colloquial term) for sporting a tattoo. He reminded them, however, that "tattoos are generally inconsistent with the high standards of personal appearance associated with officers of the Naval Service" and that those who had tattoos visible in regulation PE gear (T-shirt, gym shorts, tennis shoes, and crew socks) should be prepared to tape over the tattoo. In the future, applicants with visible tattoos would be disqualified from applying. He went on to warn of a yard-wide inspection of the brigade of midshipmen:

> For us at USNA, we need to learn what we look like. Right now, we have some anecdotal information about this mid or that and his/her tattoo. Not good enough. Accordingly, in the near future we will schedule a Brigade wide inspection in reg PE gear. It will NOT be a "strip search." You may be asked if you have other tattoos and to describe them. There is no intent to embarrass anyone, just to gather some data. Those with visible tattoos may be advised to cover them up. We have an obligation to help such midshipmen figure out how best to do that. Let me emphasize that tattoos are "our" problem, not "your" problem.
>
> Finally, since tattoos are "discouraged," I want to discourage you from getting one (or more). I am told Spring Break has become a time when mids are prone to get tattoos. Let's cancel that tradition now. Team captains are asked to support the policy and to strongly discourage team tattoos.
>
> Tattoos are tribal in origin and have become associated with gangs and prisons (inmates, not the guards). USNA is not a tribe.

Nor are we a gang; and although the wags among us may think otherwise from time to time, this isn't a prison either, and mids are not inmates.

BEAT ARMY! The Deputy.[5]

I'm not sure whether Navy did beat Army in 1997, but I do know that it collected data on the various tattoos and their locations on the bodies of all midshipmen. Despite such efforts, come spring break, new tattoos were secretly inscribed.

Such concern over tattoos marks a new post–cold war fussiness regarding officer bearing, which contrasts sharply with an earlier acceptance. As a lieutenant in the Philippines in 1899, Smedley Butler proudly had the Marine Corps emblem, the globe and anchor, emblazoned on his body: "I selected an enormous Marine Corps Emblem to be tattooed across my chest. It required several sittings and hurt me like the devil, but the finished product was worth the pain. I blazed triumphantly forth, a Marine from throat to waist. The emblem is still with me. Nothing on earth but skinning will remove it" (Edwards, 1961: 154). Butler was not skinned. He later became a major general of the Marine Corps.

If bodies are a contested domain for branding and blazing, clothing is not. Every piece of clothing in the military is marked and identified as belonging to a single soldier or sailor. If stray clothing is found on the ship or in the barracks, its owner will be immediately known. Reason enough for female students at the Naval Academy to black out the alpha codes on their bras to protest the installation of James Webb as secretary of the Navy. Those women knew Webb as one of the most vocal opponents of women at the service academies, someone who had charged them with "poisoning" the environment for male cadets. Before dawn on the day of the Webb's installation as secretary of the Navy, a ceremony held at the Navel Academy in Annapolis, the female mids unmistakably announced their presence by lacing their brassieres through the trees like Christmas decorations, an action the authorities did not treat with the respect due to such an inspired instance of installation art. Before Webb arrived, the groundskeepers had cleaned the trees of lingerie. Whether the brassieres were ceremoniously presented to Webb as trophies of victory is not known.

In war or peacetime, whenever the military admits women into its ranks, it must decide whether to outfit them so they resemble their male counterparts or whether to set them apart by their dress. We tend to assume that gender has always defined the salient differences in styles of dress, but until the eighteenth century, class, not gender, prescribed the strongest contrasts in attire in European societies. Upper-class men and women of that era selected a wardrobe composed of velvets, silks, and laces, and both wore face makeup and coiffed hair (Davis, 1992: 38). By the latter part of the nineteenth century, substantial differentiation had occurred at home and in public gathering places, but in the sporting life of the elite, crossover fashion prevailed: women who rode, sailed, or hunted wore garb almost indistinguishable from men's above the waist but gender-coded below.[6]

Ordinarily, military uniforms make distinctions based on service, rank, and merit. Distinguishing groups by other criteria is plainly discriminatory, a sign of less than full membership in the corps. The famous "colored" 33rd Civil War Regiment offers a stunning example of a group whose marginal status was graphically advertised by an exotic uniform. Segregation by skin color was not deemed sufficient, so instead of the general-issue blue jackets and trousers of their white Union counterparts, these black soldiers were assigned red jackets and trousers. Their proven hardiness in arduous campaigns and bravery under fire subsequently earned them release from those throwbacks to British regimentals; and one of the most moving incidents of a palpable outburst of unit morale survives in the account of the cheers with which those troops greeted the replacement of their scarlet stigma first by the standard blue coat and later by the blue trousers (Joseph, 1986: 70).

Set apart because of their gender, women enter the military uneasy about their full membership in the uniformed ranks. During World War II, when women belonged to auxiliary services like the WACs, WAVEs, and SPARs, their uniforms attested to their temporary affiliation. Throughout World War II female naval officers were not permitted gold braid on their uniforms to designate rank; instead they wore pale blue braid. As long as they were isolated in separate units doing separate jobs, the military could preserve an idealized realm where femininity would be preserved, a domestic sphere within the armed services, supposedly untainted by contact with GIs and unruffled by the rigors of training or of war. Writing of British women in uniform in World War II, Russell Birdwell notes: "Even in these field posts, there is no attempt to restrict the girl soldiers to 'dreary barracks life.' If they want to brighten their quarters with their favorite pictures, with flowers, with personal comforts, they are at liberty to do so. By no means do they surrender their femininity when they become soldiers . . . I suspect that many a girl soldier whom I met at that Command Post had a powderpuff tucked in the pocket of her uniform" (Birdwell, 1942: 24).

In recent years, women have slowly taken their place alongside men in regular units. Desegregation has not been easy, but in most cases it has been easier to move bodies than to retailor outfits. The Pentagon has struggled to design uniforms that neither deny nor enhance gender attributes. The experiment of dressing women in uniforms "naturally" designed for the V shape of the idealized male body (square broad shoulders tapering to a slim waist and hips, a triangle that points to the male genitalia) produced outlandish results.[7] Replacing the tie of the male uniform with an oversized bow in the late 1970s created an awkward and unmilitary appearance according to some women. And removing the breast pocket from women's uniforms (to call less attention to their breasts) baffled female officers' best efforts to conform to the proper alignment of insignia. Although the breast pocket was eventually returned to the female dress jacket, the solution to the neck finish remained a gender stereotype: men with the tie and women with an inverted V at the neck.

Uniform committees in all branches of the military have historically endorsed uniforms that reinforce conventional ideals of bodily form, always with the presumption that those ideals are masculine. In these days of an all-volunteer force, the uniform becomes a recruiting tool to assure that personnel goals will be met. Recruiting posters sell young recruits on the image of the straight and slim, uniform-bedecked, handsome male. The Marines have been particularly successful with such advertising campaigns by morphing civilians into the uniform of the corps and by dramatizing a hormonally robust youth brandishing his terrible swift sword in computer simulations that hybridize Dungeons and Dragons with Indiana Jones.

Marines make men and uniforms make Marines. However, uniform modifications that might enhance female sexuality create deep unease and generate troublesome contradictions. The military encourages women to maintain a feminine appearance through recommendations on makeup and jewelry: don't look like a man. Yet the same authorities interdict uniforms that accentuate female anatomy. The alternative, outfitting women in clothing designed to flatter male bodies, generates caricatures of soldiers—at best, women who look like boys, diminutive imitations of their male peers.[8] If female recruits are to complete the transition from civilian to soldier, their uniforms must identify them as one among equals. The policy of each branch of the armed services is uniformly ambivalent, at once encouraging women's incorporation and stigmatizing them as military monsters, part soldier or sailor and part civilian.[9] Erasing the stigma is an urgent issue for women who have undertaken military careers and for those services that in recent years have had difficulty meeting their manpower goals.

Some distinctions seem trivial. But the devil of gender inequity lives in the details of routine discrimination. Both the Army and the Marine Corps permit women to carry umbrellas when in uniform but prohibit men from doing so. In the fall of 1997, Colonel Vickie Longeneker, the Army's director of human resources, called the bluff of those critics who always complained about the different standards expected of men and women in the military by proposing that both men and women be allowed to carry umbrellas, as they are in the Navy and the Air Force. Those in command positions would have nothing to do with it, fearing, no doubt, that they would be charged with participating in feminizing the Army. Is it the concavity of the open umbrella that excites a Freudian frisson among the brass? Then why not focus on the masculine thrill of carrying a loaded stick? Couldn't the guys be encouraged to pretend that they are carrying a rain sword?

Although the military has modified the uniforms of women (by permitting them to wear pants, for example), it has continued to stoke the institutional appetite for gender anomaly by singling out the head as the part of the body that says "man" or "woman." Unlike police officers and firefighters, military men wear different hats (or "covers") from military women.[10] And hats don't just keep off the sun or the rain; they are freighted with traditions. If a flirtatious girl, for example, were to remove the hat of a uniformed male midshipman on the streets of Annapolis, she would expect a kiss as ransom for its return. Although women have been part of the brigade of midshipmen since 1976, no corresponding game targeting female midshipmen has hit the streets. A furtive variant has emerged in Bancroft Hall, the academy living quarters, however. Female midshipmen report that they have been surprised when male friends have come by their rooms soon after the women have received their regular uniforms (following probationary Plebe Summer, the six weeks they spend dressed like sailors). The guys ask to try on the gals' hats. The female midshipmen report no reciprocal urges.

The military has strict regulations regarding hair. Male hair—pate, chin, and cheeks—must conform to specific parameters. At times and in different armies, beards or mustaches have been as much a part of the regulation uniform as belts and sashes.

Wigs or powdered hair has been required of officers. The style or length of a soldier's mustache, often waxed and blackened with boot polish, was once an index of tenure. American independence plays itself out in protests against official hair regulations. Thomas Butler, a lieutenant colonel of the 4th Infantry, refused to follow regulations issued in 1801 announcing the abolition of powdered hair and queues, remnants of aristocracy that no longer fit in our fledgling democracy. Despite the threat of arrest and punishment, Butler maintained his powdered hair and queue for four years. Although he was ultimately court-martialed and pronounced guilty of disobedience and mutinous conduct, he died of natural causes before his sentence could be imposed.

From "Army Regulation 670-1."

According to legend, he was buried with a hole cut in his coffin large enough for his queue to protrude.[11]

Long, full sideburns, muttonchops, and ringlets on both sides of the face replaced the dapper twist of the queue. Regulations promulgated in 1835 dictated that whiskers could not extend below a line from the curve of the mouth to the lower tip of the ear, a line sometimes measured by barbers by running a string through the mouth and up under each ear (Todd, 1955: 167). Although the Department of the Army tried to standardize the hairstyle of its troops, enforcement was left to the local command. Some exercised that authority; some looked the other way. As later wars necessitated the drafting of civilians and the swelling of reserve ranks, hairstyles became laxer. In 1973, even hairpieces were permitted for reservists, and that concession to vanity continues for those serving in the Army National Guard and the U.S. Army Reserve.[12] Although today's regulations stipulate short, neat, clean haircuts that affect a blunt renunciation of style for both men and women, certain groups manage to fashion haircuts promoting collective identity: the high-and-tights of Marines, the shaved heads of trainees, the clipped brush of the ensign's mustache.[13] Sideburns, reluctantly tolerated and carefully mapped by the Army's tonsorial cartographers, must not extend past the lowest part of the ear opening, nor can they flare at the base.[14]

Facial hair typically distinguishes boy from man. By shaving fresh recruits, the military lowers them to the status of boys, to be schooled by more mature male overseers. Shaving also has the unintended consequence of subduing gender differences, which often play themselves out through beautifully or annoyingly metamorphic hair. Left untended, hair grows unkempt, greasy, and limp, but with a few bobby pins, rigorous back-combing, and lots of hairspray, it can be poofed and piled, twisted or teased into miracles of rare device. It can be kinked, curled, crimped, teased, waved, konked, braided, dyed, waxed, made to stand up straight or to lie slinkily and smoothly across the shoulders, shaved altogether, even ironed. It can reveal or disguise a person's age and class. It can say, "I'm hip" or "I'm reg," "I'm me" or "I'm you."

In some cultures, long hair connotes sexual vitality.[15] In others it signifies a social partition behind which the wearer retreats. Short hair can be a badge of self-elected celibacy or submission to impersonal regimentation.[16] With the large influx of women into the military during World War II, military planners and the general public had to reconcile the image of sleek, efficient military uniforms, clothing previously associated exclusively with men, with female hairstyles. Long hair, which in men was considered slovenly and eccentric, was tolerated in women as long as it was kept out of sight (in a "neat roll" [Birdwell, 1942: 24]). In fact, women's long hair was more welcome than the alternative: "boyish" haircuts, which suggested deviancy.

Susan Brownmiller roots this Western dichotomy between long and short hair in women and men in the fact that Caucasian men, more than those of other racial groups, tend to inherit the gene for baldness, and by age fifty, nearly 60 percent of them exhibit some form of hair loss. Because other cultures are less afflicted by baldness, they maintain other gender distinctions, according to Brownmiller. Male members of the Masai as well as other African and Indian tribes sport long hair ornamented with shells, feathers, or beads as a sign of their masculinity, à la the lion's mane or the plumage of exotic birds, while the hair of female members of the tribe is cropped short or shaved (Brownmiller, 1984: 59). But Brownmiller's provocative thesis fails to take into account considerable evidence that such a dichotomy is relatively recent. Both in civil society (for example, the curled wigs of barristers) and in military society, European and American men have sported (and in some cases continue to sport) long hairstyles. The male homesteaders who first plowed the Great Plains let their hair grow to shoulder length without considering, let alone fearing, the charge of effeminacy.

Just a few decades ago, young male hippies and their imitators wore hair flowing down their backs. The hippies found themselves in a world defined by their crew-cut fathers, a world in which short hair was identified with machismo and militarism and could be hidden by a helmet. This world was afflicted by rigid gender notions that required young men to fight a war that lacked widespread popular support— a war that brought with it no imminent threat to their homeland, a war whose rationalizations failed finally to justify to the majority of Americans at home the vast numbers of Americans killed abroad. The hippies' long hairstyle represented freedom from the strictly defined world of the 1950s, which prescribed certain hairstyles for women and others for men, and signaled gender ambiguity and the rise of feminism.

Through the 1990s soccer players, rock stars, and biker aficionados carried on the long-hair tradition. Even Christian doctrine and iconography are not always in harmony on the subject of hair. Art often depicts Christ and male saints with long hair, yet the apostle Paul condemns long hair on men. Long hair, he preaches, is the proper style for women, for it covers them and represents subjection. In I Corinthians 11:3–15, hair explains the proper hierarchical relationship among God and men and women:

Now I want you to realize that the head of every man is Christ, and the head of the woman is man, and the head of Christ is God.

Every man who prays or prophesies with his head covered dishonors his head.

And every woman who prays or prophesies with her head uncovered dishonors her head—it is just as though her head were shaved.

If a woman does not cover her head, she should have her hair cut off, and if it is a disgrace for a woman to have her hair cut or shaved off, she should cover her head.

A man ought not to cover his head, since he is the image and glory of God; but the woman is the glory of man.

For man did not come from woman, but woman from man; neither was man created for woman, but woman for man.

For this reason, and because of the angels, the woman ought to have a sign of authority on her head.

In the Lord, however, woman is not independent of man, nor is man independent of woman.

For as woman came from man, so also man is born of woman. But everything comes from God.

Judge for yourselves: Is it proper for a woman to pray to God with her head uncovered?

Does not the very nature of things teach you that if a man has long hair, it is a disgrace to him, but if a woman has long hair, it is her glory? For long hair is given to her as a covering.

In early Christian Corinth, some women began to pray openly and to prophesy, asserting that in the eyes of Christ, women as well as men, slaves as well as free men, have souls and as such can be recognized by God (Derreth, 1973:101). Paul's epistle cautions the Corinthians against this practice on the part of women. Their hair, according to Paul, is a sign of their sexuality and therefore must be covered. Although he says that men's hair is naturally short, Assyrian reliefs show that Israelite men in the period before the exile wore full beards and long hair (Achtemeir, 1985: 934). The style that the epistle calls natural is in fact a

Roman fashion. Paul thus adopts a fashion in the service of a new disciplinary ideology.

Deuteronomy 21:10–14 contains the only other Biblical mention of shaving women's heads:

> When you go to war against your enemies, and the Lord your God delivers them into your hands and you take captives
>
> If you notice among the captives a beautiful woman and are attracted to her, you may take her as your wife.
>
> Bring her into your home and have her shave her head, trim her nails,
>
> And put aside the clothes she was wearing when captured. After she has lived in your house and mourned her father and mother for a full month, then you may go to her and be her husband, and she shall be your wife.
>
> And if you are not pleased with her, let her go wherever she wishes. You must not sell her or treat her as a slave, since you have dishonored her.

Taken captive, women are shaved and made sexually available to their male captors. The shaving, like the sexual appropriation, is a brutal means of humiliation. If done voluntarily, close-cropping or shaving women's heads symbolizes submission to a greater purpose, as in becoming a nun or a female warrior (the classic example is Joan of Arc; the popular version is the female Seal played by Demi Moore in *G.I. Jane*). If compelled, head-shaving shames. Some institutions have routinely shaved the heads of both male and female inmates as part of an induction process. Sometimes defended as a sanitary practice, this is also designed to strip away from the individual all physical remnants of an autonomous past. Colonial American accounts depict the threat to punish an Indian woman in Timucua, a mission province in central Florida. Accused of living apart from her husband, behaving "unquietly," and aborting pregnancies with poisonous herbs, the woman was subjected to unspecified public shame and warned that if she persisted in her scandalous ways, she would be whipped and have her hair cut

(Bushnell, 1983). Head-shaving was a frequent form of punishment in liberated France in 1944. A woman believed to have been collaborating with the Germans had her head shaved and was paraded through the town to the jeers of onlookers (Brownmiller, 1984: 61). Shaving a woman's head renders her sexless and thus, by the logic of gender, powerless.

In 1996, the Citadel, the all-male public military college in South Carolina, was ordered to admit its first female, Shannon Faulkner, despite the college's attempt to renege on a commitment made in the mistaken belief that she was male. The administration made no effort to reconcile itself or the student body to the court decree. Instead, conditions were arranged so that Faulkner would experience maximum discomfort and alienation. At first the college prohibited her from wearing the cadet uniform and living in the dorms, relegating her to the status of day student. The courts eventually ordered the Citadel to grant her full membership as a residential cadet, and soon the Internet chat rooms and radio talk shows were abuzz with discussion of whether women's heads should be shaved. As college authorities debated whether or not to subject Faulkner to the same debasement the male students suffered, reactionaries on the airwaves and in cyberspace cheered at the prospect that she would get what she deserved—that head-shaving was a fitting retribution for her uppity feminism. "If women want to enter male professions, then shouldn't they be prepared to submit themselves to the traditions that are part and parcel of training for those professions?" some said. Those familiar with the Citadel mentioned that the name for first-year cadets, "knobs," referred to their shaved heads, and therefore to be without the characteristic "knob" was to be singled out for special treatment. Others argued that military academies of the major services had been admitting women for years, and although they stipulated short hair for cadets, women had been regularly exempted from the shave.

The issue of women's hair situates them in a limbo between soldier and civilian. Because they are not fully integrated through ritual shaving like male recruits, they are stuck with looking like girls. Simply arguing that a tradition is valuable because it has always existed does not prove its current utility; however, the military could have initiated a rigorous examination of its traditions—from the barbershop to the drill field to the mess hall—to assess their effectiveness in preparing all officers, both men and women, for leadership in today's armed services, where Guadalcanal is a proud memory but hardly an active possibility. Instead, they chose the easy way out, exempting women from some initiatory rites that have been retained for men, thereby inviting those resentful of women in the ranks to echo the chronic complaint of a double standard. Indeed, there *is* a double standard, but it is not one drawn up in secret by a coterie of power-hungry feminists and imposed by force on compliant, emasculated military policymakers. If head-shaving is essential in making the transition from civilian to soldier, then women should be subject to it.[17] If, however, head-shaving is just one of many options for the ritual humiliation deemed necessary to erase a former self and impress a military identity, the military could no doubt adopt a revised standard set of humiliations that apply equally to men and women.

Such a policy of gender equity has precedent. In World War II, when the Army and the Navy called on women to perform a variety of tasks that had formerly been the responsibility of men, such as engine repair, supply service, intelligence, and signal operations, they gave them coveralls and comfortable shoes or boots—the same kind of work clothes their male predecessors had worn. No one complained about the work. No one complained about the clothes. Functional equivalence disappeared in the late 1950s and early 1960s, though, when manpower needs declined and the military could afford to be choosy. It adapted its selection procedures not according to utilitarian standards but to perceived cultural norms, tracking changes in the culture at large. All branches of the military began selecting women for their physical appearance and correspondingly dictated that they wear only feminine clothing and be coifed like ladies.[18] What those who criticize the slow and steady advancement of women into positions of greater responsibility and authority call "tradition" is actually only policy implemented for nonmilitary considerations and justified as tradition.

If the true purpose of uniforms and associated rituals is to erase individual difference and inculcate corporate identity, then the military must institutionalize those forms and practices that function alike for both men and women. It would be a relatively easy matter to invent a gender-neutral uniform, one that accentuates neither male nor female attributes. Indeed, today's popular battle dress uniform fits the bill. Its loose-fitting pants, untucked and unbelted jacket, and railroad worker's hat or beret appear equally soldierly and practical on both men and women. The field of battle is not handicapped. Mettle must be proved before medals can be pinned. Why not make the uniform a truly competitive field instead of adhering to a tradition that honors untested soldiers simply because they are male?

7. Military Speech

When freshmen, or "plebes," at the U.S. Naval Academy finish their summer basic training, they trade in their Dixie cups (sailor hats) for covers (officer hats) and begin the toughest year in their careers, a year in which "flamers" "ream them out" in front of their peers for minor infractions. Those who receive the harshest abuse are the "shit screens"; those who ingratiate themselves with upperclassmen, the "smacks." In World War II, a pilot would rev up his "coffee grinder" (plane engine) and, with permission of the "madhouse" (control tower), take off toward his target, where he would "hang out the laundry" (drop parachutists), lay a few "eggs" (bombs), or make a "split S" (combat maneuver) and then hightail it away from the "junior prom" (hot mission), "flak happy" (suffering from combat fatigue) and hoping to get home without a "panting virgin" or a "ruptured duck" (injured plane).

Members of the military, like other occupational groups, maintain their own informal vocabulary, one that serves to distinguish them from civilians, to add humor to what is often a tedious job, to relieve anxiety when the tension of war replaces the tedium of peace, and to express their frustration with the hierarchical institution of which they are a small part. In their close-knit communities they pass along inherited and often humorous turns of speech while coining colorful new expressions that comment on the particular experiences of their unit. Some of these never make their way out of basic training and some flourish only during a particular mission, but others become firmly established in a unit's lexicon and foster a sense of exclusivity. The expressions that survive do so both because they entertain and because they embody shared enthusiasms or resentments.

The folk speech of military units has little in common with correct speech (the formal interchange in a receiving line, for example); it is the speech exchanged in the barracks, in the ship's engine room, among coworkers often of fairly equal rank. It celebrates the salty, the blunt, and the crude and may reflect attitudes that those in positions of power have officially condemned. In times of universal draft, when a wide spectrum of the population enters the military to serve its term and return to civilian life, slang tends to move back and forth from popular culture to military culture.[1] In an all-volunteer force, with its more homogeneous and professional staff, military slang becomes the speech of insiders.

Upon entering the Navy, any recruit learns through a semiofficial policy of redescription that a floor is no longer a floor; it is a "deck." A wall is a "bulkhead," a set of stairs a "ladder," a hallway a "passageway," a window a "port," and a bed a "rack." Although basic training takes place on shore rather than on a ship, language orients the recruit to the world of the Navy by transforming a training camp into a ship. Those in positions of power within the military endorse the use of language in this way because it serves, along with other methods of indoctrination, to transform the individual. To force recruits to refer to themselves only in the third person helps them make the transition from the individualistic, selfish, "me" culture of civilian society, according to their commanders. Compelling them to punctuate every sentence addressed to a superior with the appropriate "sir" or "ma'am" facilitates their adjustment to a rigid hierarchy and inculcates the readiness to obey orders automatically on which a successful mission or the survival of a ship may one day depend.

The recruit learns not only the technical terms that apply to the many parts of a ship but also the colloquial terms for naval personnel, those who sail the "Blue Water Navy" and those who navigate smaller craft on channel ways and rivers in the "Brown Water Navy." Within the "surface community," an experienced officer who takes a rookie ensign under his wing is a "sea daddy." "Blue jackets" (sailors) who employ more brute force than mental agility are "anchor clankers" (British), "deck apes," and "knuckle-draggers." On board the "bird farms" (aircraft carriers), complete with their "coffee pots" (nuclear reactors), "airedales" (pilots) don their "bonedomes" and "brain buckets" (helmets) and slide into their sleek aircraft. For relaxation on long deployments, carrier personnel leave their chores for the "steel beach" (deck), where they listen to shipmates play the latest tunes and the mess staff serves up barbecued burgers and franks. A "chicken of the sea" (ballistic missile submarine) "drills holes in the water" as it navigates a clandestine course, and its crew champions the motto "We hide with pride."

Military units invent names for themselves, for their rival units, for their enemies, for the shirkers among them, for those out of reach who give the orders, for those they regard as inferior, for the food they eat, for the games they play, for the missions they complete, and for the suffering they endure. "Snake-eaters" are Navy Seals. Graduates of the Naval Academy, according to their rivals, are alumni of "Canoe U." RAP is short for "rear area pussy,"[2] those safely out of the combat zone working to supply the frontline troops, like the "wagon dogs" of Civil War days. The stress of a situation is measured by its "pucker factor." A soldier who steals something commits a "five-finger requisition." One goes "stick fishing" with dynamite. Since the Civil War, soldiers have carried their "housewives"(sewing kits) into every war. "Joe Shit the Ragman" or "J. S. Ragman" is a major screwup. Some terms enjoy multiple meanings in the same war. A proven pilot, one who has downed several enemy aircraft, is affectionately called an "ace," but "to ace," according to the Marine Corps, is to kill. The practice of laying an ace of spades on the body of a dead enemy soldier was more talked about than practiced in Vietnam, but, eager to demonstrate its support for the troops, an American card company provided soldiers with packs of cards containing nothing but aces of spades. The recent deck of playing cards showing targeted Iraqi leaders distributed to troops in Operation Iraqi Freedom is an interesting spinoff.

Names often distinguish the novice from the old hand. In the Civil War, recruits were called "palefaces." Those burnished by the trials of combat or tough training missions label newcomers "cherry boys," "twinks," "FNGs" ("fuckin' new guys"), and "blister bandits." Freshmen at the service academies for generations have suffered the humiliation of being lowly "plebes" ("rats" at VMI), destined for their virgin year to be ordered about by seasoned upperclassmen. During the Vietnam War, when the need for officers required that large numbers be trained in short officer training programs rather than through the four-year alternatives of service academies and ROTC programs, those from conventional programs referred to one of their newly commissioned counterparts as "Shake 'n Bakes," "Nestlé's Quiks," and "Redi-Whips."

In the absence of official names, troops invent their own. Although the Army, Navy, Air Force, and Coast Guard coined acronyms for the active-duty women who served in World War II (WACs, WAVEs, SPARs, and WAFs), the Marine Corps had no such designation. Early in their service, women Marines found themselves called "Lady Leathernecks" and the derogatory BAMs (broad-assed Marines).[3] In retaliation, they invented the term HAMs (hairy-assed Marines) to refer to their male counterparts. Nurses in World War II were called "bedpan commandos," a term passed on to their Vietnam War medic counterparts. "Boonie rats" were members of the infantry who spent time "in country" (or "in Indian country") engaging the enemy. A song whose lyrics were written by an M-60 machine gunner of the 101st Cavalry who was allegedly killed in action immortalized the expression:

Boonie rats, Boonie rats, scared but not alone,
One hundred days more or less, then I'm going home.[4]

Divisions sometimes receive their nicknames from the insignia that identifies their membership. Troops serving in Vietnam came to refer to the 25th Infantry Division, which sported a shoulder patch shaped like a strawberry with a streak of lightning across it, as "Electric Strawberry." The Fourth Army Division, which donned a shoulder patch with four ivy leaves, was called "the Poison Ivy Division." The AAs on the shoulder patches of members of the 82nd Airborne won the division the pejorative nicknames of "All-American," "Air Mattress," "All-African," "All-Afro," and "Alcoholics Anonymous." Members of the 101st Airborne called themselves the "Screaming Eagles" after the eagle on their shoulder patches, but scoffers, regarding such a name as ostentatious, took the division down a peg or two with nicknames like the "Screaming Chickens" and the "Puking Buzzards" (Reinberg, 1991: 73, 77, 7, 193).

Not only did divisions see their nicknames knocked from the heroic to the humble, but soldiers in Vietnam saw their mission called into question by a significant portion of the American public. American combat soldiers, who in World War I had been "doughboys" and in World War II and Korea "GIs," found themselves "grunts" in Vietnam, close to the ground, mired in the muck of war: "They call us 'grunts' cause that's what you do when you shit," according to one soldier (Cragg, 1980: 168). Some of these young soldiers began their tours in Vietnam as timid soldiers but became "Audie Murphyed" (after the World War II hero) into enthusiastic warriors, those who swore by the soldier's prayer, a variant of the Twenty-third Psalm: "Though I walk through the Valley of the Shadow of Death, I shall fear no evil, because I am the meanest motherfucker in the valley." Others did their time with little enthusiasm, putting up with the daily "Mickey Mouse" that issued from "Disneyland East" (the Pentagon). In a folklore tinged with cynicism, they told stories of units who were so fed up with the practical incompetence of freshly minted junior officers that they "fragged the Lieuie" (tossed a fragmentation grenade into the lieutenant's quarters—a crime allegedly repeated recently by a soldier in Operation Iraqi Freedom). According to the folklore, there were "Bell Telephone hours," interrogation sessions in which electric jolts were administered, to captured VC sympathizers, which ended in the prisoners taking their "first flying lesson" out of a helicopters. Soldiers spoke of the "newbies," "fresh meat," and "Gomers" who would arrive each week to replace those killed and wounded in action, fighting a war that, ironically, was never officially acknowledged with the title of "war" but left to linger in the linguistic limbo of an "era."[5]

Although more macabre humor was reported from Vietnam than from any other war, it was not invented in Vietnam. Civil War soldiers, for example, called the list of the dead the "butcher's bill" (Myers, 1990: 8). In Vietnam the casualties, referred to as "Kool-Ade" (killed in action), were "bagged and tagged" and sent off to the "big PX in the sky" (Reinberg, 1991: 21). Soldiers not only invented names for dissidents at home; they also coined terms for South Vietnamese dissidents. A "Buddhist barbecue" was a Buddhist monk who set himself on fire to protest the war. "Crispy critters," from the sugary children's cereal of that name, were napalm victims, civilians who made their way to MASH facilities for treatment. The term eventually traveled stateside into emergency room lingo to describe burn victims.

Like their predecessors, soldiers in Vietnam complained about the food they were served: the "beans and baby dicks" (beans and franks), the "beans and motherfuckers" (lima beans and ham), and the "baby shit" (mustard) spread on their sandwiches. But no matter how bad the "C-rats" (combat rations) were, none produced the dreaded "Saigon quickstep" as impressively as the local street food. There was always some time, though, for rest and relaxation, a little I&I (intercourse and intoxication) or B&B (booze and broads), to be arranged through one of the "Saigon cowboys" (pimps). Some on liberty contracted for a "steam and cream" from one of the "boom-boom girls" or "chocolate bunnies" (prostitutes who preferred black soldiers to white ones). Others sought more conventional dates with the "roundeyes," American and Australian women in Vietnam as nurses, camp followers, or USO workers ("doughnut dollies," "biscuit bitches," and "jelly doughnuts"[6]).

The names heard most often in the Vietnam War were those for the enemy. American soldiers fought an elusive enemy with the commonest of names, "Charlie," short for Victor Charlie, the military alphabetical terms for VC or Viet Cong. Charlie could be a North Vietnamese regular, a rice farmer, a small child, or a grandmother. In the face of unmapped difference and the uncanny Other, soldiers' speech articulated a theme of uniformity. Charlie could appear with an AK-47 on a well-traveled enemy path through the jungle or hide underground in the long network of tunnels, only to sneak out at night in dark clothing. Charlie was both military and civilian, here and there, the ever-elusive enemy. Above all, Charlie was a "gook," a category of racial Other used to describe both friendly and unfriendly Asians. Although lexicographers disagree about the precise route this expression took before making its way into contemporary slang, most agree that it bears considerable similarity to the Korean "kuk" (pronounced *kook*), used to describe a person of a specific nationality.[7] A "Chungkuk" is a Chinese citizen, for example. In the 1940s, American soldiers used the term to describe friendly Asians. In the 1950s, they labeled Koreans in this way.

The origin of the term is less important than the function of dehumanizing the indigenous people. To kill other human beings, a prospect most Americans are raised to abhor, a soldier must psychologically imagine the enemy as something other than human beings with wants and dreams similar to his own, with families who love them and for whom they may be fighting. Language helps to reclassify the enemy, and even innocent civilian casualties, as less than human: "And when you shot someone you didn't think you were shooting at a human. They were a gook or a Commie and it was okay."[8] The enemy is reduced not only by racist nicknames but also by an array of curses. Out of frustration, the soldier meets the threat of aggression with a verbal aggression that diminishes the feared adversary. In the barracks, at least, cursing the enemy imaginatively mutes his threat.

The language of soldiers in Vietnam fighting an unpopular war not only gave voice to their fears and anger; it put a humorous cast to their cynicism. An interview between an Air Force captain and a journalist poignantly articulates the disjunction between the captain's frank, creative, bawdy folk speech, punctuated by profanity and metaphor, and its translation by an attendant information officer, one of the service's many spin doctors, into bland, printable, official comments. It brings together two cultures, the media and the military, and shows how they translate and countertranslate into each other. This example of "Xerox" folklore circulated widely among military personnel serving in Vietnam because it amusingly illustrated the two Vietnam wars, the one in which pilots sought to destroy cabbage patches and swinging footbridges and the other brought to the American public by the American government.[9]

Correspondent: What do you think of the F-4?

Captain: It's so fuckin' maneuverable you can fly up your own ass with it.

IO [Air Force information officer]: What the captain means is that he has found the F-4C Phantom highly maneuverable at all altitudes and he considers it an excellent aircraft for all missions assigned.

Correspondent: I suppose, captain, that you've flown a certain number of missions over North Vietnam. What did you think of the SAMs used by the North Vietnamese?

Captain: Why, those bastards couldn't hit a bull in the ass with a bass fiddle. We fake the shit out of them. There's no sweat.

IO: What the captain means is that the surface-to-air missiles around Hanoi pose a serious problem to our air operations and that the pilots have a healthy respect for them.

Correspondent: I suppose, captain, that you've flown missions to the south. What kind of ordnance do you use, and what kind of targets do you hit?

Captain: Well, I'll tell you, mostly we aim at kicking the shit out of Vietnamese villages, and my favorite ordnance is napalm. Man, that stuff just sucks the air out of their friggin' lungs and makes a sonovabitchin' fire.

IO: What the captain means is that air strikes in South Vietnam are often against Viet Cong structures and all operations are always under the positive control of forward air controllers, or FACs. The ordnance employed is conventional 500- and 750-pound bombs and 20-millimeter cannon fire.

Correspondent: I suppose you spent an R&R in Hong Kong. What were your impressions of the Oriental girls?

Captain: Yeah, I went to Hong Kong. As for those Oriental broads, well, I don't care which way the runway runs, east or west, north or south—a piece of ass is a piece of ass.

IO: What the captain means is that he found the delicately featured Oriental girls fascinating, and he was very impressed with their fine manners and thinks their naiveté is most charming.

Correspondent: Tell me, captain, have you flown any missions other than over North and South Vietnam?

Captain: You bet your sweet ass I've flown other missions. We get scheduled nearly every day on the trail in Laos, where those fuckers over there throw everything at you but the friggin' kitchen sink. Even the goddamn kids got slingshots.

IO: What the captain means is that he has occasionally been scheduled to fly missions in the extreme western DMZ, and he has a healthy respect for the flak in that area.

Correspondent: I understand that no one in your fighter wing has got a MIG yet. What seems to be the problem?

Captain: Why, you screwhead, if you knew anything about what you're talking about—the problem is MIGs. If we'd get scheduled by those peckerheads at Seventh for those missions in MIG valley, you can bet your ass we'd get some of those mothers. Those glory hounds at Ubon get all those missions while we settle for fightin' the friggin' war. Those mothers at Ubon are sitting on their fat asses killing MIGs and we get stuck with bombing the goddamned cabbage patches.

IO: What the captain means is that each element in the Seventh Air Force is responsible for doing their assigned job in the air war. Some units are assigned the job of neutralizing enemy air strength by hunting out MIGs, and other elements are assigned bombing missions and interdiction of enemy supply routes.

Correspondent: Of all the targets you've hit in Vietnam, which one was the most satisfying?

Captain: Well, shit, it was when we were scheduled for the suspected VC vegetable garden. I dropped napalm in the middle of the fuckin' cabbage patch and my wingman splashed it real good with six of those 750-pound mothers and spread the fire all the way to friggin' beets and carrots.

IO: What the captain means is that the great variety of tactical targets available throughout Vietnam makes the F-4C the perfect aircraft to provide flexible response.

Correspondent: What do you consider the most difficult target you've struck in North Vietnam?

Captain: The friggin' bridges. I must have dropped forty tons of bombs on those swayin' bamboo mothers, and I ain't hit one of the bastards yet.

IO: What the captain means is that interdicting bridges along enemy supply routes is very important and a quite difficult target.

The best way to accomplish this task is to crater the approaches to the bridge.

Correspondent: I noticed in touring the base that you have aluminum matting on the taxiways. Would you care to comment on its effectiveness and usefulness in Vietnam?

Captain: You're fuckin' right, I'd like to make a comment. Most of us pilots are well hung, but shit, you don't know what hung is until you get hung up on one of the friggin' bumps on that goddamn stuff.

IO: What the captain means is that the aluminum matting is quite satisfactory as a temporary expedient but requires some finesse in taxiing and braking the aircraft.

Correspondent: Did you have an opportunity to meet your wife on leave in Honolulu, and did you enjoy the visit with her?

Captain: Yeah, I met my wife in Honolulu, but I forget to check the calendar, so the whole five days were friggin' well combat-proof—a completely dry run.

IO: What the captain means is that it was wonderful to get together with his wife and learn firsthand about the family and how things were at home.

Correspondent: Thank you for your time, captain.

Captain: Screw you—why don't you bastards print the real story instead of all that crap?

IO: What the captain means is that he enjoyed the opportunity to discuss his tour with you.

Correspondent: One final question. Could you reduce your impression of the war to a simple phrase or statement, captain?

Captain: You bet your ass I can. It's a fucked-up war.

IO: What the captain means is . . . it's a *fucked-up war.*[10]

Whether the salty bravado of a fighter pilot, the playful putdown of another unit, or the witty derision of a superior (one well out of earshot), the informal language of the military offers a way of letting off steam, galvanizing group identity, and acting out a mastery of what is feared, hated, or resented. When that group is all male and has been trained to think of war as men's work, it is not difficult to understand that the construction of a hypermasculine mystique requires casting out all things feminine (see Chapter 5, "Sex, GIs, and Videotape"). The desire for women must be suppressed, sublimated within the group, or satisfied through dramatic conquest. Women are threats to this pure masculinity, polluting forces to be subdued.

Since Western militaries have looked to service academies to provide new members for their officer corps and since these elite institutions have ceased to be populated by sons of the upper class, they have come to see themselves as places to remake farmers and city kids into officers and gentlemen, as well as places from which all pleasures and all punishments issue. Cadets, both here and abroad, today still see the service academy as a place that forges men as well as officers. Isolated from the rest of society for a longer period of time than other military trainees (three to four years rather than the two or three months of most boot camp and officer candidate school programs), they pass on a male-centered, youthful, and inventive body of slang that gives voice to their frustrations as members of a repressive and restrictive society. They create an aggressive masculinity in the form of violent and cartoonish speech.

In *A Lexicon of Cadet Language,* Bruce Moore collects and defines the words that constituted the private vocabulary of cadets at Australia's West Point, Duntroon, from 1983 to 1985.[11] Rich in its variety, the speech of members of this closed institution illustrates an overwhelming interest in the domination of underclassmen and women. Gathering responses from student surveys, underground cadet publications, and interviews with cadets, Moore presents an abundant collection of terms associated with the general practice of "bastardization," the hazing visited on freshmen by upperclassmen. Despite highly publicized scandals and official censure of bastardization, cadet speech continued to be richly sprinkled with references to it. Defended as "necessary to get all fuckwits out of the corps," upperclass cadets hazed freshmen by "fagging" (requiring them to perform servile tasks), ordering "leaps" or "splits" (repeated uniform changes in rapid succession), issuing two contradictory commands at once, "bishing" their rooms, depriving them of food and sleep, and other "fourthie games" (hazing rituals directed toward freshmen or "fourthies"). The victim of a bishing (from a clipped form of "rubbish") would discover his room in a shambles. If he suffered a severe bish, or a "depressurization," a cadet would return and find the contents of his room strewn on the ground outside his window.

Deprived of an ordinary social life, cadets invoke an erotic life through lavish language and tall tales. Australian cadets bring to the military academy bawdy expressions common to the larger civilian public (such as "Mrs. Palmer and her five daughters," a euphemism for masturbation) and coin terms that apply to the occupation they have joined (a "mag" is a weapon's chamber and a woman). Anxious about their prowess as warriors and lovers, cadets flaunt a sexual bravado in their speech, talking tough in an institution that is always calling their toughness into question in order to produce it on demand. Talking about sex is more important than performing the act, because sexual banter welcomes one's mates as coparticipants, cementing fraternal bonds with shared homoerotic fervor—homoerotic not because they talk only about homosexual sex, which in fact they do a good deal, but because even their talk of heterosexual encounters becomes in the retelling a shared erotic experience within the all-male group. The cadet rarely recounts sexual exploits with someone he truly cares about; rather, he shares with the group intimate details (both real and imagined) of encounters with women he has no attachment to, women he speaks of as if they were disposable. In this way, heterosexual sex is simply the pretext for fraternal bonding, for the homosocial.

In her book *Fraternity Gang Rape,* the anthropologist Peggy Sanday argues that fraternity brothers both enact and expunge their sexual attraction for one another through the gang rape of a coed who has passed out on too much liquor. The unconscious victim, a blank slate according to Sanday, plays the ritual scapegoat "who received the brunt of collective male sexual aggression that would otherwise turn a group of privileged heterosexual males into despised homosexuals. By degrading and extruding the woman who has been the ostensible object of their mutual sex act, the men degrade and extrude forbidden sexual feelings from the group" (Sanday, 1990: 59).

In the service academy, heterosexual liaisons threaten the power and solidarity of the group, so men must learn to talk about sex in ways that diminish the attractiveness of women and affirm the importance of the male group. According to Australian cadets, even seduction is a group mission. The legendary "Gary Groundwork" first engages a woman with casual conversation; "Simon Superstructure" softens her with flattery; then "Ivan In-there" loosens her with a "leg opener" (liquor); and finally "Eric Endaway" scores.

Cadet speech has no word for a fulfilling and romantic sexual relationship. The closest thing to a neutral term is "dayboy," a cadet who sleeps at his girlfriend's home every night and sneaks back into the academy in time for morning formation, and even a dayboy is often also called a "thumbprint," a cadet whom others believe to be too much under the control of his girlfriend. Most cadet talk of sex casts women as abject objects of pollution or as mechanical replacements for masturbation. A girlfriend is a "wanking machine," a "handbrake," a "toe rag," or a "dragon" (the latter a controlling woman). Like the mythological beast, the cadet's dragon is a girl who "breathes fire." According to legend, the knight must slay the dragon in order to win the other vision of femininity, the damsel in distress. Derived from the British, the term "dragon" for woman surfaces across another ocean as "drag," the term for a date at the U.S. Naval Academy.[12] Official memos preceding a Naval Academy event usually inform students whether they can "drag" (bring a date) or not. Both "drag" and "dragon" are pejorative terms. Australian cadet speech also presents women in Freudian fashion as castrated males: "Show us your 'axe chop' [vulva]" or "where the chainsaw bit" (Moore, 1993: 20). When one cadet kids another about his girlfriend, he calls her a "fugly," a blend of *fuck* and *ugly* (more properly, a portmanteau word).

Unflattering terms for women whom cadets are supposedly fond of are surpassed only by those to whom they have no special attachment. Most women, according to cadets, are "exercise bikes," "dick warmers" or "willie warmers" (a term that may have evolved from the knitted tea-cozy covering for the penis men could order from girlie magazines). An unattractive woman is a "slag" (waste or refuse), a "maggot bag," a "bush pig," a "horrorbag," or a "bush mag" (from the term "bush magazine," a rifle magazine in battered condition used for target practice rather than for parades). Just as each cadet maintains both a highly polished "parade mag," a rifle magazine in perfect condition for formal parades, and a "bush mag" or "fid mag" (short for "field mag") to use out in the bush, he seeks a "parade mag," a girlfriend suitable for formal occasions, and one or more "bush mags" or "fid mags," townies he sees merely to gratify his sexual desire. Cadets speak of these women in even less flattering terms as "semen receptacles," "sperm banks," "root rats," and "night deposits for sperm." These women, in legend at least, play the role of victim while cadets play the part of aggressive predators in such sex acts as "ripping the eyeballs out" (aggressive and sadistic sex) and "skull fucking" (fellatio). In the world of cadets, women are defined by the sexual acts they perform. An "eleven" is a "ten that swallows," one who willingly performs fellatio and swallows the cadet's discharge.

The ugly or polluted woman enjoys great popularity in military slang, particularity cadet slang. The "grogon," the ugly pickup handy for sex but never acceptable as a girlfriend, reigns as a grotesque queen of cadet speech. "Grogon," according to Moore, is also a slang term for excrement: "The dogs have deposited grogons all over the lawn" (Moore, 1993: 176). This meaning certainly jibes with other terms for women. Women, say cadets, are either waste themselves ("slags"), feed on waste ("maggots" and "buzzards"), or serve as containers of waste ("slime bags"). The Australian "grogon" may have also descended from the gorgons of classical mythology: Medusa and her two sisters, who are most commonly represented with snakes for hair, wings, and claws, and whose stares turn men to stone—phallic women.[13] As a way of transforming their lack of success in winning beautiful women, the corps turns disadvantage into advantage through the celebration of the casual pursuit, aggressive conquest, and indifferent disposal of ugly women. Companies give an award to the cadet who dates the ugliest girl: the "grogon hunting award" in Australia and the "brick" at Annapolis. The process is formal at both service academies. In Australia a grand high wizard presides over the "Morals Patrol," a group of cadets dressed in long coats and helmets with "Morals Patrol" emblazoned on them; he initiates investigations into acts of moral depravity and presides at an "atrocity trial," at which he calls for the charges to be read publicly and evidence brought forth. If the cadet is found guilty of having sex with the ugliest woman (or, in most instances, merely of dating a woman), the grand high wizard presents him with a varnished board with the picture of a grotesquely fat woman. Such practices have a way of effectively diverting attention away from civilian women and back into the close bonds of brotherhood.

Cadet slang also conflates both subject and object, or in some cases subject, object, and act itself. In the 1980s, Australian cadets expanded the meaning of a popular slang expression for either masturbation or intercourse so that it was also a term for a woman. The act of copulation and the partner in the act are one and the same. To masturbate, to fuck, or to screw is to "boff," and a "boff" is also the woman the cadet has sex with ("Is that your boff over there?"). A sleazy woman is a "boff bag," one to be slain with a cadet's "beef bayonet." The slang term "cum" refers both to the act of ejaculation and to the semen itself, as it does in American usage. Australian cadets call women who are easy marks "cum bags," "cum buckets," and "cum catchers"; they call their girlfriends "cum kittens." Cadets employ the term "cunt," which signifies both female genitalia and the female herself, as both a derogatory term for males (as in "cunt head," "cunt face," and "drill cunt") and a term of male fellowship ("C'mon, you cunt, let's get going"; "What were you up to last night, cunt guts?"). A "cunt crusher" is a large penis and by synecdoche the possessor of such an organ. Cadets do not possess penises, they sport "pork" ("Me and my pork are off to the Bin [bar], the old fella's raging to go"), and they have sex with "pork," or women ("I feel like poking some pork tonight"). As a verb, "pork" refers to sex ("Bill porked his girlfriend"). Conceivably, you could hear a sentence that would integrate all three meanings: He porked some pork with his pork tonight. In such a way the word functions as agent, recipient, and act in a quintessential linguistic masturbation. Its phallocentric magic manifests it with the power to be, to do, and to receive.

In his social history of swearing, Geoffrey Hughes distinguishes two forms of obscenity: one consisting of references to the pudenda and the other of references to the anus and excrement. Cadet speech links both these forms in a homoerotic exuberance. A girlfriend becomes a "front bum" or "split arse" because, according to Australian cadets, female genitalia resemble an anus. A "pillow biter" is both a gay man and a woman who bites the pillow in sexual ecstasy while "doing the doggy." One who initiates either heterosexual or homosexual anal intercourse is a "Captain Cadbury." His sexual exploits take him up the "chocolate channel," the "shit shoot," the "chutney passage," or the "clay road," where he goes "dirt tracking." The American equivalent is, of course, "the Hershey highway."

The hypermasculine culture of the service academy demands constant demonstrations of a cadet's manliness and constant displays of trim, tight, manly bodies. It encourages powerful bonds between members, proscribes the feminine, and breeds desire for a temporary release of repression, mutual affection, and desire between male cadets. Cadets litter their conversation with references to homosexuality; Moore lists seventy slang terms for anal sex alone! Someone who is gay is a "freckle puncher," "poo pirate," "turd burglar," "bung-hole buster," or "bum puncher." To be "goat-fucked" is to be required to perform an unpleasant task. Generally, first-year students are the most likely to find themselves in this predicament ("Okay, round up some fourthie goats— there's work to be done"). "Southern Comfort" is a West Point cadet from the South. To "dirk" is to knife someone in the back, along the lines of "being dicked" "dorked up the arse," and "getting shafted." The writers of an underground student newspaper lampoon a fellow student: "Richard, is it true that you wear your PJs backwards for convenience?" A combat unit is "butt-fucked" when the enemy has approached and fired from behind. The fear of anal penetration—to be "butt-fucked" by the enemy—and its attraction as a sign of ultimate male bonding ("he's my butt-fuck buddy") go hand-in-hand at service academies, not only in Australia. A freshman at the Virginia Military Institute and the senior whom he attends as valet and assists in his dressing serve as "dykes."[14] VMI personnel explain the term's derivation from the white cross-belts worn in formal parades, called "cross dykes," which are impossible to don without help. Dressing in this way is called "dyking out." The term "dyke" has no clear etymology. It may have appeared as a clipped form of "hermaphrodite," or it may have evolved from the expression "diked out," like "decked out." Regardless of its origin, it continues to enjoy wide acceptance today despite the contemporary meanings of this slang word.

More than anything else, cadet sexual speech is about breaking taboos. Two Australian underground student papers, *The Bastions' Bugle* and *The Pussy Rag,* produced by two companies of cadets, poke fun at fellow cadets and describe in lavish and outrageous detail acts of violence, sodomy, and rape. They attribute deviant sexual practices to fellow cadets. On the cover of one issue, a small naked boy sits on the lap of a naked man; beside the photo a caption reads, "MACMASTERS at age 5 playing 'games' with daddy."[15] One page sports an ad for a lifesize sex doll in the likeness of a fellow cadet. Narratives depict cadets fornicating with animals, beating children, killing crippled women, and having sex with their male civilian instructors, their officers, freshman cadets under their control, and young boys. One first-person narrative details the kidnapping, torture, and killing of a young boy in sadistic cartoonish fashion:

> As I withdrew my member the little boy screamed in terror and pain, vomiting profusely. This gross slight on my hospitality caused me much anger and I hurled him across the bathroom. He crashed into the sink and subsequently emptied his bladder all over the floor. Outraged, I placed one foot firmly on his underdeveloped little genitals and, heaving him upward, left his tasty testes on the floor for a delighted Woofy and myself to eat later. I then forced my clenched fist into his tiny ring [anus] and placing his head against the wall I punched my forearm in to the elbow so that his small torso fitted my arm like a glove, my fist touching the base of his neck. Spying

a tap below I swung back and punched him firmly onto it, creating a gaping hole in his head. His horrifying screams were reduced to a gurgle as I plunged my newly erect member into the hole, my violent gyrations scrambling his brains. As his tiny body was seized with spasm after spasm I reached a shattering climax.

In this bizarre violence, the speaker destroys the boy, or rather transforms him into a glove, which he wears while masturbating. One of a series of stories that run through several issues, this, like the others, is told from the perspective of a male adolescent (often with his dog, Woofy, as a sexual partner) who happens on individuals far weaker than himself—a young female child in one, a blind teenager with no hands in another—victims whom he literally tears to bits in the achievement of his passion. No woman is attractive in these underground newspapers; no cadet is less than an all-powerful sadistic force.

In 1986, the Australian Defense Force Academy (ADFA), a triservice academy built on the outskirts of Canberra, succeeded Duntroon. The integration of women took place as three cadet corps from three branches of the military and their respective military staffs were merged. Rivalries among the services have never totally disappeared within the corps of cadets, but they have abated with the formation of a new identity as ADFA cadets. Male cadets found it easier to admit officers-in-training from a rival service than to accept women into their ranks. They labeled the first women to arrive "squids" because, according to one cadet, "They're flabby, they smell of fish, are easy to get into, enfold you with their tentacles, and squeeze the moral life out of you" (Cowham, 1983: 19). "Squidwoman," a figure in ADFA cartoons, is the force who declares herself the enemy of "Kaptain Kordie," the superhero who stands for all male cadets.

Reluctance to change the unofficial speech of the institution in recognition of the integration of women reveals how closely cadets and many of their military superiors identify soldiering and masculinity. One classic example is the insistence on maintaining the phrase "use your balls" as a command to speak up. Rather than abandon the expression, upperclassmen insist on saying to lower-class female cadets, "Use your ovaries," a stab at gender equity perhaps, but by no means the same command!

Slang resists translation across gender lines. In all-male training units, instructors have called men "girls" or "pussies" as a form of humiliation. Should they then call women "boys" or "dicks"? This would obviously fail to create the same humiliation, because military training has historically sought to reinforce rigid definitions of gender that view women as outsiders unfit for military service and men fit only insofar as they demonstrate their potential for violence in nonviolent ways and submit to dominance by those up the chain of command. If women are ever going to achieve full membership, the phallocentric, hypermasculinized, homosocial speech of the military must change, not only because it is abusive and demoralizing to women, but because it simply does not work in a volunteer military that must recruit women to ensure a well-qualified and educated pool of potential soldiers, sailors, and officers.

8. Culture and Controversy

On May 16, 1996, Admiral Jeremy "Mike" Boorda, chief of naval operations, the highest-ranking officer in the Navy, killed himself at his home at the Washington Naval Yard, ending a distinguished forty-year career. The real tragedy was that Boorda was a fully capable, admirable leader of extraordinary use to the military. What his death demonstrated was the power of the honor code on an honorable man and the cynical manipulation of that code by a group of fierce opponents, politicians in khaki.

At sixteen, Boorda lied about his age in order to join the Navy. He became the only "mustang" (someone who comes into the commissioned ranks from the enlisted ranks) and the only Jew to rise to the level of chief of naval operations. Boorda was one of those rare leaders who communicate a genuine willingness to help solve the personal difficulties faced by those even at the bottom of the chain of command. No one, not even his detractors (and he had several), doubted his concern for the ordinary enlisted sailor.

Chief among Boorda's detractors was James Webb, a former Marine, secretary of the Navy for a ten-month term, and a decorated Vietnam veteran. Both Webb and Boorda spoke at the annual Naval Institute Conference a couple of weeks before the latter's death. On April 24, Boorda put aside his prepared speech to speak frankly to a large gathering of midshipmen and naval and Marine Corps officers about the problems facing the Navy in these post–Cold War, post-Tailhook days. On April 25, after Boorda's departure, Webb excoriated current naval leadership, an act that few could interpret as anything other than a public humiliation of the chief of naval operations. Although he named no specific leaders, it was quite clear that Boorda was a main focus of his attack.

Webb's address began with a long, nostalgic tribute to the Naval Academy, a place that, according to Webb, "challenged us to be men at eighteen." It was in this environment that Webb learned who real leaders were. Like the mids who came before him and those who followed him, he listened to tales of heroic deeds that magically invoked their subjects, the "giants," who came before him. Webb recollected that these sea stories fixed in him and his classmates a determination to aim for what some might call an "unreachable, romantic standard that human nature in its tilt toward accommodation cannot consistently maintain" but that Webb insisted he has lived by. By contrast, today's naval leaders, according to Webb, have repudiated such a standard in order to advance their careers. Boorda was not trained in the Navy's "leadership laboratory," an expression Charles Larson used to describe the Naval Academy, unlike Webb and most who sat before him. Webb, in effect, cast Boorda as an outsider, someone without the pedigree to lead the Navy, someone who had never been reborn in the blood of "Mother B" (the mids' term for Bancroft Hall, the single dormitory in which four thousand students spend their four years at Annapolis), someone who had not experienced the pressure of plebe year.

Webb's address was delivered on the hallowed ground of the Naval Academy, a place whose physical and verbal abuse he credits with making him a man and a warrior and memorializes in his novel, *A Sense of Honor*. Although Boorda referred to the Naval Academy as *his* academy, he was always considered an outsider by diehard "ring knockers," because he had never been a member of their "good society" and lacked a Naval Academy degree. Although Boorda had never thrown his cover in the air at graduation, in 1996 he was far more of an insider than Webb. Webb may have voiced sentiments shared by some active-duty officers and several retirees, but it had been eight years since he had held any leadership position. His military career, though distinguished, spanned only four years in the Marine Corps after graduation from the Naval Academy. Boorda's forty years in the Navy and his role as chief of allied forces in Europe granted him an intimate knowledge of the Navy throughout its ranks.

Webb acknowledged in his address that the Navy still had some worthy leaders—some of his classmates—but he insisted that they had either been passed over for promotion or were not being listened to. He singled out Charles Larson, who had enjoyed an extremely successful naval career from his days as midshipman to his term as head of the

Pacific Fleet and finally to a second stint as superintendent of the Naval Academy. Although a highly visible position, especially in the days of cheating scandals and sexual assault charges, the superintendency does not count as one of the top leadership positions about which Webb spoke. Larson had lost out to Boorda for the coveted post of chief of naval operations, and Webb's address could be interpreted as suggesting that the wrong choice had been made.[1] Larson had escaped any taint of Tailhook. His inaction in an alleged rape, however, raised questions about his willingness to take violence against women seriously. While head of the Pacific Fleet, Larson had warmly welcomed two Soviet ships docked in San Diego in July 1990. While these ships were in port and open to tourists, a female sailor in civilian clothes went on board one of them, became separated from her group, and, according to her report, was raped by members of the foreign crew. She left with bruises and went to a civilian rape crisis center, whose staff reported the crime to Naval Investigative Services. When the naval investigator took his concerns to Larson, according to Gregory Vistica, author of *Fall from Glory*, Larson dismissed the woman's story: "I talked about this to my wife, and she doesn't believe this happened and neither do I." Larson took no action to investigate further, and the Russians rolled their ships back out to sea.[2]

Many occupying the highest positions, according to Webb, achieved their status only after caving in to pressure from Congress and a critical citizenry. Those willing to stand behind the traditions of the Navy, which to Webb meant saying no to demands for change, were by-passed. They had caved in to political correctness rather than demonstrate moral courage. Those who didn't, many of them skillful leaders, were passed up for promotion.

The charge that opponents have attained their rank through preference rather than merit is one that Webb made before this speech and would make after it. In his famous 1979 *Washingtonian* article on women at the Naval Academy, Webb declared that no senior female in a leadership position at the academy won her rank by merit, thereby impugning the accomplishments of every female midshipman and throwing fuel on the smoldering resentments of a vocal minority of disgruntled midshipmen. In a 1999 article, Paul Roush, fellow Marine veteran and graduate of the Naval Academy, concludes that Webb's views "are based on the politics of resentment" (Roush, 1999: 99).

Webb enjoys considerable company in his attacks on women and on male leaders who advance the cause of expanded roles for women. Along with others on the military right, he finds it hard to believe that leaders could genuinely feel that moving women into more nontraditional non-supportive roles and taking seriously the lessons learned from Tailhook might actually be good for the Navy. Such sympathies Webb and others regard simply as capitulations calculated to advance these officers' own careers. For these outspoken conservative critics, Boorda played handyman in a feminist conspiracy begun by Congresswoman Patricia Schroeder. As Schroeder advocated an expanded role for women in the U.S. military in the 1980s and early 1990s, Elaine Donnelly, a protégé of Phyllis Schlafly's, organized a concerted effort to inhibit women's advancement into nontraditional roles. Through her Center for Military Readiness, Donnelly staunchly fought any progress in this area and singled out for special attack the Defense Advisory Committee on Women in the Services (DACOWITS), an institution she referred to as a "tax-funded feminist lobby."[3] DACOWITS has served as the Department of Defense's watchdog on behalf of women, pointing to persistent inequities and arguing for the opening of more positions to women. In 2002, after considerable lobbying, Donnelly, the *Washington Times,* and like-minded supporters persuaded the administration of George W. Bush to eliminate DACOWITS' watchdog role.

For Donnelly, Schroeder and anyone who advocated expanding women's roles in the military threatened military "readiness," or the military as we have known it. In an op-ed piece in the *San Diego Union-Tribune,* Donnelly criticized Schroeder and Boorda in the same breath:

> Judging from the debut of Adm. Jeremy Boorda, the new chief of naval operations, the biggest threat to the U.S. Navy is not our nation's enemies, or even brutal budget cuts leaving the service on the "ragged edge" of readiness. Rather, the greatest threat to the Navy is the extraordinary effect of sexual politics, an artful technique used

by Democratic congresswoman Patricia Schroeder to manipulate Pentagon officials in pursuit of her ideological goals.

Rep. Schroeder of Colorado, a senior member of the House Armed Services Committee, is a mistress of sexual politics. The technique works because it excuses Schroeder and her allies of the responsibility to make their case with rational arguments and empirical evidence that radical change is in the best interests of military women, the Navy, or the armed forces in general.

The real enemies for Donnolly and Webb were not foreign enemies but domestic ones, those who insisted on making an issue of Tailhook.

Webb faulted naval leadership with its unwillingness aggressively to defend officers who had attended the 1991 Tailhook Convention and whose promotions were delayed by Congress. Naval leaders had failed to prevent civilian interference in the Navy's "sacred promotional process" and allowed the interference of Senate staffers. What Webb missed is that the Senate is in fact obligated to confirm (or refuse to confirm) these appointments. Was it of no consequence to him that the Navy's own investigation reported that "closing ranks and obfuscation" were the rule among the aviators who attended Tailhook? When questioned, many displayed the attitude "What's the big deal?" The infamous gauntlet, a gathering of drunken aviators on both sides of the third-floor hallway in the Las Vegas Hilton, had gone on in similar fashion for several years (at least back to 1986), and many attendees who were questioned felt that women who chose to walk down that hall should have expected and accepted what they got. Even the secretary of the Navy, Lawrence Garrett, expressed his dismay at the extraordinary lack of cooperation among those attending: "The conduct of certain of our naval aviators during the Tailhook convention last September, and during the ensuing investigation, has stained the fabric of this institution. We know from the reports of victims that a significant number of naval aviators participated in or witnessed assaults. . . . However, relatively few naval officers provided information to the investigators, and those who did generally minimized their own involvement and/or failed to identify others who were present."[4]

The Navy's efforts to investigate itself only obscured the path toward justice. One of the original Naval Investigative Service investigators was taken off the case for propositioning Lieutenant Paula Coughlin, a helicopter pilot and Tailhook's most outspoken victim, and for calling her "Sweet Cakes."[5] A subsequent inquiry conducted by the Department of Defense assistant inspector general's office concluded that "many attendees viewed the annual conference as a type of 'free fire zone' wherein they could act indiscriminately and without fear of censure or retribution in matters of sexual conduct and drunkenness. Some of the Navy's most senior officers were knowledgeable as to the excesses practiced at Tailhook 91 and, by their inaction, those officers served to condone and even encourage the type of behavior that occurred there" (U.S. DOD, 1993: I-1).

The scandalous behavior displayed by aviators at the 1991 Tailhook convention was in keeping with previous gatherings. After the 1985 event, the board of directors recommended: 1) that duty officers be assigned to monitor the suites and be responsible for any misconduct, 2) that the number of suites and their hours of operation be limited, and 3) that commanding officers of the squadrons sponsoring the suites be held responsible for the activities that took place in and around their unit's suite. The president of the Tailhook Association continued to request that commanders assign duty officers to the hospitality suites and that they curb lewd behavior. These warnings were largely unheeded. Some squads did assign duty officers, but these officers did little to restrain behavior. Even before the news media got wind of Tailhook 91, F. G. Ludwig, the organization's president, delivered his annual post-mortem to the secretary of the Navy on "the Mother of All Hooks." In an October 11 letter to Garrett, Ludwig reported that $18,000 would be required to replace damaged hotel carpeting and that disaster was narrowly avoided when "a pressed ham [a naked rear end] pushed out an eighteenth-floor window which subsequently fell on the crowd below." He also relayed accusations of physical assault and physical abuse toward women who walked through the third-floor gauntlet. "Most distressing was the fact an underage young lady was severely intoxicated and had her clothing removed by members of the gauntlet," he noted (Zimmerman, 1995: 36–37).

Throughout the inquiry into the charges of unlawful behavior, Navy Secretary Garrett vowed that demeaning behavior toward women would not be tolerated and that instances of this kind would be dealt with "swiftly, fairly, and effectively." But the Navy's response to the Tailhook allegations indicated nothing of the sort. Garrett also pledged that commanding officers would bear the responsibility for the activities that occurred in and around their units' hospitality suites.[6] Garrett declared a new zero-tolerance policy with regard to sexual harassment, but his actions were too little, too late. No one was convicted of any of the ninety acts of assaults committed during the three-day conference: eighty-three against women and seven against men.

What if the drunken aviators at Tailhook had staged minstrel shows in the hospitality suites, had dressed in white KKK robes and hoods and harassed all African Americans, military and civilian, who happened to appear on that floor? Would leaders passing by be forgiven for saying nothing? The story of Tailhook details not only the debasement of and physical attack on women; it also tells about all those who turned a blind eye to such behavior. Daniel Howard, the undersecretary of the Navy, declared in a *New York Times* interview that "Americans don't want a naval officer to behave like just any person in society. They expect a higher standard of behavior."[7] In fact, when critics insisted that those responsible be prosecuted, they invoked no "higher standard of behavior." When they condemned those who witnessed a crime but failed even to notify the police, they demanded no superior moral standard than the decency and responsibility that come with citizenship. What happened at the Tailhook reunion was both traditional and criminal. The Navy failed to punish the perpetrators and others who sought to inhibit the truth from getting out, and people like James Webb minimized the significance of Tailhook and its deep-rooted misogynistic traditions, which breed such behavior.

In his 1996 address to the Naval Institute Conference, James Webb praised naval aviators as the best the Navy has to offer and asked why the Navy's leaders did not step in to defend aviators and their "unique culture" when the Tailhook scandal gave aviators and the Navy a bad name. Webb questioned how the acting secretary of the Navy at that time, who Webb insisted had never donned a military uniform, could characterize the events that took place at the Tailhook convention "a culture problem—culture, as an ethos, as in the overall body of traits that constitute an institution's history and traditions." He reserved his harshest criticism for the chief of naval operations, who, according to Webb, stood by at the news conference and failed to defend that culture.

In the question-and-answer period that followed this address, former undersecretary of the Navy Dan Howard stood up to point out errors in Webb's speech, not least of which was that Webb had attributed to someone else Howard's statement about the Navy's culture problem. Webb couldn't remember the name of the acting secretary he insisted had made the remark, but as proof he insisted that Howard could look up a *New York Times* article that Webb himself had written, attributing the statement to someone else. After Howard had spoken a few diplomatic but critical sentences, Webb stopped him in midsentence and told him that he hadn't been invited to address the audience and that if he wanted to present a point of view, he should write an article: "That's what I do."

In this address and in other writing, Webb persists in refusing to blame the Navy and Marine Corps officers who participated in the abuses of Tailhook, who failed to raise a hand to stop them and stonewalled the investigation that followed. Certainly the tales of naval heroes he heard as a midshipmen must have affirmed the values that those in charge should take responsibility for things that go wrong on their watch and that an officer is an officer whether on duty or off. The Naval Academy's chair of leadership, the retired admiral Bud Edney, did not hesitate to invoke the latter in his 1998 congressional testimony on the impeachment of President Clinton: "The fact is, core values for military leaders and their civilian commander-in-chief remain in effect no matter where they are or what they are doing twenty-four hours a day. When observed by anyone, they must reflect the institution's core values of respect for decency, human dignity, morality, and doing what is right, in or out of uniform, on an off duty" (Edney, 1998). One wonders what sort of defense Webb would have had Admiral Kelso, the chief of naval operations at the time, make in response to the acting secretary of the Navy's characterization of Tailhook as a "culture problem." Should Kelso have said, "The Navy stands proud of the culture of our aviators and applauds their 'party hardy' attitude. We defend the gauntlet as a time-honored tradition in the Navy, one that has enjoyed a prominent part in past Tailhook conventions and one that ships' crews reenact in 'crossing-the-line' ceremonies performed each time one of our ships crosses the equator"? Senior officers knew about these abuses from past Tailhooks but did nothing to prevent them. Although most officers were technically on leave to attend Tailhook 91, the Navy extended administrative support to its planners and provided military flights and even military aircraft for some officers.

The reason *this* Tailhook became a national scandal and former ones did not is that a female officer ultimately went public with the story of the assault she suffered while walking down the hall on the third floor. That officer, Lieutenant Paula Coughlin, first took her complaint to her commanding officer, Jack Snyder. According to Jean Zimmerman's book *Tailspin*, Coughlin repeatedly complained to Snyder, but Snyder's only reply was "That's what you get when you go to a hotel party with a bunch of drunk aviators" (Zimmerman, 1995: 40). Zimmerman goes on to claim that after a month of insisting that what happened to her at the Las Vegas Hilton was wrong, Coughlin told another officer that she was ready to quit her position as Snyder's aide. The friend arranged a meeting between Coughlin, Snyder, and himself at which Snyder agreed to forward her complaint. In the face of a subsequent delay, Coughlin forwarded her own letter. Snyder's soon followed.

Despite this, Webb insisted that a Navy leader should have defended Jack Snyder on the basis of his outstanding skills as a pilot and as a commander of a superior fighter squadron Webb criticized the admiral (Boorda) who dismissed Snyder without giving Snyder an opportunity to explain himself. Although Boorda was indeed the one to enact Jack Snyder's transfer, it was his predecessor, Admiral Kelso, who actually made the decision, with the backing of then secretary of the Navy Garrett. Even Snyder agreed that Boorda was simply following through on a decision that had already been made. As to Webb's assertion that Snyder was without a chance to explain his actions. Kelso insists that he in fact had a personal meeting with Snyder to discuss the matter (Kotz, 1996).

Webb was not alone in efforts to "turn the Navy over to new leaders." Three others participated in efforts to denounce Boorda in the final weeks of his life: Commander John Carey, USN; Roger Charles, a contemporary of Webb's at the Naval Academy and a fellow retired Marine; and David Hackworth, a highly decorated Army veteran turned writer about whom Webb had written an adulatory article in a 1989 issue of *Parade*. In December 1995, John Carey was relieved of his six-week command of the *Curtis Wilbur*, a Navy destroyer stationed in the Persian Gulf, and transferred to a desk job in San Diego. Vice Admiral John Redd, commander of the Navy's Fifth Fleet, made the decision to relieve him of his command after investigating complaints by sailors and officers that Carey had mistreated those under him. Although his behavior was visited on men as well as women, Carey clearly resented having women on board, claiming, "I didn't sign up to go to sea with women" (Kotz, 1996). He blamed the Navy's treatment of him on political correctness and cast his resentment on the most senior officer, Admiral Boorda. Carey learned from Robert Caldwell, editor of the Sunday "Insight" section of the *San Diego Union-Tribune*, that Webb was preparing an address to deliver at the annual Naval Institute Conference in April. To reinforce Webb's call for new naval leaders, Carey approached the *Navy Times* about publishing an anonymous letter from him calling for Boorda's resignation. In spite of the fact that the *Navy Times* had twice reported on his dismissal from the command of the *Curtis Wilbur*, it printed his defamatory letter without mentioning that he was a disgruntled officer who had just been relieved of his command. The letter appeared in the May 20, 1996, issue, but it was available to subscribers on May 13, three days before Boorda took his life. Like Webb, Carey found fault with the Navy's senior leaders. He called for Boorda to resign because he had not only lost the respect of fellow admirals, who called him "Little Mikey Boorda," but he had also lost the respect of most of the officer corps.

You cannot help but notice the similarity of Webb's speech and Carey's letter. Whereas Webb asks, "What admiral has had the courage to risk his own career by putting his stars on the table?" Carey calls for Boorda to "put his stars on the table and resign." Webb blames naval leadership for an increase in the attrition of aviators, and Carey cautions that "good people are leaving the service in droves." There's a peculiar point in Carey's letter at which Webb seems almost to inject his own disclaimer, designed to free himself from any charges of defamation, a simple dependent clause, "it was his belief": "Former Navy Secretary Jim Webb pointed out that it was his belief that the admirals had let their men down." This would have read much better simply as "Former Navy Secretary Jim Webb pointed out that the admirals had let their men down." It is one thing for Webb to talk about "the admirals" in his address and to accept the likelihood that a former secretary of the Navy might be privy to the derogatory quips of admirals; it is quite another for Carey, a mere commander, to speak as if he enjoyed the banter of admirals: "Behind his back, admirals often refer to the CNO as 'Little Mikey Boorda.'" Having no indication that the printed rebuke came from an officer who had recently been removed from his command, Boorda was reasonably disturbed by Carey's letter (Kotz, 1996).

After Boorda's suicide, Carey wrote another letter to the *Navy Times*, signing this one. The letter begins in the first-person singular as a straightforward apology. He confesses that no one in the Navy would ever have suspected that Boorda would commit suicide. Shortly after this apology, the speaker's voice switches from *I* to *we*, as if Carey believes himself to be speaking for others. What begins as an apology (Carey taking responsibility for the pain he might have inflicted) soon drifts into confused self-justification and stubborn insistence that his criticism was legitimate and that James Webb was justified in his call for a new naval leadership. Although his Navy remains "militarily strong," Carey, like Webb, frets about the loss of its soul: "We must get our self in order and restore the integrity that was our hallmark. It is time to stand up for what we believe in"—stand up, as Webb advocates, in opposition to elected leaders who dare to question the military and its "clean promotion process." Though Carey's letter is not as polished as Webb's rhetoric, it nevertheless adopts a call to insurgency, urging those in the military to actively resist the changes that they are being asked to make.

Two other leaders in that insurgency, Roger Charles and David Hackworth, provided the final embarrassment for Admiral Boorda in their efforts to show that he had worn medals to which he was not entitled. After his retirement from the Marine Corps, Charles worked for the National Security News Service, a nonprofit news organization that investigates stories in which it has a political interest and shares its information with the mainstream media. A year before Boorda's suicide, Charles had filed a request under the Freedom of Information Act for details on Boorda's medals. Boorda's office learned of Charles's request and conducted its own review of the admiral's citations. It determined that he was not authorized to affix two small bronze V's to two relatively minor ribbons he had received for service in the Vietnam War, one in 1965, while serving as weapons officer on the destroyer *John Craig*, and the other in 1972, at the completion of service as executive officer on the destroyer *Brooke.*, When informed that no record specifically authorizing the addition of the two V's could be found, Boorda removed them.

Charles sat on the story until the spring of 1996, when he and the former charismatic commander David Hackworth, who at the time was serving as a contributing editor for *Newsweek*, decided to pursue the story as a possible *Newsweek* cover. Hackworth sensed the human dimension to the story and mentioned to his assistant that if it were known, Boorda "might put a gun to his head." Hackworth also scheduled an appointment with Boorda, knowing that he would have to back out because of a previously scheduled appointment for oral surgery. Instead, Charles, along with the veteran *Newsweek* reporters John Barry and Evan Thomas, met with Boorda after first meeting among themselves. Thomas harbored some misgivings about the warrior-turned-journalist duo, having assessed Charles as "too conspiracy-minded" on an earlier *Newsweek* story. He admitted: "Outsiders generally make me nervous. They're not our own people. Hackworth makes me nervous; I think of him as more of a soldier than a journalist. I wanted to have the [full-time] correspondents I most trust involved" (Alter, 1996: 8, 30).

Charles showed the reporters pictures from the 1970s when Boorda was wearing no V's and others from the 1980s with the V's. He gathered the evidence, and Hackworth ran interference with *Newsweek* and set up the meeting with Boorda, which never took place. Boorda told his aides he was leaving his Pentagon office to go to his residence at the Naval Yard for lunch, but instead, the chief of naval operations walked into his garden and shot himself in his heart, where the disputed V's had once adorned his uniform. A suicide note addressed to his sailors described the issue of the medals as "an honest mistake."

You might assume that an institution with so many regulations— one priding itself on precision—would eliminate all ambiguity in specifying which medals someone is entitled to wear. That is anything but the case, however. Criteria for awarding the same medal differ from service to service and within a given service are subject to change over time. Eager to find officers wearing medals to which they were not entitled, James Webb, while secretary of the Navy, instituted a regular practice of investigating the medals worn by all flag officers up for promotion. At that time, the awards office conducted a review of all 257 admirals and found that 30 percent, including Boorda, were wearing improper medals, but no one ever informed Admiral Boorda. Although a zealot on this issue, Webb insisted that he not be quoted in the *Newsweek* article Charles and Hackworth were preparing. Fearing that he might be suspected of being behind the story, he asked Hackworth not to quote him: "This could be a big deal . . . If you quote me on this, they'll say I'm behind it"(Kotz, 1996).

The V, although clearly defined as valor in combat by the Army and the Marine Corps (Charles had received the same medal with the authorized V), enjoyed a vaguer definition in the Navy, one that fluctuated over time. Boorda served on destroyers in the South China Sea. Although this was designated a combat zone, his destroyers, and indeed most Navy ships, with the exception of the "Brown Water Navy" river boats, did not engage in combat during the Vietnam War. Retired Admiral Elmo Zumwalt, Jr., a former chief of naval operations, told a *New York Times* reporter, "You just assumed a ribbon authorized in a combat area [as was Boorda's] carries with it the V" and affirmed that he had routinely informed sailors that they were entitled to wear the V. Paul Bucha, the president of the Congressional Medal of Honor Society, supported that position: "Navy officers had a far different standard for awarding the combat V than did the Army. In the Navy, it means you participated in a combat operation . . . It has nothing to do with being shot at."[8] The captain of the ship at the time, J. K. Jobe, was issued the same award for the same operation and was authorized to wear the V (Kotz, 1996).

Ironically, exactly a year after Boorda killed himself, ABC and CBS ran reports claiming that Hackworth was himself not entitled to several of the medals he had claimed. Subsequently, an Army investigation raised ambiguity about two of Hackworth's awards, the prestigious Ranger Tab and one of his two Distinguished Flying Cross medals. Upon learning of this, Hackworth removed them from his Internet page.[9]

At the heart of the issue of who can wear V's lies a less trivial dispute about who has the right to be called a warrior and who is entitled to lead the military.[10] Someone like Admiral Boorda, who pushed for an expanded role for women in the military and who represented to his ardent critics not a warrior but a bureaucrat, was clearly regarded by some as not entitled, despite the fact that as NATO commander in 1994 he ordered the first air strike in Bosnia. The Marine Corps, reserving for itself the last province of pure masculinity in the larger, corporate Navy, cherishes the myth that warriors are exclusively hand-to-hand combatants and resists more than any other service the mixing of men and women. Marines' training maintains separate but (purportedly) equal status for female recruits so that women will in no way "taint" the training of men and have no opportunity to achieve warrior status, or the valor that comes with it. The Marine Corps, from Hackworth's point of view, has opted for the high road of tradition and with it a higher ethical way: "All the services have serious honor and morality problems except the U.S. Marine Corps, which just goes along in its old-fashioned proud, ethical way."[11]

Webb, Charles, and Hackworth represent a contingent of retired military officers who served in Vietnam at a time when the grunts, asked to make all the sacrifices, grew to doubt the skill and integrity of those generals who were out of harm's way, leading a war not to a victorious conclusion but to weekly tabulations of body counts. They fought in Vietnam when many of their age either doubted the military's mission or boisterously protested it. Psychologically, it is easy to understand their disdain for elected civilians, who as a group are increasingly unlikely to have served in the armed services.[12] Psychologically, it is easy to understand their doubts about military leaders who seem to them too easily influenced to make changes in the military by civilians who have never put on a uniform and never made the sacrifices they have made. It is a perspective easy to understand but dangerous to support.

If we can understand their disdain for Boorda, no one should condone or accept their tactics. As chief of naval operations, Boorda was prepared to advance the Navy's interests with the political forces gathered on the Hill. He was selected in part because he could be successful in negotiating with Congress. What he was woefully unprepared for was the power exerted by another group seeking to exercise influence over the Navy: the retired officer corps, the most reactionary of whom insisted that "their" CNO, at all costs, resist the changes they sensed coming in the aftermath of Tailhook. Boorda was vulnerable to the charge of being an outsider precisely because his entire naval career had been that of an outsider getting in: the sailor turned admiral, the non-academy grad making it to the top, the Jew in the land of one-, two-, and three-star gentiles, and the ship driver among the trendy submariners and flyboys. For Boorda, being publicly denounced by a former secretary of the Navy must have smarted, but discovering that the entire audience of midshipmen, the Navy's next generation of officers, had risen for a standing ovation at the end of such a lashing must have wounded. A fact that Webb knew and Boorda probably did not is that the young and enthusiastic mids give a standing ovation at the least provocation. (I remember when a literary scholar long past his prime delivered a rambling and uninteresting talk before most of the brigade, many of whom nodded throughout, but when the lecture was finished, all the mids stood and gave him a hearty round of applause.) The day before Webb's speech, the midshipmen had sent off Boorda himself with a standing ovation.

Boorda lived with the echo of Webb's talk, as newspapers reported it and audiences questioned him at appearances in the days that followed. On May 5, Robert Caldwell reprinted Webb's address in the *San Diego Union-Tribune*. Caldwell had not only discussed the content of the address with Webb before Webb delivered it; he had also spoken with Carey about Webb's upcoming speech (Kotz, 1996).

On April 25, 1996, Webb publicly made the case to an audience of the Navy's future officers that their leaders were cowardly, that they did not deserve their positions of leadership, and that they should be replaced by new leaders, not in order to protect and defend the nation or its constitution but in order to preserve the Navy's culture: "It's time to give the Navy back to such leaders. . . . Without officers who will defend the Navy's culture and take decisive action when it is needed, there will be nothing but continuing chaos."

Webb made no claim that the naval leaders he faulted had failed to deploy their ships, their submarines, and their aircraft to the world's trouble spots; rather, they had failed in what Webb called a more important duty: defending the Navy's "hallowed traditions." Consider for a moment Webb's standard for measuring leadership: the defense of hallowed traditions. What are these "hallowed traditions" which need defense? From whom are naval leaders to defend them? From the women whose very presence in uniform threatens male exclusivity? Against the civilian government to whom the military must report? Because Webb could not imagine a position different from his own, he could not imagine that a leader might listen to civilian concerns and agree with them. For Webb, taking women seriously as full members of the armed forces was simply a bald ploy for personal advancement, not a principled position.

Courageous and true military leaders, according to Webb, will put their own positions on the line to counter civilian pressure. Webb offers an example from his own brief stint as secretary of the Navy: in the face of cutbacks ordered by the secretary of Defense, he argued that the Air Force and the Army should receive the brunt of military cuts and the Navy should continue its aggressive shipbuilding program. Unable to tolerate any diminishment of his six-hundred-ship Navy, Webb resigned rather than retire sixteen frigates, in what seemed more like an intemperate huff than an exercise in strong leadership.

Webb disappointed several, baffled some, and even prompted the columnist George Will to remark, "Webb, the warrior-novelist, is temperamentally unsuited to the culture of government. He was a man to take yonder hill. Capitol Hill is another matter."[13] Certainly other leaders have managed both to lead the military and to work within a civilian government (Boorda was one of these), but when these two cultural realms are held to be so distinct, so irreconcilable (one pure, the other polluted), defense of the nation by the military becomes in a strange way defense of the culture of the military by representatives of the nation.

In an interview with Peter Boyer, who was investigating the Boorda suicide for a *New Yorker* article on the subject, Webb rang the same bell, claiming that real leaders willingly sacrifice their own positions for the principle of the noninterference of Congress, as should have been done in the aftermath of Tailhook: "There should have been a point where the senior leadership said, 'This is beyond the authority of the Congress. We will not go along with it. Find somebody else to go along with it.'" (Boyer, 1996: 74). In his April 1996 speech, Webb likened his demonstration of the ultimate test of leadership, the threat to resign, to a 1949 struggle for the Navy's aircraft carrier program. In 1949, when Secretary of Defense Louis Johnson canceled the Navy's aircraft carrier program, Navy Secretary John Sullivan resigned, followed by the "Revolt of the Admirals." As a result, the defiant naval leadership saved the carrier program. Unlike the 1949 show of force, Webb's was a lone voice, not that of a strong leader whose commanders unite in support. Webb even admitted that he did not expect his position to have their broad support: "There was no second Revolt of the Admirals, nor did I expect one, but the lack of vigorous argument on behalf of their Navy did, frankly, amaze me." To plan so extreme a ploy while knowing you lack the support of those under you is either foolishness or zealotry. Webb's dramatic gesture resulted in little more than the selection of the next secretary of the Navy.

Ultimately, Webb's battle with the civilians in Congress was not over readiness, it was over culture. Webb was trying to protect and preserve his Navy, whose traditions he held dear, from outsiders set on changing it. Those in the conservative flanks of the culture wars often argue for purity over mixing. In defense of the status quo, they warn of weakening that will issue from the incorporation of new, previously marginalized groups.

The culture wars of the 1960s had to do with racial mixing: in the fight for voter rights and the rights of African Americans to mix with whites in restaurants, on public transportation, and in schools and universities. In the 1970s Phyllis Schlafly railed about the need for women and men to have clearly defined and distinct spheres. The crossing over of women from their traditional domestic duties to the workplace represented a mixing that was anathema to those committed to preserving the status quo. Schlafly's work continues with the Center for Military Readiness, an organization that has forcefully lobbied in the last decade against women's entrance into nontraditional roles in the military.

Conservatives like Schlafly, Elaine Donnelly, Anita Blair, and James Webb, who lay claim to a sacrosanct separate culture, do so not on the basis of race or ethnic background but on the basis of gender. Those who seek to preserve all that is unique in military culture strive to keep it free from the corruption of what is labeled "civilian culture." So often in the military, *civilian* has been synonymous with *female*. A very restrictive notion of military culture, this view depends on a macho warrior ethos. According to Webb, military culture must be maintained and defended against a very real enemy—women, those "ardent feminists [who] have focused on the military as an important symbolic battlefield." Webb charged military leaders with passivity and cowardice (Webb, 1996: A23).

One of James Webb's favorite words is *warrior*, a term of identity that excludes women. There are few words left that so desperately retain their gender-rigid fix. If women and known homosexuals could be acknowledged as warriors, Webb's fragile definition of masculinity would be shattered. The values of many Americans have changed with regard to the work that women can do, and that change is creeping into the military. Opponents of change, who hold firm to what they describe as "tradition," or the belief that women should be segregated in certain jobs, look to the military institutions of old or to the Marine Corps of today. Webb and other opponents to change would do well to listen to the words of Secretary of the Army Togo West, on his recommendation of a task force on extremist activities: "The fact is that the United States Army does not belong to me or to the Secretary of Defense. As proud as we are of them, it does not belong to our soldiers or our NCOs or our officers. It belongs to the American people. And as such, it should espouse the values of the people to whom it belongs."[14]

Admiral Boorda's suicide was many things to many people. To the conspiracy theorists who logged onto the chat lines, his death, like those of Vince Foster, the White House deputy counsel, and Commerce Secretary Ron Brown, killed in a plane crash over Bosnia, was part of a sinister plot by some threatening force, either domestic or foreign, to control the United States. Those like former secretary of the Navy John Lehman, who had themselves been singed by the press, placed the full blame on a hostile media: "Boorda's death was seen, by some of the chiefs, as the ultimate declaration to protect his service from what all the services have seen as a lynch mob that's out to break the culture of the military" (Alexander, 1996: 118).

The lynching metaphor sounds like the countercharge of the Supreme Court nominee Clarence Thomas in which he dubbed his Senate confirmation hearing and the intensive glare of the press it spawned as a "high-tech lynching." Such a rhetorical ploy allowed Thomas, accused of sexual harassment by Anita Hill, to shift position from predator to victim. Discussing the death of Admiral Boorda, former secretary of the Navy Lehman spoke as one who had felt the personal embarrassment consequent to press inquiries into the Tailhook scandal. One flamboyant example, the opening of Gregory Vistica's *Fall from Glory: The Men Who Sank the U.S. Navy*, reports eyewitnesses to

Secretary Lehman's enthusiastic encounter with a prostitute at the 1986 Tailhook convention:

> When the door to the suite at the Las Vegas Hilton opened, a prominent member of President Ronald Reagan's administration and a naked woman were clearly visible. He was lying on his back, stretched out in front of a throng of naval officers. There were probably one hundred men watching him, laughing with him and feeling there was no better place to be right then than in this room near this man, captivated by his powerful presence . . . Many knew he was married and had three children. Almost everyone knew who he was, which made the show that much more fascinating. They were standing almost shoulder to shoulder, their necks twisting this way or that so they could take in everything . . . The carpet was spongy and damp from alcohol spilled on it by drunken military men. The room itself reeked with the odor of booze and sweat. But nobody seemed to care much. All eyes were on the man and the naked woman standing over him, wagging her bare rump in a teasing motion (Vistica, 1995: 13–14).

Like James Webb, Lehman believed that Tailhook should have been only a minor story, but it lingered in the consciousness of the American public, they conjectured, not because it was so outrageous but because a press obsessed with "gutter reporting" would not let it go.[15]

Although the *Washington Times*, like James Webb, Roger Charles, John Carey, and Elaine Donnelly, had attacked Boorda for his capitulation to a feminist agenda, when he was dead, the paper bizarrely pronounced him a victim of a secret feminist campaign. On September 13, 1998, the paper opened an article with the statement, "An argument can be made that Secretary of the Navy John H. Dalton is directly responsible for the suicide of Adm. Jeremy Boorda." The article goes on to explain that the blame must rest on Dalton because he carried out "a radical feminist agenda on the U.S. Navy and then covered it up." This was an agenda that resulted in the "witch hunt"—ironic gender reversal here—that ruined the careers of some who attended Tailhook, precipitated an increased rate of aviators opting to leave the Navy, and "led directly to the death of Adm. Boorda." One day Boorda was the perpetrator of a feminist agenda; the next he was its victim. Once dead, Boorda could no longer serve as the scapegoat, so the stigma moved to Dalton and the demonized feminists.[16]

Of all of Boorda's attackers, only Carey and Hackworth admitted any remorse, but the *Washington Times*'s efforts to diminish its own heavy-handed criticism of Boorda and his stand on women in the Navy is clearly one of the strangest instances of weaseling out of any culpability. For those who live the code of honor rather than those who merely mouth it, Boorda's disproportionate response proves that he was a man of honor in the strictest sense and that the code of honor is a standard few can live by. The tragedy of this episode in naval history lies in the fact that Boorda was a fully capable, admirable leader of extraordinary use to the military. It demonstrates the power of the honor code on an honorable man and its cynical manipulation by politicians in khaki.

What many found alarming about the Boorda suicide was its disproportion and its finality in the face of what some saw as a natural mistake, others a small foible, and still others as a major embarrassment. In his suicide note, "To My Sailors," Admiral Boorda gave the most authoritative explanation of his action:

> *What I am about to do is not very smart but it is right for me. You see, I have asked you to do the right thing, to care for and take care of each other and to stand up for what is good and correct. All of these things require honor, courage and commitment . . . our core values. I am about to be accused of wearing combat devices on two ribbons I earned during sea tours in Vietnam. It turns out I didn't really rate them. When I found out I was wrong I immediately took them off but it was really too late. I don't expect any reporters to believe I could make an honest mistake and you may or may not believe it yourselves. That is up to you and isn't all that important now anyway. I've made it not matter in the big scheme of things because I love our Navy so much, and you who are the heart and soul of our Navy, that I couldn't bear to bring dishonor to you.*

If you care to do so, you can do something for me. That is take care of each other.

Be honorable. Do what is right. Forgive when it makes sense, punish when you must but always work to make the latter unnecessary by working to help people be all they really can and should be. My idea of one-on-one leadership really will work if you let it and honestly apply it. We have great leaders and I know you'll succeed.

Finally, for those who want to tear our Navy down, I guess I've given them plenty to write about for a while. But I will soon be forgotten. You, our great Navy people, will live on. I am proud of you. I am proud to have led you if only for a short time. I wish I had done it better.

J. M. Boorda

9. Prisoners of War

Military prisoners of war share the advantage that they enter prison camps already socialized by one total institution before capture. Their military training has already mortified their selves, curtailed their freedom of movement, and minutely regulated daily activities such as eating, sleeping, and dressing. Conscripts and enlistees alike have forfeited to military overseers their power to make independent choices. The prison camp deepens that forfeiture by more or less systematically stripping them of their identity as soldiers. Their captors confiscate their weapons and then undermine their discipline either by leaving them idle for days, weeks, even years, or by assigning them servile drudgery, which rewards the laborer only by relieving boredom. While confinement changes from fact to condition to fate, the war goes on; other GIs take the places of men who must invest in memory—memory as the exertion of recalling the people they were, memory as the faith that they have not been forgotten by family, friends, and country.

Despite being *hors de combat* and subjected to institutional measures designed to extinguish social memory, military prisoners form bootleg groups that vie with the institution for control, if not of the inmates' docile bodies, then at least of their contraband spirits, by reviving an eclipsed esprit de corps. By maintaining a sense of themselves as soldiers, pilots, military nurses, or Marines, prisoners defy the power of the institution to transform them into guilty civilians serving time or into mangy and desperate creatures lost to human feeling.

Often, suffering is not the fault of an individual jailer but the effect of a prevailing condition of scarcity. Because prison camps reflect the disparate cultures of the combatants and sensitively register the shifting fortunes of war, they have often lacked the appropriate food and medicine to keep prisoners from perishing from starvation and easily treatable diseases. The standard fare in a World War II German camp was warm water flavored with a little cabbage or potato and brown bread.[1] Many Japanese camp commanders maintained the attitude that it was their responsibility to provide rice; anything else was up to the prisoners. To augment their scant rations, prisoners in the larger and more stable camps organized garden crews and arranged for delivery and distribution of illegal gifts from sympathetic local residents. Prisoners without other resources reported eating whatever rats, lizards, and snakes they could find within the compounds to stay alive. One group of prisoners in a Japanese camp even removed eggshells from their captives' garbage and ground them between bricks into a powder, to which they would add water for a calcium drink.

Scarcity is the grandmother of invention. Consider the sterling example of the group of Army nurses interned in the Philippines during World War II. As the Japanese invaded the Bataan Peninsula in April 1942, most of the nurses evacuated to the island of Corregidor and set up a hospital in the Malinta Tunnel—actually not a single tunnel but a network of concrete tunnels built into the side of a hill. From that post they treated the wounded. As many as one thousand patients at a time filled the tunnels. In May 1942, Corregidor surrendered to the Japanese, who immediately transferred the male military personnel to Bilibid prison and the Army nurses, along with five thousand foreign civilians, to Santo Tomas Camp. The Navy nurses went to Los Banos, which also housed more than two thousand other prisoners.[2]

The nurses in both camps spent the rest of the war struggling to survive and to help the sick as best they could with precious little medicine, antiseptics, or bandages. Although the nurses had already abandoned their regulation white uniform as too fussy for the island's field hospitals, throughout the ordeal of their captivity they proudly and stubbornly retained a red cross carefully appliqued to an armband. But the resistance was more than ornamental. The nurses actively countered enforced deracination by constructing an alternative domestic space and compensated for systematic deprivation by ingeniously transforming even seemingly useless objects into tools of practical value. They fashioned knitting needles from straightened barbed wire, which they sharpened at the ends by rubbing it on concrete. Bullet casings doubled as thimbles. They unraveled worn-out sweaters and reknitted the yarn into warm socks. When their cotton undergarments fell apart, they picked up bits of string around the camp and knitted themselves new ones.

The reconstruction of a domestic space and the inventive application of domestic skills were not restricted to female prisoners. There is no evidence that any prisoners, male or female, tried to turn the prison into a facsimile of stateside barracks or a parade ground. Often separated from fellow prisoners for long periods of time and with few physical materials at hand, POWs in solitary confinement constructed a culture of memory through replication and reenactment. They conjured intricate buildings room by room and furnished them in extraordinary detail. They played day-long games of golf, hole by hole, on the courses they recalled. And they rehearsed an entire series of National League games play by play. One prisoner scratched out a keyboard on the dirt floor of his cell so he could "play" as he recalled his favorite concertos. Another spent hours repairing, washing, and polishing an imaginary motorcycle. Though these sound like the fabricated worlds madmen inhabit, prisoners credited the mind's ability to create weeks', months', and even years' worth of imaginary pastimes with keeping them sane. The virtual realities they constructed were a relief from numbing boredom and an escape from physical suffering, but they were also assertions of the prisoners' continued participation in a humanely ordered world and promises to themselves of an eventual return.

Despite severe privation, prisoners often managed to observe those holidays that had formerly punctuated the passing of the year. At Christmas they constructed nativity scenes out of toilet paper and bits of food and made Christmas cards from scraps of brown paper discarded by guards (Howes, 1993: 120). One Christmas, a prisoner and his five buddies hung up socks, and each shared what little he had with the others:

> Each of us had something put away for the day we would be rescued. We hung out six socks, then asked, "What can we put in our socks?" One person had a package of razor blades; each one of us got one, to shave our huge beards. I had one piece of chocolate

which I divided. One of my companions had a little bar of soap which he divided. Someone else had shoelaces. I remember I got one shoelace, a little piece of chocolate, a razor blade, a tiny piece of soap, and a couple of buttons. It is strange, but when people have less and less, they tend to hang on to crazy little things which never amount to much. Nevertheless, that served as our Christmas. I made two little flower pots from bamboo, and I put a little weed in them. I then put a holy picture with them; and that was our Christmas scene (Havard, 1991: 42).

Australians imprisoned in Singapore during World War II labored long to construct a simple chapel out of found materials. In the Vietnam War, North Vietnamese jailers of the Hanoi did their best to assure that there were no materials to be found. With nothing to make gifts from, and therefore nothing tangible to exchange, the Hanoi prisoners one year drew names and exchanged imaginary gifts; each giver lavished the recipient with an elaborate description of his present (Kathryn Johnson, 1983: 41).

Holding on to religious practices and holiday traditions, however spare, gave each prisoner continuity with his former self and a sense of community both with fellow prisoners and with those on the home front who were performing similar rites.[3] Although prisoners of war never forgot that they were captives, they struggled to maintain an identity distinct from the abject one imposed by the enemy. When American prisoners in a German camp were allowed to turn in their ragtag uniforms for new sets provided by the Red Cross, camp officials insisted on affixing a black triangle with the letters KGF (for *Kriegsgefangener,* or prisoner of war). In protest, eight prisoners painted "U.S.A." on the backs of their shirts. This infuriated the Germans, who insisted that the nationalistic inscription be removed. The Germans threatened to shoot the eight rebels for mutiny if they did not remove the offending letters by a prescribed deadline. John Young, one of the eight, described what happened: "Let me tell you how much I love those GIs. On the morning of the deadline, we had roll call, and there wasn't a single GI in the compound that didn't have the letters 'U.S.A.' on his uniform. It's one thing to make an example of eight people. Shoot them for mutiny, and it'll keep the rest in line, but it's another to slaughter 784 people. It would take quite some explaining. Those GIs saved our hides that day, or eight of us would have been shot for sure" (Havard, 1991: 59).

Although no prisoners were permitted to display national flags, Australian soldiers imprisoned in Sumatra hoisted up a flagpole a stuffed kangaroo made from scraps of brown cloth by one of the imprisoned nurses—a gesture lost on the Japanese (Clarke, Burgess, and Bradon, 1988: 136). Personal mementos, photos, and a letter that had gotten through during years of captivity were all freighted with significance and, and if kept from the hands of the guards, helped to sustain an identity. To foil confiscation, prisoners in Japanese camps secreted family photos in straw ticking, in the soles of shoes, and in the hems of shorts.

The culture of memory was also a culture of performance. The reconstruction of domesticity was, of course, home economics of the most practical and urgent kind. Yet the symbolic recreation of a former world was not merely practical; the collaborative contrivance of domesticity was a kind of theater in which nurses played at being themselves rather than accepting the brutal circumstances of their lot. That serious play, which involved miniaturization and substitution, simulation and dressing up, was just one variety of individual and collective make-believe. As dismal as prison camps inevitably were, an irrepressible theatricality invariably interrupted the gloom. Most prisoners faced each morning with the prospect of just another day, bleached of all the animating detail of everyday life. To relieve the boredom of the prison camp, they occupied themselves by telling and retelling the plots of novels they recalled, reciting poetry they had memorized as children, writing their own poems when paper was available, recounting (with glorious embellishments) the plots of John Wayne films, and improvising their own games. Most prison camps lacked enough blankets, let alone any supply of recreational materials, so soldiers fabricated their own decks of cards, chess sets, dominos, and dice. Early on in World War II, when prisoners enjoyed fairly good health, they organized softball leagues and wrestling competitions; cricket matches took place when there were enough British, Australian, or New Zealand prisoners.

Music and theater offered those interned for long periods of time in large camps an antidote to "barbed-wire fever," the general malaise of prisoners. Some camps simply organized talent shows, or a prisoner would write a script for a play—melodrama or musical comedy—and others would perform it. Larger prisons, both Japanese and German, allocated enough resources for the prisoners to mount theatrical productions; some even staged serious dramas that were rehearsed for weeks and were complete with elaborate sets and costumes inventively assembled from whatever scraps the prisoners could salvage. The most professional of these camp companies included casts, lighting crews, and stagehands. Changi, a camp in Singapore that housed nearly 17,000 Allied prisoners, at one point maintained a drama troop of thirty full-time members (Clarke, Burgess, and Braddon, 1988: 69).

Female impersonators provided comic relief at first. But as familiarity increased, hilarity subsided, and men who were practiced and plausible as women were soon accepted in serious female roles. Privileges followed. For example, actors skilled at impersonating women were permitted to grow their hair long to enhance the gender transformation they made onstage. Occasionally the feminine disguise was so convincing that it not only evoked admiration but produced serious confusion. A member of Changi's "Concert Party" cast, Slim DeGrey, recalls one performer who did a very successful impersonation of a woman. In fact, he looked so beautiful as a woman that one of their Japanese captors became hopelessly smitten. Fellow prisoners chided the performer,

"Your boyfriend's here again, Norm," one of the boys said. "He'll be bringing you flowers next."

"I wish he'd bring me a dirty big steak and a couple of eggs. I'd even let the little ugly bastard have a feel of me tits," Norm grinned at the thought. "Can you imagine his reaction if he grabbed one of my half-coconut shells? Reckon that'd dampen his ardour, or should I say, flatten his hard-on."

The star-struck guard came back for several nights to watch the dazzling performer. Then one night he ventured backstage and demanded that Norm take off his clothes.

"All right, pal," Norm said to the Jap, "so you think I'm a real girl, eh? Well, we'll soon fix that up."

Norm put his hands up his dress first of all, then tugged his shorts down. The Jap's eyes popped at that. Then, with a magnificent flourish, Norm lifted his skirt and ... whammo, "Look at that!" Norm was generously endowed by nature ... he had the biggest donga in the concert party.

The Jap was thunderstruck. He reeled backwards in amazement and hit the wall, dropping his rifle to the floor. He stood there for a few seconds as though he was paralyzed, as Norm held the pose. The Jap's eyes were riveted on Norm's anatomy, he seemed to have frozen. Whether it was the realization that Norm wasn't a female, or the shock of seeing such a whopping big doodle on this now unquestionable figure, who just a few seconds ago was a beautiful, gorgeous, desirable glamour girl, we will never know.

He stooped down and picked up his rifle, looked at us all, half smiled and nodded his head as if to say, "He's a man all right, he's not a girl, he's a man."

The Jap turned around and walked through the door and we never saw him again (DeGrey, 1991: 151–152).

Although prisoners in civilian prisons attest to the prevalence of homosexual encounters, prisoners of war avoid mention of them. With thousands of men living in such close quarters with a great deal of time on their hands, some homosexual liaisons must blossom. The dispensation of the theater in Changi enabled men to entertain inadmissable desires openly and yet legitimated evasion. Note that although DeGrey clearly accepts that Norm looks sexually attractive, he never countenances the possibility that the prison guard may in fact have desired Norm, knowing full well that he was a male in woman's clothing. How could the guard have thought otherwise? It is inconceivable that a Japanese prison guard would casually assume that Australian soldiers had smuggled a woman into a remote all-male camp and were parading their prize before the eyes of their captors. If in fact a woman did disguise herself as a male soldier in order to accompany a lover, for example, is it possible that the Japanese would think she would blow her cover by launching a stage career in prison?

For DeGrey's interpretation of the incident to be credible, we must assume, as many prisoners did, that the Japanese guards maintained a childlike hold on reality, one easily manipulated by the disguises of the theater, which to that degree were acts of symbolic aggression against the jailers. DeGrey does not offer Norm as the member of a class of prisoners called transvestites. Norm is not deviant but representative. He stands in for all prisoners. Although he appears emasculated, under his disguise he actually sports the largest token of Australian masculinity in the group, a masculinity so impressive that it temporarily disorients the enemy. Like the Medusa's head, Norm's "whopping big doodle," "the biggest donga in the concert party," effectively paralyzes the guard. DeGrey's story thus manages the sexual tension coiled in the cross-dresser's role by subsuming it in a classic dupe-the-guard story, which portrays the person in power as a simpleton easily fooled by the wily prisoner. The 1960s TV series *Hogan's Heroes* offers an extended illustration of the same reassuring premise, which promises compensation for incarceration and physical privation by the endless playing out of winning stratagems against the guards in games of the prisoners' devising.

The disorientation of institutional roles induced by theater opened for prisoners a free zone in which mildly subversive acts might be played out, not to indulge the illusory goal of toppling the prison and all its minions, but for the sake of preserving the morale necessary for survival. Toward the end of the war, the Concert Party became increasingly more explicit, until the Japanese finally put it out of business for staging a production allegorizing the triumphant reassertion of Allied masculinity. A female impersonator played the part of an Asian maiden courted by a British sailor. In this inversion of *Madame Butterfly*, the sailor wins the girl only to become completely dominated by the Asian *belle dame sans merci*. Imprisoned beyond endurance, he rebels and asserts his dominion by slaying her, a climax accompanied by exuberant crescendos, crashing cymbals, and enthusiastic applause from the audience. The message was so transparent that even those guards who knew no English got the point, and the authorities promptly outlawed any more productions.

Generally, humor, not hatred, gave prisoners relief from the overwhelming awareness of a confinement that was at best indefinite, at worst terminal. They joked about their lot ("We're the forgotten men of Bataan/No mama, no papa, no Uncle Sam"), but they reserved much of their humor for their guards. In German camps, prisoners practiced "goon-baiting" spoofs on their guards. A group of British prisoners, for example, designated several huts in a row as a train that departed from one of the London stations. At designated times they would assemble, present their tickets, and board the train. A few coming a little late would hurry to their car, lugging their imaginary suitcases, arriving just in time to present their ticket and board before the whistle (made by the prisoners) blew. After a week of this playing, the Germans thought these prisoners were going stir-crazy, so they created more recreation space and organized more activities to prevent the captives from going further around the bend (Clarke, Burgess, and Braddon, 1988: 29). A group of three hundred American prisoners in Korea all pretended to go insane: they woke in the middle of the night and ran to the latrines; some rode phantom bicycles and shaved their hair in peculiar styles.

POWs in Vietnam sought to reverse the dehumanization process by giving their guards animal nicknames or the names of simpletons. In his memoir, *In Love and War*, James Stockdale, a Navy pilot who was a prisoner of war for eight years, recalls the nicknames that stuck with the Americans' captors during their long imprisonment. "Dipshit" was a stretcher bearer, "Dog" the commander, "Rabbit" the interrogator, "Pigeye" the torturer, and "Cat" the officer who approved the severity of punishment. Stratton, a fellow prisoner with Stockdale, referred to

some of his captors as "Vegetable Vic," "Straps and Bars" (the chief torturer), and "Dum Dum" (Blakey, 1978: 96). Prisoners passed the time by
embellishing the nicknames with legends about the guards:

> Camancho and I amused ourselves with jokes and made-up stories
> about the guards. We would assume that Walter Brennan actually
> acted like Walter Brennan when nobody was watching, that he came
> from the same kind of mountain background, a sort of Vietnamese
> hillbilly. One of the guys with him had a sporty red hat, and we
> made up some kind of story about him—that he was one of the cats
> from Saigon. We just caricatured each of them according to his ap-
> pearance, made a joke out of it some way—how they happened to
> get there, what they would rather be doing than babysitting four
> Americans on this damned island in the middle of a swamp (Smith,
> 1971: 91).

The prison and its parts acquired their own nicknames. Prisoners
divided the "Hanoi Hilton" into "Heartbreak Hotel," "New Guy Village," and "Las Vegas," the latter with cell blocks called "Desert Inn,"
"Stardust," "Thunderbird," "Golden Nugget," and "Riviera."

Unlike gallows humor, which wittily turns on the last moment of
life and toasts the imminence of death, camp humor responds to the di-
lation of time that is the death-in-life of indefinite imprisonment. The
archetypal captivity joke: "I hear that the first hundred years of internment are the worst." Gallows jokes are short and sweet or short and
bitter, but short. Prisoners have time to tell stories, often stories about
time. In one joke that circulated through a Japanese camp in the Philippines, seven old men with long white hair and long beards sit on a bench
just inside the gates to the camp. One day a unit of Marines arrives and
bangs on the gate. There is no response. They bang again. Still no response. Finally the Marines break through the gates and ask the men,
"Is this a prisoner-of-war camp?" One of the men nods. They say, "We
are the United States Marines!" Another man nods. "We are stationed
in the South Pacific," says one of the Marines. There is no response.
Finally one of the Marines says, "We are from General MacArthur's

headquarters, and he sent us to find the teenagers." All the men look up and say, "We are the teenagers."[4]

The culture I have been describing had practical and symbolic consequences for World War II prisoners, compensating for physical privation, helping them pass the time in meaningful and pleasurable activity, reviving memories of home, affirming a sense of solidarity with other prisoners and with the forces in combat. But beyond its importance for morale, communication among prisoners, out of earshot of authority, could seriously threaten the stability of the institution. German and Japanese officials took extraordinary steps to suppress communication; yet such measures proved futile, defeated by the massive numbers of prisoners congregated in one place and their resourcefulness. O'Donnell, a Japanese camp in the Pacific, for example, housed more than 40,000 prisoners, less than one fourth of whom were Americans, in a facility designed for far fewer. The proportion of inmates to guards and the primitiveness of available technology made the surveillance to monitor, let alone suppress, communication impossible.

During the Vietnam War, the situation was dramatically different. Because the North Vietnamese and the Viet Cong took prisoners in a relatively small proportion to combatants, they could afford to dedicate a higher proportion of guards to prisoners in places designed for misery and equipped for torture by the French, who built them during their colonial rule. In an effort to extinguish all vestiges of esprit de corps, authorities systematically and brutally interdicted all normal forms of prisoner contact. Even so, they could not completely suppress communication. Even segregating prisoners in isolation cells and threatening to torture those who sent messages did not work. The threats steeled the prisoners' determination to break the silence and spurred their ingenuity in finding ways to do so. The Americans who were interned in Hanoi—largely officers and aviators whose planes had been shot down on bombing raids over the north—created "whisper holes" and efficient tap codes, complete with alphabets, to confound their captors. Torture would force a pause. But when the broken bodies mended enough, the tapping would begin again.

Prisoners were vigilant to avoid detection by guards. They watched for shadows and created small reflecting pools of urine near their doors in order to spot the authorities. They put the openings of their porcelain drinking cups up to the eight-inch thick wall and tapped with a fingernail to begin their secret communication. James Stockdale describes the way in which communication humanized the hell the prisoners found themselves in:

> As we worked the wall together, we learned to be sensitive to a whole new range of acoustic perception. Our tapping ceased to be just an exchange of letters and words; it became conversation. Elation, sadness, humor, sarcasm, excitement, depression—all came through. Sam and I would sign off before dark with abbreviations like GN (goodnight) and GBU (God bless you). Passing on abbreviations like conundrums got to be a kind of game. What would ST mean right after GN? Sleep tight, of course. And DLTBB? I laughed to think what our friends back home would think of us two old fighter pilots standing at a wall, checking for shadows under the door, pecking out a final message from the day with our fingernails: "Don't let the bedbugs bite" (Stockdale, 1984: 186).

Stockdale also recalls his elation at discovering his best friend seated across from him in a truck transporting them to another prison. Both were shackled, blindfolded, and seated toe to toe. Feeling an exposed toe across from him, Stockdale tapped, with a soft pressure of his toe, the characteristic conversation opener ("shave and a haircut"); the other American pushed his toe twice back to signal "two bits." Stockdale tapped out his initials; the other American followed with his, and Stockdale instantly recognized that the prisoner with the postnasal drip sitting across from him was his old friend:

> What a moment to savor! Here I am with a guy I love as much as any man. I know his wife and kids, his father and mother. They've been to our house to have dinner with Syb and me. . . . As the truck driver grinds gears and chugs along through crowded city streets for twenty minutes or so, and as guards move among us in the bright

light, clicking their pistols, checking blindfolds, and shouting "No!" to suspiciously shifting prisoners, Harry and I go into high (but motionless) gear, "tapping" with mere pressure through our foot soles. In this heady, fresh, January air, balmy and free of all that cell-block clamminess, I am transported into another world—the world of the aircraft carrier and its pilot ready rooms full of good and highly respected friends (Stockdale, 1984: 187).

The code that Stockdale used to recognize his friend and, under the suspicious eyes of the North Vietnamese, transport himself to the world of the aircraft carrier was an instrument that the cadre of prisoners at the Hanoi Hilton had developed and deployed to overcome separation and subvert North Vietnamese control. They recreated the bonds of a culture already formed. Unlike the inmates of the prisoner-of-war camps in World War II, which threw together enlisted men and officers, soldiers and pilots from diverse units, and men of several nationalities, the prisoners incarcerated in the Hanoi Hilton were a homogeneous group to start with. They did not rely on the code to get to know someone and develop trust in a situation calculated to produce paranoia; rather, they used it as a means to recognize someone they already knew (or knew about) and either trusted or did not. Propagation of the tap code fused this cohort of officers and aviators into a clandestine force with which the enemy seriously had to reckon. Prisoners cheered one another, passed along information about other prisoners, coached each other on what to expect from interrogators, and spread any news about what was happening in the war without uttering a word.

Like prisoners before them, the Vietnam POWs debated how to reconcile what they were trained to expect after capture with actual life in the hole. In all wars since World War I, the U.S. military has attempted to prepare at least those members of the armed services it regards as prospective combatants for the possibility of capture by providing some instruction in appropriate behavior once taken prisoner. A booklet entitled "Prisoner Sense," issued by the Navy's Bureau of Aeronautics in 1943, instructs aviators who are shot down to divulge only name, rank, and serial number: "Once you've delivered yourself of your name, rank, and serial number, pipe down. You can, according the Unofficial Military Law, Section 284 B, grunt, whistle, wheeze, or cluck, but don't SAY anything else. In short, SHUT UP" ("Prisoner Sense," 1943: 1). It warns that the enemy will try to extract more information by claiming that fellow prisoners have already talked and that cooperation will insure a more comfortable prison-camp stay. It cautions against taking along any documents that might provide information to the enemy—not only maps and orders but also theater ticket stubs, laundry markers, diaries, and letters, which might tip off the enemy about the location and strength of the prisoner's unit. It instructs the aviator to set his downed plane on fire if possible.

"Prisoner Sense" assures aviators that threats of torture are simply that, threats: "Violence is NOT going to be used on you. Keep that firmly in mind, no matter how grim the preparations for it get." "Don't worry about threats of violence. The enemy, and particularly the Japs, may try to scare you into talking. The Japs have been known to tell prisoners they were condemned to death, and then make all sorts of elaborate gestures to break down their morale. These gestures have taken various forms, all pretty corny. Sometimes the Japs trotted out what was presumably a firing squad and marched it up and down in front of the prisoners. Again, they made a great fuss of sharpening up swords, meanwhile carrying on a lot of patter built around dark hints of torture." In the face of such threats, prisoners are advised to "sit quite still and let your mind dwell on random topics." They are cautioned against the friendly fellow prisoner who may actually be an Axis sympathizer (likely to be an Australian, cautions this publication). Prisoners should likewise greet friendly and attractive nurses with suspicion. They too may be enemy agents out to entice some vital information from the prisoner ("Prisoner Sense," 1943: 7–8).

Such advice proved dead wrong. Japanese captors did more than make a show of violence and torture; they routinely and openly brutalized prisoners in order to deter and to punish. The story was much the same during the Korean War—and far better publicized. Korea was the first foreign war in which the United States failed to win a decisive victory. It was the first foreign war in which ideological contestation was fully as significant as combat on the battlefield. It was also the first televised war. The overmatched enemy hoped to exploit television as a medium of ideological war directly linked to the American home front by broadcasting the spectacle of penitent GIs compliantly denouncing the aggression of their own government—a scenario calculated to pierce the hearts and disturb the minds of the American people sufficiently to require adjustment of the terms by which cost-benefit analysis was conducted in Washington.

By the Vietnam War, the American military admitted that prisoners might be tortured and, through torture, turned into agents of the enemy. The Korean War had fundamentally altered the coordinates of what to fear from enemy captors and what to expect from American captives. Numerous well-publicized instances of American POWs who buckled under the enemy's regimen of mistreatment and indoctrination and became mouthpieces for Chinese propaganda had shattered military and civilian confidence in American invulnerability. Many stateside commentators interpreted the televised images of "brainwashed" GIs not as deplorable yet understandable human responses to inhuman treatment in the prison camps but as evidence of something degenerate in American culture. Eugene Kinkead, an American journalist, disproportionately influenced debate by attributing prisoners' capitulation to their captors to moral and political rot in the armed forces. Intent on branding American behavior as craven and symptomatic, Kinkead concocted invidious comparisons between American capitulations and the intransigence of Turkish prisoners. Kinkead's comparison was not pertinent, however. The Koreans captured fully half of the 229 Turkish prisoners in April 1951, after the worst was over for the prisoners (Biderman, 1963: 159). The Turks were an elite corps of volunteers, not draftees like the Americans. Not one Turkish prisoner died in captivity; 2,701 American POWs perished. The failure of the Communists to reeducate the Turks was practically insured by their difficulty in finding translators adequate to the job of indoctrination. More important, the Communists undoubtedly calculated the exchange value of a POW for propaganda purposes in terms of the influence his collaboration would have in discrediting and embarrassing their chief enemy, the United

States. What would be the propaganda value of coerced confessions by Turkish POWs? Why waste time demoralizing Ankara?

Ignored by Kinkead, such nuances were lost on an American public uncertain of the military mission in Korea and goaded into cold war hysteria. Communist spectacles and journalistic oversights had a cumulative effect. Government embarrassment at the public display of American POWs parroting the anti-American line of their captors, as well as the military's belated realization that American soldiers had been inadequately prepared to resist the kind of physical and psychological pressure applied to them, led to the establishment and promulgation of the U. S. Prisoner's Code of Conduct (Executive Order 10631) in 1955.

The 1949 Geneva Conventions defined the proper treatment of prisoners. The new U.S. code of conduct sought to standardize earlier directives regarding prisoner behavior in light of the Korean experience. An attempt to fight foreign ideology with homegrown ideology, the code stipulates the following six affirmations as the credo of the cold war combatant:

1. I am an American fighting man. I serve the forces which guard my country and our way of life. I am prepared to give my life in their defense.

2. I will never surrender of my own free will. If in command I will never surrender my men while they still have the means to resist.

3. If I am captured I will continue to resist by all means available. I will make every effort to escape and aid others to escape. I will accept neither parole nor special favors from the enemy.

4. If I become a prisoner of war, I will keep faith with my fellow prisoners. I will give no information or take part in any action which might be harmful to my comrades. If I am senior, I will take command. If not I will obey the lawful orders of those appointed over me and will back them up in every way.

5. When questioned, should I become a prisoner of war, I am bound to give only name, rank, service number, and date of birth. I will evade answering further questions to the best of my ability. I will

make no oral or written statements disloyal to my country and its allies or harmful to their cause.

6. I will never forget that I am an American fighting man, responsible for my actions, and dedicated to the principles which made my country free. I will trust in God and in the United States of America.

Although the drafters of the code of conduct no doubt intended it to guide the behavior of captured personnel, its inadequacy in the real-life circumstances of POWs was dramatically exposed during the Vietnam War. The code was an anachronism. It reiterated World War II directives that instructed troops, if taken prisoner, to "make every effort to escape."[5] Although prisoners' histories are filled with accounts of failed escape attempts, they tell of few successes. The injunction to attempt escape meant death to many of the POWs who tried and were caught. If they spoke reasonable German, prisoners who escaped from German camps at least stood a chance of making it to Allied lines. Most British, American, and Australian prisoners in Japanese camps had no hope of passing for Japanese soldiers or Filipino locals, and they could look to no friendly encampments. As Allen Washington, an African American infantry soldier captured by the North Koreans in 1950, summed it up, "I did contemplate escaping, but I knew I had no chance of success due to the fact that I'm a black man. I would have been one black man in a whole country of people with yellow skin."[6] Because prisoners in German camps were more likely to attempt escape, their German captors contrived to detect plans before escapes actually happened. In large camps they designated "ferrets" who scoured the grounds for any evidence of tunnels. In some instances, the Germans even planted officers proficient in English among the prisoners. The Japanese never had recourse to that method of preventing escapes; they found that the terrain, the lack of Allied lines anywhere near, and the public beheading of captured escapees were quite effective deterrents.

Although efforts to escape misfired far more often than they succeeded, planning escapes did excite hope in many dispirited POWs and gave them a project that surreptitiously defied the enemy. In German prisoner-of-war camps, many men organized so that a few could dare. Numerous bed slats were redeployed to support underground tunnels, and many a prisoner sewed long pockets the length of his trouser legs to fill with dirt for clandestine removal from the excavations. Known as "penguins," these dirt carriers would casually loosen a drawstring, and dirt would fall to the ground from a pant leg or a long coat. Excavators gave the tunnels American names so that they could discuss their plans without detection and devised codes so that they could communicate while working on different sections of a tunnel. Before their attempted escape, prisoners were instructed in practical German terms to aid them on their journey back to friendly territory. They were issued fake identity papers, forged in one prison by an extremely proficient draftsman, who affixed stamps carefully created to replicate the originals. They often glued a map into another item, like the inside flap of a book.

The most popular stories of escape celebrated cleverness rather than tactical expertise and logistics. In one story, a group of Allied prisoners walked out of a German camp dressed as a German general and his staff. John Castle, imprisoned by the Germans in World War II, recalls a Pole who managed to escape, only to be turned in by his brother-in-law and returned to prison. The clever Pole escaped a second time, this time to kill the brother-in-law and return before he was noticed missing, insuring the perfect alibi (Castle, 1963: 54).

The drafters of the 1955 code of conduct failed to account for situations in which escape attempts were almost certain to fail, leading to the death of the principals and, worse, to jeopardy for fellow prisoners, who might be interrogated under torture to reveal the organizational infrastructure and would certainly be subjected to harsh punishment. In light of the trauma of the Korean War, the codemakers concentrated their attention on preparing prisoners to resist manipulation by their captors in a propaganda war. In line with the code, the military modified training to prepare combatants for wars in which a demonstration of ideological commitment would have strategic importance. Planners foresaw that the televised front would inexorably increase in importance as an arena where foes could use coerced confessions to challenge the legitimacy of the American war effort directly before the American people. Moreover, strategic planning for increased U.S. involvement in brushfire wars had to take account of the fact that opponents in the field and in the command structure were likely to be indifferent to the Geneva Conventions. Certainly the recent unwillingness of the United States to observe the Geneva Conventions in its detention of prisoners taken during the war in Afghanistan call the future of this international accord into question.

To prepare its aviators for the possibility of capture by the North Vietnamese, the Navy assigned its aviators to survival school, where they were reminded of the prisoner code of conduct ("If I am captured I will continue to resist by all means available") and where they endured a mock prison camp complete with corporal punishment applied by enlisted instructors dressed in foreign uniforms. Navy planners aimed to eliminate surprises and inure combatants to the kind of physical and psychological duress they were likely to undergo.

Although Vietnam had signed the 1949 Geneva agreement, the North Vietnamese refused to abide by it, holding that they were engaged in neither a declared war nor an "armed conflict" (also covered under the accord) but an undeclared war of aggression. The North Vietnamese followed the pattern set by their North Korean and Chinese predecessors. Prison interrogators did not seek information—there was little the aviators could supply that the Vietnamese did not know. They wanted confessions—confessions of war crimes, which could be used as propaganda to bolster the dissatisfaction with the war fomenting stateside. Many of the American prisoners had gone to survival school, but the simulations conducted by amateur torturers utterly failed to prepare them for the ingenuity and practiced brutality of the enemy jailers.

James Stockdale recalls that throughout most of his internment, he yearned for the tidy, rule-governed prison camp created for his survival training. In the hands of the real enemy he encountered horrendous conditions, frequent torture that surpassed any person's endurance, severe deprivation of food and water, and maddening solitary confinement. When he entered the prison, Stockdale was greeted by the following scene: "The floor of the short hallway I faced was littered with debris, including a goodly batch of blood-and-pus-soaked bandages.

The ceiling of this building was very high, the walls a dirty white, and four bolted cell doors were on either side. All were padlocked except the first door on the left. . . . Inside were two crumbling cement-slab bunks, one on either side of a very narrow aisle, leg stocks at the foot of each slab by the door" (Stockdale, 1984: 151).

In survival school, Stockdale had been taught that if a prisoner held fast against pressure to capitulate for the first month or two, the enemy would conclude that it was a waste of time to bother and leave the prisoner alone. On the contrary, he found that "that might be the way an efficient American would run a propaganda farm, but that wasn't the way things worked in North Vietnam. They were neither that efficient nor that impatient" (Stockdale, 1984: 149). Torture had its own logic. Ridiculously small infractions would often provoke brutal punishment. Once Stockdale accepted a cigarette from an inmate who didn't smoke. When his North Vietnamese jailers spied the exchange, they bound Stockdale's hands behind his back and shackled him in leg irons. The next morning they simply retied his hands in front of him, then repeated the procedure for several days.

The severe conditions in North Vietnam were no worse than those in prisoner-of-war camps in the South, where the Geneva Conventions were similarly disregarded. Indeed, comparative mortality rates indicate that those in the north were actually less brutal. Systemic violations of the Geneva Conventions by the South Vietnamese were resolutely ignored by the South's major ally, the United States, as similar infractions by the South Koreans in their treatment of prisoners from the North had been ignored. In *POW: Two Years with the Vietcong*, George Smith describes the treatment suspected Viet Cong soldiers received when captured by the South:

They brought back prisoners, too, if they happened to catch somebody on one of these patrols. Anyone captured was declared a VC. How's a guy going to deny it? If you say he's one he's a VC. If he's not on your side, if he's not in the army, he must be on the other side.

All the time I was at the camp we had so-called VC suspects, prisoners of war. The LLDB [Luc-Luong Dac-Biet, or Vietnamese

Special Forces] kept them in two little barbed-wire cages, one about five feet high that people could walk around in at a crouch and a smaller one about three feet high. You couldn't even sit up in the small one: those POWs lay down. They were out in the sun, with no shelter whatever, and they were in there day and night. I don't know how often they fed them. I'm not sure that they even *did* feed them, or give them water for that matter.

We withdrew from that, even though we were paying for the whole shebang. "This is the Vietnamese's project," we said. "They're their prisoners. They caught them, they can take care of them. This is not our concern."

One night I went into the dispensary to give a patient a shot. Lieu and one of our officers were inside with a bunch of other people. One of the LLBD non-coms had a guy in black pajamas on the floor, and he was smashing his knee into the guy's back. Of course the guy would yell like hell, and the NCO would just wham the hell out of him with his fist and beat the guy up. Then they'd ask him some questions, and you could see the guy was refusing to answer them. They were just whaling the hell out of the poor guy and I asked somebody, "Hey, what's going on here?"

"It's none of your business," he said. "That guy's a . . . a VC. A VC squad leader."

"How d'you know he's a VC squad leader?"

"Oh, you know, they *said* he was."

"Well, *who* said he was?"

"Well, it's none of your business, just pretend you didn't see it" (Smith, 1971: 58).

Of course, the American prisoners in the North had neither knowledge of nor responsibility for the allied conduct toward Viet Cong prisoners in the South. They understood their obligation to maintain military discipline and unit cohesiveness in the face of concerted efforts by the enemy to break down individuals and recruit them for purposes that would undermine the U.S. war effort. The key, the aviators believed, was to preserve the chain of command despite isolation and interdiction of communication. Faced with a system designed to divide and silence, James Stockdale and other senior prisoners in Vietnam asserted the chain of command to unify prisoners into a force for opposition. To the extent that prisoners maintained a strong military structure within the camp, they infiltrated a hostile institution with the form of another. The Hanoi Hilton was the scene of an extended struggle between competing authorities for control of the inmates. That struggle played out on the bodies of inmates in the form of brutal torture; the only thing that stood between the captor's will and the prisoner's resistance was the prisoner's flesh, bones, and nerves. When the body broke down, the captor prevailed. It is reasonable to ask why, if torture ultimately induced cooperation, as it always did, the prisoners endured the torture in the first place. For leaders like Stockdale, the willingness to submit to torture, to make the North Vietnamese work for what was extracted, offered a degree of control and the image of themselves as a force with which the enemy must contend.

Stockdale, the highest-ranking officer imprisoned in Hanoi in 1967, realized that although the notorious Hanoi Hilton was the permanent residence of higher-ranking officers like himself, it was merely a holding point for those of lower ranks, who were to be transferred to outlying prisons. He therefore devised a set of standing orders which he believed were more likely to be obeyed than the official code of conduct and which would demonstrate a unified resistance to the North Vietnamese. These rules were communicated via the tap code to all who passed through the Hanoi Hilton and from there to the network of outlying prisons by those who moved on. Stockdale issued his first rule, "Do not bow in public," because he reasoned that although POWs found the practice of bowing to their captors demeaning, they had been bowing in prison camp for a couple of years and if they were to stop, they would simply invite repeated physical abuse. If the men reserved their refusal to bow for public occasions when the North Vietnamese coerced prisoners to appear before the press (an American prisoner bowing to his captor being a powerful message of propaganda), the North would register the forceful but limited defiance of the Americans.

Stockdale realized that the code of conduct's prohibition against confessions was insupportable; under torture, any prisoner would eventually confess. Instead, he instructed prisoners to avoid the use of the word *crime* in confessions, making the admission less sensational when publicized. Thus he formulated his second rule: "Admit no crimes." His third, "Don't kiss them goodbye," reminded prisoners to remember the injustices committed against them and others and not to part as friends. The fourth, and perhaps the most universal—certainly the rule with the widest interpretation—instructed prisoners to put "unity over self." In practice, this simple maxim compelled prisoners who were made to confess by torture to admit whatever they had divulged to the enemy to senior officers. Thus, in place of a ruined military hierarchy, Stockdale and other ranking officers established a system well adapted to their penitential situation: commanding officers assumed the authority to hear confessions, absolve the prisoner, and assign penance (Howes, 1993: 66).

The system was less than perfect. Because there were no witnesses to torture other than the victim and his torturers, fellow prisoners sometimes raised doubts about whether a prisoner had in truth been tortured to the breaking point or, in the face of the inevitable, had yielded with little real struggle. Not all prisoners would criticize such anticipatory capitulation; some disagreed with the strategy of resistance on the practical grounds that if in the end torture would produce the submission sought by captors, suffering was worse than pointless, because it was certainly futile and would weaken the physical ability of the prisoners to survive their captivity.

Stalwarts like Stockdale were committed to resistance, but they were unable to keep all prisoners in line. Although Stockdale issued an order that all prisoners refuse to read articles from American newspapers critical of the military operations in Vietnam, some dissidents continued to participate in propaganda broadcasts rather than undergo renewed torture. The collaboration may have been self-interested, but it was not necessarily abject. Most who cooperated attempted to subvert the occasion by interjecting into their broadcasts terms like "Horseshit Men" for Ho Chi Minh."[7] When the North Vietnamese first proposed their "Make a Choice Program," which promised early release to some willing to cooperate, Stockdale christened it the "Fink Release Program" and issued orders that no one was to accept early release. Several Hanoi prisoners ignored that order. In the jungle camps, many more accepted early release for themselves rather than insist that the release of any prisoner be contingent on the release of all, as Stockdale and other senior officers commanded (Hubbell, 1976: 517).

News of the torture of POWs finally played in the international press in the late 1960s. That publicity and the death of Ho Chi Minh in 1969 created a climate in which treatment of American prisoners improved. Near the end of 1970, American prisoners in outlying camps were gathered together in the Hanoi Hilton. Increased population meant less isolation; less isolation meant increased communication; and more communication narrowed the scope of Vietnamese control. As more prisoners bedded and exercised in proximity, they developed the kind of community culture characteristic of previous wars: singing sessions, plays and musicals, and classes taught by those with particular expertise or skills.

Control was less easily exercised on the American side as well. Although senior prisoners continued their efforts to unite all under a disciplined military regimen, some prisoners, eager for the whole nightmare to end, became increasingly disaffected with both the prison command and U.S. policy in Vietnam. The most outspoken collaborated with antiwar activists stateside and formed what came to be known as the Peace Committee, a group willing to protest the U.S. bombing of North Vietnam vocally. The American senior officers who had commanded absolute resistance to the end equally vocally urged that those who cooperated with their captors in any way should be court-martialed upon their return to the United States. The imperative "Don't kiss them goodbye" turned out to apply not only to the enemy but also to those prisoners who refused to comply with directives from the senior officers. In 1973, the U.S. government, uncritically eager to present POWs as heroes in a war that had produced none, stifled all initiatives by Stockdale and others to launch prosecutions of former prisoners for violations of the code of conduct or for disobeying the order of a superior while in prison.

In the Korean War camps, captors had also worked to prevent the reconstruction of the chain of command among prisoners. They segregated prisoners by rank and required them to select new squad leaders. When prisoners selected the highest-ranking among them, their captors often removed that spokesman and installed a lower-ranking soldier. The policy was highly unusual, if not unprecedented. Armies the world over have assumed that in the event of capture, their forces would maintain military hierarchy and discipline, and in previous wars captors had generally recognized the military hierarchy prisoners brought with them. This was not courtesy but pragmatism. In the large World War II camps, the Germans and Italians discovered that controlling prisoners was impossible without some mode of organization, and the existing chain of command was made to order. Ordinarily, if a prison commandant conferred with the highest-ranking officer, he was spared the task of exhorting the mass of prisoners. Without the discipline that Allied officers imposed on their fellow prisoners, German and Italian captors would have had to pull far more of their own soldiers out of combat to serve as prison guards. The opposing officers' shared commitment to rank and discipline occasionally induced a commonality that trumped national allegiance—what might be called the *Bridge Over the River Kwai* effect. Some Allied officers went so far as to turn in subordinates to prison officials for crimes like stealing and disrespect.[8]

Instances of spontaneous complicity of imprisoned officers with their opposite numbers are not the only evidence suggesting that an inflexible commitment to a hierarchy can be a problem. Consider the difficulty of constructing a chain of command out of assorted personnel from multiple branches of the service. Do the senior-ranking Air Force and Army officers share command? What sounds like a simple directive in the code of conduct, to take command if senior and to obey those in command if junior proved to be very complicated in practice. Having analyzed Vietnam POWs, Craig Howes concludes, "An ugly fact therefore lurked behind Article IV as the key to POW survival. Disputes over rank, authority, and obedience were frequent, widespread, bitter, and at times divisive" (Howes, 1993: 26).

The emergence of conflict around rank should have surprised no one. POWs (not to mention ordinary GIs) have always questioned the perks of rank, which in wars before Vietnam included better quarters and occasionally better food for the officers. If the privileges are not offered by the guards, they are often invented by the captives. POWs in Vietnam on occasion disputed the utility of rank in prison camps, where such distinctions served no function except as a pretext for goldbricking. Howes cites the example of George Smith and his enlisted buddies, who refused to defer to the one noncommissioned officer in their group:

> Cooped up in that tiny space with nothing to do, Roraback really got on our nerves. He wouldn't draw water or wash his plate because he said his feet hurt too much, but his feet didn't keep him from taking trips to the latrine. He even tried to make me take his KP. We had servants at Hiep Hoa, and of course at Fort Bragg the NCOs didn't have to pull KP because we had the lower-ranking people doing it. But Roraback apparently thought he was going to be an NCO in the jungle—he seemed to think McClure and I should cater to him because he was a sergeant first class and outranked us. I should wash his plate, I should go carry water from the well, I should do all these things. "Bullshit, buddy, you wash your own damned plate! I'm not going to be your KP!"
>
> "You better watch out what you're saying. Do you realize who you're talking to? I'm a sergeant first class, and I'll have you court-martialed when we get back to a court."
>
> "Go get your damned court and try me right here! Otherwise, you son of a bitch, you keep your mouth shut. I'll punch you in the goddamned nose. You wash your own plate." Camancho would interrupt when I was about ready to burst Roraback wide open. Roraback remembered those POW training films where the NCOs supervised while the lesser men got the picks and shovels and went out to do the work. Maybe if there had been two hundred of us that might be true. But there were only four of us, and everybody would do his own share (Howes, 1993: 116).

The aim of North Vietnamese and North Korean prison camp commanders was not simply to manage prisoners and prevent their escape but also to break each prisoner down so that he could be of use in a propaganda war. It made sense, therefore, that unlike German and Japanese prison commandants, the Vietnamese and Koreans would act to destroy any alternative structure of authority. Not only did North Korean jailers substitute a lower-ranking soldier for his superior as squad leader; midway through the war, guards began segregating officers from enlisted men. Dissidents nevertheless managed to organize themselves into solidarity groups nerved to resist the enemy's indoctrination. One group performed skits that, under the guise of light entertainment, communicated anti-Communist messages to fellow prisoners. Others, including the Non-Benedict Arnold Club, the Progressive Tea Party, the Un-American Activities Committee, and two African American groups, Black Robe and Black Diamond, secretly encouraged fellow prisoners to avoid collaboration (Biderman, 1963: 61).

Although most American POWs struggled against their Communist captors, the popular image of American prisoners who survived the war was of brainwashed, craven turncoats and collaborators. The picture was painted by such journalists as Eugene Kinkead, who, in *In Every War But One,* claimed that fully one third of American POWs collaborated with the enemy. If we accept Kinkead's narrow definition of *collaboration,* which includes any information yielded to the enemy other than name, rank, and serial number, then 100 percent of Americans interned by the North Vietnamese surely collaborated. Yet when the Vietnam vets returned, not a critical voice like Kinkead's was heard in the land. The heroes' welcome accorded these returning officers, their moving memoirs published in the years after their return, and the recent documentary film on their experiences, *Return with Honor,* create the impression of men who were deprived of almost everything and subjected to continual inhuman treatment but who nevertheless courageously asserted their humanity and their military identity in defiance of an enemy determined to break them.[9]

It is a sad irony that public memory has forgotten many of the generation of American prisoners who preceded Vietnam War POWs and who displayed similar determination and defiance in Korean prisons. Most prisoners in Korea who did divulge information to their captors did so only in the face of extreme hunger and severe torture. The information they divulged was either untrue, already known, or of scant use to the enemy.[10]

The treatment of POWs in both conflicts had the effect of individualizing war in ways unfamiliar to students and survivors of World War I and World War II. Exposed to broadcast scenes of public confessions and barraged by exploitive commentary, by the end of the Korean War the public had developed an unprecedented awareness of the conventions of the propaganda theater and a fascination with the performances of prisoners in ritualized scenarios. In one well-known episode, the Chinese engaged in a propaganda campaign charging the United States with using germ warfare in Korea. Few in the United States or Europe took the charge seriously. Some POWs succumbed to pressure and signed "confessions," taking responsibility for crimes the men could not have committed because they never happened. Others would not confess; they endured torture, and some died.[11] It would be difficult even now to judge who made the right choice (if *choice* is the right word for the way the mind is moved under torture) or suffered the worst fate. At the end of the Korean War, 21 of the more than 4,439 American POWs who lived through their captivity chose not to be repatriated, fearing that charges would be brought against them for their collaboration. Nineteen of these later returned, when the threat of court-martial lapsed. American prisoners in Korea suffered greatly at the hands of the Communists, enduring unheated, ramshackle barracks, inadequate clothing for the below-zero weather, untreated war wounds, poor food, and rampant dysentery, which, together with outright killings of prisoners between 1950 and 1951, contributed to an appallingly high death rate (Sandler, 1995: 272).

In memoirs of their captivity, prisoners often credit their faith in God for pulling them through. Some describe consoling visions that convinced them that a greater power was aware of their despair.[12] They also attributed their survival to the support of other prisoners, to the

Red Cross packages that occasionally made it through, and to a simple and unquenchable will to live. Through the Great War, World War II, Korea, and Vietnam, the experience of imprisonment forms a vast fraternity of survivors. Theo Baudoin, Jr., a prisoner of the North Koreans for thirty-three months, summed up what helped him survive: "I lived with sickness and death every day, but I survived as a result of a will to live, my belief in God, and a desire to go home" (Havard, 1991: 12).

The differences among wars were perhaps felt most keenly not in the prisons but when the prisoners returned to a nation more or less gratified by the war's conclusion, more or less grateful for the sacrifices made. Of all American POWs, the Korean veterans had the most difficult homecoming. The end of the war was not so much the end of their ordeal as a transition to a new phase, for they returned to an America that saw in their highly publicized capitulations to a foreign enemy and an alien dogma the mark of an unsuspected weakness in the national character. It was an America desperate to distance that humiliation and willing to accept the scapegoats that the Chinese offered in order to allocate some blame on some men for the disgrace that an equivocal end to an equivocal war had visited on a nation. It was a nation that had so recently achieved victories in European and the Pacific, and it was confident that its nuclear monopoly would assure a prosperous and tranquil Pax Americana.

With the experience of the Korean POWs fresh in their memory and the perception of an unpopular war vivid in their minds, many Vietnam POWs returned home in the grip of anxiety. Would Americans see them as those who failed to complete their missions and sometimes spent the war sitting in dreary camps, simply waiting for release? Those imprisoned in North Vietnam knew that they would be returning to an America very divided about the war itself. They feared that both they and their families would suffer ridicule. Instead, they received a carefully orchestrated heroes' welcome and the exuberant praise of President Nixon, who exploited the rhetorical possibilities of a contrast between their steadfast patriotism and the easy virtue of antiwar activists.[13] Nixon hit the right note when the Vietnam POWs were released; the press and the American public were hungry for any good news associated with the long and unpopular war, and seeing the last of the prisoners come home offered Americans their only real closure on the war: the heartfelt tribute to its victims.

In World War II, Axis powers imprisoned 130,201 American men and women, 11 percent of whom died in captivity. North Korea and its Chinese ally imprisoned 7,140 Americans, 38 percent of whom died in captivity. Although the number of Americans imprisoned and the number counted as missing in action in the Vietnam War tended to blur, reliable estimates indicate that fewer than 800 prisoners were taken and 114 died in captivity (Gruner, 1993: 14). The American military personnel who, under compulsion, served their country in the prison camps of the enemy had a vastly different experience of war from that of their comrades in the trenches and jungles, at sea or in a flying hotel. The knelling welcome of the captor to his prisoner, "The war is over for you, soldier," was never quite accurate. Although prisoners were taken out of combat, removed from the front, and deducted from the computation of forces made by each side, the battle continued— whether as the fight to fight, to continue to contribute in some way to the war, or as the fight to keep body and spirit intact until liberation, victory, or negotiated release.

10. Jane Fonda, the Woman the Military Loves to Hate

Before going to bed at the U.S. Naval Academy, a plebe shouts "Goodnight!" to the senior midshipman in the company, and the company commander answers "Goodnight!" in reply. A litany of goodnights then passes down the chain of the company's command. At the end of this ritual courtesy, the plebe yells the final goodnight: "Goodnight, Jane Fonda!" and the entire company shouts its enthusiastic retort: "Goodnight, *bitch!*"[1] Until that point, the performance has simply closed the day with an homage to hierarchy, the lowest in the company, the plebe, showing deference to upperclass leaders. But the final exchange, a unanimous curse of the former actress, former workout queen, and former antiwar activist, serves quite a different end. The first part of the performance reminds everyone of the rigid service academy structure, inherited from British boys' schools like Eton, in which upperclassmen dominate their juniors. The plebe plays the role of a child performing nightly valedictories to parents. The final episode, the mock goodnight to Ms. Fonda, reassures even the lowliest plebe of his insider status by expressing collective disdain for an outsider.

But why Jane Fonda? Why not Ho Chi Minh or even Tom Hayden, Fonda's ex-husband, who helped found Students for a Democratic Society, who wrote the first draft of the radical Huron Statement, and who in fact made more visits to North Vietnam during the war than Fonda? Why not a more contemporary adversary? Naval Academy midshipmen weren't even born when Fonda spoke out against having U.S. troops in Vietnam; what's more, many of them don't even know who she is until they are introduced to the mythic Jane at the academy. Soldier folklore during the Vietnam War and for several years after made fun of Ho Chi Minh, his "gooks," and the notorious VC, but those figures of ridicule stepped aside in the Gulf War, to be replaced by Saddam Hussein and his fellow Iraqis ("ragheads" in the jokes, songs, and stories) and most recently by the terrorist leader Osama bin Laden. All, that is, except Jane Fonda, who even as a grandmother in her mid-sixties continues to attract a seemingly endless steam of abuse. Thirty years after her trip to North Vietnam, veterans fill cyberspace with their resentment, and new recruits learn that being a real warrior and hating Jane Fonda are synonymous.

Along with fresh recruits, both commissioned and enlisted, in other branches of the military, these naval officers-in-training learn that just as military identity prescribes adulation for heroic military figures, it also encourages the ridicule of despised civilians. In their plebe year, freshmen make the dramatic transition from civilian status to military, from home to barracks. They leave a world in which mothers have played a large part in their lives and enter an institution that remains largely male in numbers and traditions, despite opening its doors to women in the late 1970s. The goodnight ritual articulates the need to repudiate the civilian life they have left behind and to embrace the spartan life of tight bunks they hunker in alone.

The Navy certainly has no monopoly on hatred of Jane Fonda; active-duty members and veterans of all the services freely express their disdain for the sex-kitten-turned-dressed-down-radical, and veterans' Web sites provide forums in which contributors vent their anger toward the actress: "She should have been shot, and will never be forgiven."[2] One vet posting to a hate-Fonda Web site describes going to see her film *Coming Home* and his disappointment that her character wasn't killed.

They rail at "Hanoi Jane," belittle "Jane Fondle," and castigate her as a "pinko slut" who "appeared nude in movies, smoked pot, smuggled drugs, used profanity publicly, and, worst of all, was aiding and abetting the enemy during wartime." A self-identified twenty-year vet who flew patrol aircraft opens his site with the statement, "Why I Hate Jane Fonda." A veteran who served in Vietnam in 1966–1967 recalls working as a security guard in California while going to college on the GI bill. In nearby Santa Rosa, a film crew was shooting *Steelyard Blues*, starring Jane Fonda and Donald Sutherland, and this vet's employer lent some of the security guards to serve as extras in the film: "We played the cops that drive up to the airplane that Jane Fonda and Donald Sutherland are about to take off in, but they escape and blow up the plane. And there

I am . . . one of the movie cops shooting at Jane Fonda—and I wouldn't have missed!" Fortunately for Fonda and Sutherland, the vet was only shooting blanks.[3]

Some statements on these Web sites border on the felonious:

> If I meet her and can get away without notice, her long term
> future is not, not, not bright.
> Even though she has apologized, she still is owed a hanging![4]

In a 1988 interview with Barbara Walters, Fonda defended her opposition to the war but apologized to vets and their families for the "thoughtless" and "careless" things she might have said and done in her political enthusiasm. Referring to this apology, one vet states his anger simply: "I will forgive Jane Fonda when the Jews forgive Hitler."[5] These sites sport bumper stickers with NUKE JANE FONDA and the more tepid HANOI'D WITH JANE.

Internet critics routinely direct their hostility to Fonda in the form of virtual and real urinal targets. Some sites boast such targets available for download; others advertise them as stickers that can be purchased and affixed to public urinals. One of these targets features Fonda with legs lifted and spread apart (a promotional shot for one of her exercise videos). This image rests in the center of a bull's-eye. Superimposed over other images of the actress are cross hairs, as if she were the sole enemy from an unfinished war. One target reproduces the notorious 1972 photograph taken during Fonda's visit to North Vietnam: helmeted, smiling, seated at an antiaircraft gun. Just as soldiers then saw her actions as "taking aim" at her fellow Americans serving in Vietnam, many vets today take aim at her on the Internet. In an interview for *O, the Oprah Magazine,* Fonda told a reporter that she'd "go to my grave" regretting that photograph.[6] Indeed, those who view her as the enemy ritually exterminate her with each visit to the john. After explaining why Fonda's 1972 appearance in North Vietnam was so repugnant, one vet recalled his pleasure at urinating on her face: "[The] only addition I might add to these sentiments is to remember the satisfaction of relieving myself into the urinal at some airbase or another where 'zaps' of Hanoi Jane's face had been applied."

The cleverest of the Fonda hate sites features an animated soldier walking across the top of the screen toward an image of Fonda as Barbarella. When he gets to her, he pulls out his penis and urinates on her.

If the animated pissing soldier and the urinal targets offer the fantasy of retributive justice, accounts of Fonda's visit to the notorious Hanoi Hilton charge her with conspiracy. These word-of-mouth and Internet stories circulate widely among active-duty soldiers and veterans. One version features a pilot who refuses to meet with the visiting star, only to receive severe torture in return. When American POWs came back to the United States as part of Operation Homecoming, the media carried stories of the torture they had received. Although U.S. officials had known about this torture for years, they managed to keep it secret from the press. They feared, no doubt, that such reports would cause even more Americans to call for U.S. withdrawal.

When Fonda visited American prisoners in Hanoi, she saw no sign of mistreatment and naively took the situation at face value. Even when the returning POWs reported the horrible treatment they'd received, Fonda refused to believe their stories and voiced her disbelief publicly. She was wrong. But revisionist tales lay blame where the tellers and their audiences would have it rest: on Fonda as the deliberate agent of torture. Although she didn't tighten the ropes and inflict the blows herself, she is somehow their direct cause.

An oft-told variant of the torture legend depicts a single prisoner (generally considered to be POW Jerry Driscoll) who is forced to meet with Fonda and registers his defiance by spitting on the star: "Dragged from a stinking cesspit of a cell, cleaned, fed, and dressed in clean PJ's, he was ordered to describe for a visiting American 'Peace Activist' the 'lenient and humane treatment' he received. He spat at Ms. Fonda, was clubbed, and dragged away. During the subsequent beating, he fell forward upon the camp commandant's feet, accidentally pulling the man's shoe off—which sent that officer berserk. In '78, the AF Col still suffered from double vision (which permanently ended his flying days) from the Vietnamese colonel's frenzied application of wooden baton."[7] This story, like most spat-upon stories, is pure fiction. The specific prisoners to whom it is attributed, although no fans of Fonda, have nevertheless flatly denied that it happened. What's more, the account defies credibility: what propaganda-conscious regime would actually club a prisoner in front of cameras at an international press conference?

The most popular of all these legends is by far the most dramatic:

He [Larry Carrigan] spent six years in the "Hilton"—the first three of which he was "missing in action." His wife lived on faith that he was still alive. His group, too, got the cleaned/fed/clothed routine in preparation for a "peace delegation" visit. They, however, had time and devised a plan to get word to the world that they still survived.

Each man secreted a tiny piece of paper with his social security number on it in the palm of his hand. When paraded before Ms. Fonda and a cameraman, she walked the line, shaking each man's hand and asking little encouraging snippets like "Aren't you sorry you bombed babies?" and "Are you grateful for the humane treatment from your benevolent captors?"

Believing this *had* to be an act, they each palmed her their sliver of paper. She took them all without missing a beat. At the end of the line and once the camera stopped rolling, to the shocked disbelief of the POWs, she turned to the officer in charge . . . and handed him the little pile. Three men died from the subsequent beatings. Col Carrigan was almost number four.[8]

Such stories travel from vet to vet and soldier to soldier by word of mouth, across the back fence into the cyber fields, and even in print. One popular biography of Fonda recounts them not as legend but as truth, as does the *Washington Times* and William F. Buckley, Jr., in a syndicated November 1999 article.[9]

Vietnam POWs have tried to debunk the stories falsely attributed to them. Mike McGrath, the president of NAM-POWs and a prisoner of the North Vietnamese from 1967 to 1973, has denounced these libels. Speaking for specific POWs named in the stories, McGrath has tried to set the record straight:

They had nothing to do with the article attributed to them. They ask that we get their names off that bunch of crap. Tonight I talked with Larry Carrigan. He asked that we get his name off all that crap as well. He never left a room to talk to anyone like that. No torture or beatings to see Fonda. He was living with Bud Day, John McCain and a bunch of hard-nosed resisters during the Fonda visit . . . lots of witnesses if you want to question him (or them). Larry was never near Jane. There were never any POWs killed on account of Jane. (Did anyone ever provide a name of one of these tortured fellows?) That story about the notes has a nice theatric touch, but no such thing ever happened. The only ones who met with Jane willingly, to my knowledge, were CDR Gene Wilber and LCOL Ed Miller. One NAM-POW was forced to go before the Fonda delegation. And I think that was only to sit at a table for a photo opportunity. I doubt he ever got a chance to talk to her, let alone slip her a note. To my knowledge, the worst that happened to the rest of us was that we had to listen to the camp radio (Radio Hanoi and Hanoi Hannah) with the Fonda propaganda. It pissed us off, but I doubt you can call that "torture." So, if you get a chance to SHUT THIS STORY DOWN to the groups who are forwarding it, PLEASE DO SO.[10]

Despite the efforts of McGrath and others to stanch the flow of such legends, they continue to circulate, because they satisfy their tellers and audience as a protest against one of the most outspoken critics of the military.

The spat-upon story constitutes the perfect rebuttal to the enormous legacy of spat-up legends. Executing the same anger as that implied in the urinal targets, the soldier sprays bodily fluid on the antiwar activist as an act of protest against a protester, and by proxy against the brutal captors with whom she sympathized. But Fonda is not just any antiwar activist; she is a civilian woman—*civilian* and *woman* being terms that in military culture tend to collapse into each other.

For the Vietnam War soldier, more than for his counterparts in any previous war, the lines between civilian and military became increasingly ambiguous. The Vietnamese who appeared one day as harmless civilians (women, children, and the elderly) might on another day behave as agents of the enemy. Soldier songs, chants, jokes, and stories gave voice to the soldier's fear of a civilian population capable of transforming itself into the dreaded enemy. A version of that uncanny transformation took place stateside as well. Civilians at home, who in past wars had shown steadfast support and offered a grateful welcome to the returning soldier, became increasingly outspoken in protesting the war America had sent its soldiers to wage. These protesters grew loud in their denunciation of dropping napalm and carpet bombing, which targeted civilians, they claimed, rather than enemy troops. They called soldiers "baby killers" and chanted, "Hey, hey, LBJ, how many kids did you kill today?" At the end of their tour, soldiers returned to condemnation rather than congratulations.

The military has traditionally done an effective job of transforming the fresh recruit into a government-issue soldier capable of executing violence on command. It has done very little to reverse the process and return the soldier to civilian life. Historically, the civilian population has assumed that role by ceremoniously welcoming home its soldiers with an acknowledgment of their suffering, thereby absolving the individual soldier of personal responsibility for acts performed in the name of the nation. When the civilian population refuses to accept this burden, it falls heavily on each soldier to handle as best he can. Thus we saw a proliferation of "rap groups," group therapy sessions in which vets sought the confidence of fellow participants, fellow sufferers, after the Vietnam War.

It was sadly ironic that so many who watched the war on the nightly news selectively embraced and even heroized prisoners of war while ignoring the sacrifice and courage of others. The prisoners of war were certainly brave men, but their status as heroes was won not by aggressive acts against the enemy but by years of passive resistance. It was to them that many Americans extended the warm welcome home they had denied others. And it was stories of them and their fictional encounters with Jane Fonda that enjoyed such a long life and such wide circulation among members of the military. Those stories rebuke the civilian who inflicts greater pain on the war's unambiguous victims. In a war in which the enemy was not clearly defined, it sometimes seemed to the unappreciated soldier that the real enemies might be back home. And in an important sense, Vietnam was a war of America against itself.

The choice of Jane Fonda as the woman soldiers love to hate didn't arise solely from her highly publicized antiwar stance. Other American women were just as active in the antiwar movement. Denise Levertov, like Fonda, made a trip to North Vietnam to protest the war, and Joan Baez was every bit as much a staunch critic as Fonda. No, Fonda engendered such anger in part because of her dramatic transformation from the girl who stood for the girl they had once known. Vietnam-era soldiers had come to know her first as the cute ingenue of *Tall Story* and as the daughter of a famous and admired Hollywood star and then as the sex kitten Barbarella, always ready and willing to please. In the 1968 film of that name, directed by Fonda's then-husband, Roger Vadim, the president of a futuristic country deploys Barbarella on a search-and-rescue mission to find a missing scientist. Eager to serve her country, the sci-fi bombshell heads out in her one-woman, shag-carpeted space-ship, the interior of which looks more like Graceland's jungle room than any U.S. craft currently circling the globe. Along the way Barbarella discovers what is to her a new method of making love—intercourse—and spends the rest of the film in a series of sexual adventures: one with an angel who has lost the will to fly but who regains it through sex with our heroine.

Within three years of playing this part, Fonda appeared regularly in primetime news clips condemning U.S. involvement in Vietnam. She and other actors and writers (Donald Sutherland, Dick Gregory, Fred Gardner, and Jules Pfeiffer among them) performed in shows that satirized the U.S. military and its role in Vietnam in coffeehouses near U.S. bases. They intended their traveling review, named FTA for "Fuck the Army," to be an antidote to the performances of entertainers who traveled from base to base to lend their support to the troops.[11] Fonda described this effort in 1971: "It is disturbing that Bob Hope, Martha Raye, and company seem to have a corner on the market in speaking to soldiers in the country and Vietnam. The time has come for entertainers who take a different view on the war to reach the soldiers" (Anderson, 1990:238).

For those who condemned Fonda, it was not only her efforts to win the hearts and minds of U.S. servicemen through these performances and through her longtime support for Vietnam Veterans Against the War that so disturbed; it was not only her support for the North Vietnamese propaganda campaign that so angered. They saw in Fonda the American female uncannily, as if by sabotage, turned feminist. While touring North Vietnam, she attended performances of theater and dance, spoke with "the blushing militia girls," retreated to a bomb shelter when the shells began to drop, and voiced her strong opposition to the war on North Vietnamese radio.[12] The ever available, innocent Barbarella had transformed herself into Hanoi Jane, an outspoken critic of the war. The figure of a woman who appears to be one thing but turns out to be something more sinister or monstrous inhabits centuries of folklore. She makes her way into soldier lore as the apparently innocent but seductive foreign woman who turns out to be extremely menacing—for example, the Vietnam-era legends of pretty and inviting Vietnamese women who secretly laced their vaginas with broken glass, fishhooks, or barbed wire in order to castrate GIs.

The Jane Fonda stories, the urinal targets, and even the goodnight ritual at the Naval Academy function in military culture to stabilize and punish the dangerous female. Fonda is seen as the ultimate shapeshifter, a woman who has remade herself many times over, as ingenue, sex kitten, exercise queen, wife of Ted Turner, and born-again Baptist. In the face of this fluid civilian female, the military traditionally promises a one-way transformation from civilian to soldier, from boy to man, a process intended to fix a new identity, one that will travel with the soldier long after he has left active service. During the rapid rotations, massive antiwar demonstrations, and challenges to traditional gender roles that characterized the period of the Vietnam War, when a majority of soldiers didn't see combat, the military failed to make good on its promise of transformation for many who served. Caught in the predicament of a transformation gone awry, many found themselves neither the innocents they were before going off to war nor the respected warriors their fathers had become when they returned from World War II.

For Fonda, no amount of self-transformation will save her from being cast in legend as the figure of the seductive woman who turns out to be a snake. It's the oldest story in the world.

11. Fighting the Digital War

Old warriors express their anger about an old war—one lost but not forgotten—by exchanging legends about an outspoken critic. New warriors ready themselves for a novel kind of war, one that raises even more questions about the place of masculine exclusivity. Software wizards from the entertainment industry, working with engineers and scientists from the Defense Department and affiliated private contractors, are inventing and fine-tuning new technology that will transform the way our armed forces prepare for and fight wars. They are computerizing more and more weaponry, making it easier for commanders to issue orders through cyberspace, and, having already revolutionized the training of pilots and submarine drivers, they are introducing computer simulation to other forms of warfare training. The new technology promises instant intelligence, increased accuracy, and diminished vulnerability for U.S. troops. But those promises will be realized only when military planners begin to rethink training, logistics, command strategy, and field tactics. As long as the military holds fast to the old ways of thinking, the old organization of separate branches clinging to separate cultures, and the old procurement practices, the trumpeted transformation will not occur.

SIMULATION

For years, military aviation has successfully employed computers to mimic the cockpits of different aircraft. Today's sophisticated simulators combine actual terrain footage, complex adjoining computer labs, and expensive hydraulic lifts to make flying a simulator feel amazingly close to flying a real plane or helicopter. While live training boasts the "feel of the real," simulation offers important advantages. First, it permits beginning pilots to learn in a safe environment and experienced pilots to practice risky or emergency maneuvers without endangering life or equipment. Second, it saves money. Flying an F-16 can cost as much as $5,000 per hour, whereas a simulator runs about $500 per hour. Driving a tank costs $75 per mile, driving a simulator $2.50. Operating an Apache helicopter costs $3,101 per hour, operating a simulator of that aircraft $70.[1] Before simulators, it was estimated that fighter pilots used three air-to-air missiles per year for training purposes; now it is roughly one every four years. In the recent wars in Afghanistan and Iraq (Operation Iraqi Freedom), pilots even deployed some cutting-edge weapons for the first time on actual missions. That field use would have been impossible without the use of simulators in training.[2]

Simulators can alter the terrain with the click of a mouse, saving the millions it would cost to transport troops to new training locations. "We've now modeled the majority of the world," according to Scott Davis, the director of the manned flight simulator at Patuxent Naval Air Station.[3] On one simulated flight a helicopter pilot can be flying over mountains; in the next she can be swooping under the Golden Gate Bridge. If a submarine driver changes depth too quickly, the simulated hydraulic system will respond just as a real sub would. Though such full-motion simulators have proven costly to operate, programmers are beginning to design cheaper software to use on personal computers. Simulations of simulators, these programs enable a ship driver to hone basic skills so that time spent in the costly full-motion simulator is used more productively.

Simulation may in fact prove more versatile and efficient than on-site field exercises staged at training facilities both here and abroad, like those that take place at Fort Bragg's Camp All-American each year. Simulation permits far-flung units to train together: ground troops conduct maneuvers in one location while operators of weapons systems engage their simulators at another location and pilots fly their simulators in yet another, creating a virtual theater of war. Although simulators do break down and they do require sophisticated operators, the setup and takedown time for simulated exercises is significantly less than that required for traditional field exercises, which call for the transportation, maintenance, and repair of large war-fighting equipment. In war games, simulation also allows instant feedback: commanders can issue critiques and rerun the mission. Additionally, simulators can put the ground soldier, the pilot, and the ship driver through extreme situations that they would never rehearse in reality because of the risk involved. Increasingly, simulation has taken on the "feel of the real": troops walk, crawl, and run through specific terrain in real time. In today's simulators, pilots fly through downloaded satellite imagery of actual terrain and feel the tilt of the plane as they turn.

Simulation has become increasingly important in training pilots and testing new aircraft. Nowhere can its importance be more dramatically demonstrated than at the Navy's test center. Since its establishment in 1942, the Naval Air Station ("Pax Air" to pilots) has occupied the broad peninsula in southern Maryland where the Patuxent River reaches the Chesapeake Bay. At this 6,400-acre base, the Navy and its industrial partners develop and test new aircraft. Young but seasoned pilots attend a one-year course to become test pilots, and many stay on for two additional years to "stress" new aircraft—that is, to force them through extremes of speed and maneuvers so the Navy can either decree them fit for the fleet or mothball them back to the manufacturer. Some test pilots even go on to become astronauts (including four of the first: Glenn, Shirra, Shepard, and Carpenter). Just outside the gates of the Naval Air Station, prominent new office buildings gleam with turquoise windows the color of liquid crystal screens. Their prominent logos—Raytheon, SAIC, Hjford, VSE, Veridian—advertise the intimate connection between the Navy and industry.

If the Navy or the Marine Corps wants to add any new components, such as a clearer digital readout, to the controls of an aircraft, it tries them out first on the simulators. Trained engineers and test pilots work the controls. Of course, the pilots would certainly prefer to be in the clouds above the Chesapeake rather than in the dark surrounded by video screens, no matter how lifelike the simulators are. The controls may be designed to feel like the real thing (simulators duplicate one type of pull for digitally controlled aircraft and another for the hydraulically controlled helicopters), but for a pilot, nothing is as glorious as flight. Nevertheless, although they would rather be banking out over the Patuxent River, even the most veteran pilots admit to respect for the work of the manned flight simulator.

Every door in the simulator locks and unlocks with a code, and on the stairwell from the first to the second floor, lights the size of traffic signals indicate whether classified or unclassified work is under way. Once you are inside the classified portion of the building, you learn that there is only one real wall in the main building, a wall infused with white noise to insure that when business "higher than classified" is being conducted in the meeting rooms and computer rooms behind, nothing can be deciphered. Proud of both the technical expertise of his workplace and its practical design, Scott Davis stresses the efficiency of the manned flight simulator's interchangeable bays, which accommodate the trolley-mounted cockpits of eight different aircraft. In twenty minutes, one aircraft can be rolled out and another moved into its place and connected to the adjacent computer room. Like an abandoned soapbox racer after the derby, an F-14 simulator sits outside its bay in a large hallway.

When a crash that involves a Navy or Marine aircraft occurs, engineers at the manned flight simulator review the data and reenact the aborted flight to determine whether pilot error or equipment malfunction caused the mishap. For example, computer operators and engineers conducted such a postmortem on a crash of a V-22 Osprey, which in one mode performs like a helicopter and in another flies like a conventional airplane. At their computer screens and aboard the chilly, dark V-22 Osprey simulator, the technicians reenacted the flight that killed nineteen Marines on April 8, 2000, on a training mission in Arizona. The forensics of aircraft tragedies, particularly with aircraft that are still experimental, can be complicated. Although the verdict of pilot error or mechanical failure sounds like a simple one, in practice it may not be quite so black and white. The process of perfecting a new aircraft involves more than insuring that it is mechanically fit; accidents highlight passages in the flight manual that need clarification and tragically illustrate where rewriting can prevent future disasters. According to test pilots, the flight manual becomes an instruction book rewritten in blood.

Pilots have a love/hate relationship with simulators. Whereas army pilots once logged 800 hours of actual flight time per year, they now take three to five years to log that much time in the air.[4] "I didn't sign up to dress in flame-proof pajamas [pilots' uniforms, otherwise known as 'poopy suits'] and sit in simulators," one test pilot said.[5] Although most pilots prefer the roar and thrust of the engines to countless hours in a dim control box, most agree with Lieutenant Tom Tenant, a test pilot, that simulators are invaluable, because they permit pilots to "practice, practice, practice" scenarios too risky to stage in actual flight.[6]

Current simulators incorporate an actual cockpit with instrument panels that respond in real time to every act of the pilot. In pursuit of cost-effective miniaturization, the Navy has experimented with helmet-mounted displays. Once these devices are perfected, the pilot will be able to take a virtual flight from his helmet. Pilots will train to fly unmanned aircraft on these cost-effective helmet-mounted displays, whose advanced fiber optics allow them both to see the images and to see their hands at the controls.

Simulators allow pilots to practice what they call "switchology," the careful hand-eye coordination required to respond instantaneously, and also to perfect their "cadence," the verbal interchange that accompanies any flight. In warfare, a pilot not only has to keep the aircraft on course but also has to navigate (in a one-seater) and to target other aircraft (in an attack craft). This requires an efficient, clipped communication between pilot and copilot, between pilot and other friendly aircraft (even the pilot in a solo aircraft must often communicate with two other planes), and between pilot and ground or ship control. In addition to sometimes dealing with as many as six different people providing information over their earphones; they must keep in mind the rules of engagement while navigating. The pilot's mantra, "aviate, navigate, communicate," highlights the need for precision control. Realizing that an extra word or phrase could decrease efficiency, pilots practice the banter to make sure it is as efficient and effective as possible.

Good pilots must develop perfect hand-eye coordination and learn to master multiple tasks simultaneously, and they must learn to think fast enough to "stay ahead of their plane, to control their aircraft rather than letting it control them," according to one pilot.[7] Pilots concede that simulators sharpen a thought process that involves split-second tactical decision-making and therefore better prepare them for the heat of battle. Most pilots believe that those who follow in their footsteps, having logged in so much time on computer games, will demonstrate even greater dexterity at aircraft control panels. The coming generation will, after all, have practiced their "switchology" from grade school. They will have imagined themselves in wars not by playing soldiers in the back yard with other kids but by practicing their battle craft in computer games.

Pilots keep in shape on simulators during down time. During protracted deployments at sea they risk becoming dangerously rusty if they don't have the opportunity to practice extreme or emergency procedures on a simulator. Newly developed portable simulators that can go out with the fleet enable carrier pilots to tune themselves on routine maneuvers and run through actual missions before firing up the engines. Through computer simulation, trainees practice for war in a controlled environment that every day more accurately mimics reality. Helicopter pilots flying in a simulator can look out the window and see fog, haze, clouds, city lights, even battlefield smoke. Counterterrorism teams practice their missions in studios whose floors and walls are transformed with 3-D graphics recreating specific combat environments.

In the mid 1990s, those who were responsible for training, such as General William Hartzog, the commanding general of the U.S. Army Training and Doctrine Command, championed the breakthrough of computer simulation: "Today, with the linking of virtual and constructive realities, we never have to go back to surrogates, because you can constructively generate a real picture of what this future battlefield might be."[8] Brigadier General William Bond, commander of the U.S. Army Simulation, Training, and Instrumentation Command, imagined a simulated training future that adds smells and textures to virtual environments:

> What I would like to be able to do is create an environment that when you pull the lanyard on that Paladin you smell the cordite. You crank up the M1A2 and you smell the diesel and you feel the chunks in the road as you go down there, or the bumps of the air turbulence when you're flying the helicopter. Those subtleties, I think, are going to enhance the realism and help the soldier forget, really, where

he's at to put him into those tactical situations and really, I think, enhance the training environment.

Bond goes on to describe his experience of getting into a tank simulator:

Compared with the last time I drove a tank, the time when I got in to drive it in the CCTT [Close Combat Tactical Trainer), it was as real as it was then, at least as much as it could be without having all the dirt and the dust and the smell of diesel and all those kind of things, and the cramped quarters. But I think we were working on that. I mean, anybody who's ever been to Disney World or to Universal Studios or whatever lately knows that that experience is pretty fulfilling.[9]

Disney fantasy-makers have already lent a practiced hand to the military to design an environment that will blur the distinctions between the facsimile and the real thing. But Disney is not the sole Hollywood connection. In August 1999, the Pentagon established a $45 million Institute for Creative Technologies to bring together screenwriters, special effects people, engineers, and computer scientists from the University of Southern California and the entertainment industry to create Army training simulations. As conceived, the center will benefit both the Army and the entertainment industry by inventing special effects of use to the warfare, computer game, and theme park industries and by devising the plots for war games and military training scenarios.

With such an intimate connection between the gaming industry and those writing the scripts of future wars, actual war and simulation merge: first computers train pilots and now computers can fly crewless bombers. The incredible success of unmanned aerial vehicles (UAVs) was dramatically demonstrated in Operation Iraqi Freedom, a conflict that marked the transition of the UAV from reconnaissance craft to offensive weapon capable of dropping precision bombs on the enemy. The role of the pilot as a joy-stick buccaneer will only increase. A joke exchanged among pilots gives voice to such a possibility: A plane carries a pilot and a dog. The pilot is there to feed the dog. The dog is there to bite the pilot in case he tries to do anything else.

Computers now train tank drivers, but someday these computers, operated remotely from a computer, may maneuver tanks alone. In the past twenty years, computers and their applications have altered our sense of reality. In the twenty-first century they will certainly transform our conception of war. As the U.S. military becomes the world's special forces and military police, deploying specialized units to maintain a fragile peace, extinguish a spark that threatens to ignite full-blown war, protect refugees, or fight terrorists, military planners and a voracious defense industry will increasingly plot the virtual global war. This is a war that may in fact never be fought in deserts, under the sea, or in the air but on the screens of computers. New warfare will therefore require the sophistication to extinguish the enemy's communications systems and protect our own.

THE SOLDIER OF 2010

If the cyberwar seems imminent to the pilot, it is just emerging from the stuff of science fiction for the average infantry soldier. In its effort to make the individual foot soldier the center of its modernization crusade, the Army launched the Land Warrior 2010 program in 1993. This program aimed to equip each soldier with a radio system, a computer, a global positioning system, a helmet-mounted display, and a weapons system complete with thermal and video sights. After three different designs, three field tests, and a critical GAO report, the initial projection of equipping 34,000 soldiers by the year 2000 was modified. Part of the problem, according to some, was that the Army had set about procuring the system in the same way it procures a tank. Planners came up with the concept and defined it for industry, and industry invented the whole system from scratch, producing the first working model in 1998. The result: a cumbersome metal frame with an embedded forty-pound laptop computer, called the "turtle shell" by the soldiers who tested it, because if a soldier fell with the equipment on his back, the rigid frame would be shoved up and bang the back of his head. It was less waterproof than a turtle shell, however.

After three redesigns and extensive field tests, the Land Warrior system replaced the twenty-five pounds of body armor with sixteen pounds, but it put the weight right back on the ground soldier in the form of new high-tech equipment (portable computer, thermal weapons sight, laser range finder, digital compass, video camera, and display), totaling a burdensome ninety-two pounds. For the infantry, the economies that digitization promises have a way of remaining virtual. The projections of featherweight uniforms and gear deserve to be treated with the same skepticism as the promise of a paperless office.

The Army concluded that it needed more than just a new design; it needed a different way of designing, acquiring, and testing this equipment. Colonel Bruce Jette, the project manager of soldier systems at Fort Belvoir, Virginia, who holds a Ph.D. in astrophysics, came to salvage the project. Jette broke with the old way and acquired individual components off the shelf at lower cost. "I can't afford to compete with the electronics industry," he said. "Pentium, after all, spent more than the Army's entire budget developing the Pentium chip."[10] (Since the army's budget for fiscal year 2000 was a whopping $67.4 billion, Jette indulged in a bit of hyperbole. The development of the Pentium chip was costly, according to Intel's George Alfs, but nowhere near the army's annual budget. Government-sponsored research and development simply couldn't compete with Silicon Valley.) Instead of asking industry to develop an entirely integrated system from scratch, Jette and his staff shifted to a modular system, one with access to multiple vendors and that relied on commercial off-the-shelf equipment that would work with the latest version of Windows. Jette kept repeating his mantra: "If you can't buy it at Fry's [a famous California computer store], we don't want it." Whereas previous systems had half of their components coming off the shelf, Jette's version integrated 80 percent off-the-shelf components and linked to a Windows operating system.

Although Jette and his crew managed to make the equipment

rugged, weight continued to be a problem. Can a 120-pound soldier walk through a war zone with 90 pounds of gear and still be agile and effective? Military planners imagined the Land Warrior system as the next generation of gear, designed to extend the senses of the ordinary ground soldier. Intelligence acquired by any ground soldier's thermal weapon sight (TWS) or by any surveilling aircraft would instantly upload in to the Land Warrior System. By looking through a helmet-mounted display, the ground soldier would immediately know the locations of fellow friendlies and enemies. They would also see symbols specifically designating any civilians in the field. Ground units have always had to stop and plot their location and their destination on paper maps with compass and protractor, but the Land Warrior would simply click his mouse to display his coordinates on a computer map. Sophisticated thermal sensors would be so sensitive that if an enemy soldier hid behind a brick wall, he would throw a detectable thermal shadow off nearby bushes and be visible even though he was out of the line of sight.

With such powerful sensors, the Land Warrior's weapon would be his prosthetic eyes into the beyond; his night sensor display would see through smoke and render even the dark visible. With his new gear, the ground soldier would point his weapon, not his eyes, around the corner, and the weapon's display would reveal any enemy. Alerted, he could line up that enemy in his cross hairs and shoot from the side of his weapon as well as from its rear, and thus stay safely behind cover. If an enemy were to travel down a hallway and a soldier followed with a thermal sensor, he could detect the thermal "footprint" of the fleeing enemy and maintain his advantage. Thus, the Land Warrior system would apply high technology to the deadly game of flight and pursuit.

That was the intent. The problem came when this system was tested in the field, where it proved unreliable. Frequent rebooting, while a nuisance in the office, proved a real problem in the heat of combat. Having moved from single-vendor to commercially available technology, the Army found it necessary to circle back on itself. In January 2003 it awarded a contract to General Dynamics to develop the next iteration (scaling back use of off-the-self components to 50 percent), shifted supervision of the project to another Department of Defense lab, and gave the program a new name: Objective Force Warrior.

In 2000, soldiers began preparing for combat by playing Delta Force II, a video game produced by Nova Logic Systems. According to retired general R. Springer, the president and CEO, the software his company developed doubles as an entertaining game and an effective training device. The advantage of the PC game world, according to Springer, is that gamers become so absorbed in the game that they stick with it till they have mastered the skills it teaches. "If we can take that motivation with young soldiers and induce them to continue training," he suggests, "the process will be more interesting." During deployment, skills honed in distant training sessions slacken when not practiced. The solution: take the right computer games to Bosnia, Afghanistan, and Iraq. Although Springer is quick to say that computer-based simulation is not a substitute for conventional training but strictly an add-on, he does claim that keeping soldiers busy playing computer games in the home and garrison will lessen the time and cost of training in the field.[11]

Just as the Army is playing a video in which Special Forces "Delta boys" play the heroes, it can learn other lessons from Special Forces. In the aftermath of the cold war, Special Forces, deployable within eighteen hours, have played a large role in conflicts in Afghanistan and Iraq. With the heavy reliance on proxy forces, with specially trained units of Special Operations soldiers and rangers, and finally with military police (both male and female), the Taliban regime was destroyed in Afghanistan. At the time of this writing, Special Forces continue to subdue the remaining Baath Party loyalists resisting U.S. and British forces after the overthrow of the Iraqi government.

At Fort Bragg's Special Operations headquarters, on Desert Storm Drive, just off Kuwait Road, military and civilian planners for what is often called "the fifth service" express the frustration that comes from trying to prepare an elite, high-tech force within a military setup to protect the interests of the other four services. They boast of their crack teams, whose eight to twelve members work closely together over a relatively long period of time. They undertake special, sophisticated assignments, often behind enemy lines and increasingly in urban terrain. Typically, the smaller the unit and the longer it spends together, the more it develops an autonomous esprit, identifying itself as distinct from the regular military.

In the move toward a lighter and more lethal military, Special Forces offers a compelling model, one designed for discrete operations and informed by a global perspective. Rather than organize troops around special weapons systems, Special Forces designates geographical specialties for its units. Army units prepare for deployment to any part of the world; Special Forces teams learn foreign languages and concentrate on a specific region. Before "jointness" rang as a mantra down the halls of the Pentagon, Special Forces, out of necessity and by definition, acted jointly with other organizations, including conventional American forces and the forces of friendly nations. Special Forces know that they are often deployed at the request of the host nation, that they must complete their job as inconspicuously as possible, and that they are sometimes the senior U.S. representatives in a foreign country. As American troops increasingly put out international brushfires, troops with a knowledge of regional cultures and languages and a familiarity with nongovernmental organizations (such as relief and refugee aid agencies) have become vital.

Like their counterparts in mainstream Army infantry, armor, and artillery as well as in the Marine Corps, Special Forces troops are preparing for the digitized war. But Special Forces planners have concluded that trading maneuverability for increased information makes no sense. Rather than opting for the Army's Land Warrior system, Special Forces has concentrated on miniaturized technology. Lieutenant Colonel Daniel Moore, the assistant chief of staff for force integration, Special Forces Command, reasons that if cell phones can hook up to the Internet, download data, and pass situational information back to commanders, then ground forces do not need to carry around cumbersome computing systems. Instead, he anticipates that hand-held computers will communicate by spreading messages across multiple frequencies, keeping communications between soldiers "down in the noise clutter," where they will be undetectable.[12] This would offer them a far less costly alternative to burdening every ground soldier with a heavy computer and batteries.

The accelerated pace of technological change demands the adoption of a tactical mindset by all planners. A sluggish procurement process requires planners to request sophisticated equipment years in advance of its implementation. Such a tedious procedure might have sufficed in the past, but it will never keep up with the rapid development of faster, more powerful, and lighter equipment. "The system is broken," according to Colonel Moore, "when planners must predict eight to twelve years out in the military while industry plans only two to three years ahead."[13] Each branch of the military has evolved a procurement system ill-equipped for today's technology and incompatible with that of the other branches. If the Pentagon is to succeed in the construction of a digital force, it must streamline procurement and at the same time reorganized to eliminate redundancy and incompatibility. Although the current secretary of defense, Donald Rumsfeld, has embraced the concept of "jointness" and championed the need to reorganize, some in the defense industry suspect that his solution to the procurement problem will probably result in even more bureaucracy and a longer rather than shorter procurement process. Although separate procurement systems for each branch of the military reflect the culture of independence that still prevails in the Pentagon, they inhibit the integration of technology. Rather than dismantle this, Rumsfeld may simply weigh down an already sluggish system with an additional layer of oversight.

Not only is the procurement of equipment likely to remain a problem, but the recruitment and retention of skilled individuals will challenge operations for years to come. Current high-level officers commanding technology operations may be skilled leaders, but they often lack sophisticated technical expertise. Once they acquire real, usable knowledge of this complicated area, they come up for rotation, taking their experience with them and leaving an empty chair to be occupied by another high-ranking rookie.

FEEDING AND EQUIPPING THE
GROUND SOLDIER BEYOND 2010

To see what lies in wait over the next ridge, the ground soldier of the future will deploy an unmanned aerial vehicle (UAV, or "drone") small enough to fit in the palm of a hand or strap onto a belt buckle and equipped with a video camera that will transmit vital reconnaissance up to five miles ahead of his unit. If the enemy shoots down one of these golfball-sized reconnaissance helicopters, the ground unit will simply send another in its place. UAVs equipped with thermal sights will spot enemy soldiers as they hide behind a tree or crouch under a camouflage net. According to Air Force predictions outlined in "Spacecast 2020," the weather will cooperate fully (at the behest of "counterforce weather control") to befuddle the enemy and give our forces the advantage.

Locating large groups of soldiers in the field for extended periods of time demands huge influxes of energy to operate the field mess, the communication system, and the medical facilities. Today's generators are large, cumbersome, and noisy. The heavy batteries carried by today's soldiers will be replaced by lightweight miniatures weighing less than a pound and run by nonpetroleum fuel sources. Ground troops may not even need to carry the power sources with them, but may rely instead on energy beamed in from satellites or from Navy ships offshore.

Ground forces will not only deploy lethal weapons, they will also have an arsenal of nonlethal devices, which the Pentagon calls "calmatives"—immobilization devices like stick foam. With one zap of stick foam, approaching enemy soldiers will stop in their tracks, engulfed in foam. Stick foam elevates the game of freeze tag to a warrior's sport.[14] If war's imaginative thinkers have their way (and their funding), other nonlethal weapons will make their way into the ground-war arsenal. Bacteria cultured to corrode parts of the enemy's weapons system will be released in the vicinity of their equipment. We can admire such ingenuity and still note that such designer bacteria do not come with a guarantee that they will go only where intended. What if they turn tail and work their corrosive darnedest on the metal parts of friendly weapons?

As news reports of recent conflicts show, wars displace people, and the management of refugees has become an increasingly pressing concern for military leaders as they plan for situations in which the boundaries between the political and the military dissolve. Thanks to FedEx, the Pentagon has a model: code refugees and track them the way you track packages. As people move from an initial safe haven to a refugee camp, and then on to another camp, scanners and software will chart their location. A system for personalizing populations of disoriented and desperate victims who may speak no familiar language will obviously help reunite families and ultimately help return refugees to their homeland.

Unfortunately, the civilian world offers no ready-made models for efficiently feeding and clothing soldiers. Military labs in Natick, Massachusetts, that have been assigned responsibility for the soldiers' food, clothing, equipment, and shelter advertise themselves collectively as the "Army's one-stop soldier-support organization."[15] They invent new fabrics to protect against chemical warfare, lightweight field kitchens to feed more people with less expenditure of energy, and nutritional, high-calorie meals that soldiers can carry into combat. Their concern is the soldier's body—"the ultimate weapon"—and they often work jointly with scientists at other government labs and research universities.

Courtesy of DOD-funded scientists at Rutgers and Clemson universities, soldiers of the future may slap on a patch or suck on a lozenge of "nutriceuticals" designed to reduce stress caused by exertion, cold, or high altitude. Current experiments employ green tea extract, on the premise that it will "clear the fog of war."[16] Along the same lines, future soldiers may swallow or have implanted under their skin a dime-size microchip (variously referred to as a "pharmacy on a chip" or a "grocery store in a chip") that will deliver needed drugsduring combat. With a small electric charge, a self-administered jolt from a power source the size of a belt buckle, performance enhancers, adrenaline, wound healers, and nutrients will enter the bloodstream. The chip will contain several highly concentrated drugs, released separately as needed by the individual soldier. No more downtime: soldiers in short-term intensive conflict will get the nutrients they need when they need them.

An army lives on its stomach. Remaking the stomach means remaking the soldier. Behind enemy lines, a downed pilot will be able to choose between insects (ants actually taste lemony, grasshoppers crunchy but sweet) and the digested gelatinous mass issuing from Natick's "portable stomach." To partake of the latter, he will simply pick leaves and bark and put them in a sealed bag. Bioconverter enzymes will transform these inedible foragings into an edible, if unsavory, meal. When the "digestion" in the portable stomach is complete, the pilot has only to turn on the spigot at the bottom of the bag and open wide. This may sound far-fetched, but the U.S. Army Soldier and Biological Chemical Command undertook a cellulose conversion program in the late 1960s that worked to convert newsprint into an edible substance and whose science led to the portable stomach.[17]

To promote futuristic possibilities like the portable stomach, the Department of Defense's Combat Feeding Program at Natick has produced a CD entitled *The Care and Feeding of the Starship Trooper*. According to the program's director, Gerald Darsch, "The soldier is the ultimate weapon, and we fuel the ultimate weapon."[18] Those given the task of inventing the future soldier's fuel, or food, predict that it will be "stealthier": traditional rations but invisible to infrared. The food will also turn digestion into a means of camouflage. Like polychromic packaging that turns beige in desert terrain, white in snowy regions, and jungle green in tropical climates, soldiers will consume food additives that temporarily alter the cast of their skin. (This of course presumes a light skin tone to begin with.) The face-painted soldier we see stalking an invisible enemy in television commercials may soon be an image of the past, as the GI's camouflage will be the sign of a good meal. Well fed means well hidden.

Given the strategic priority of field rations, future terrorists will probably target a foe's food source with the intention of spoiling or secretly contaminating it. To plan for such a contingency, the military has commissioned university scientists to invent a biosensor the size of a hand-held beeper that will scan food for harmful biological agents— no mean task, considering that it must distinguish healthy biological agents from foreign contaminates.

At the Combat Feeding Program, scientists work to develop new combat rations and packaging that will facilitate longer shelf life, ease transportation, and insure edibility at extreme temperatures of 115 degrees or 50 below. Not all their inventions remain in the world of the military. Many have made their way onto grocery store shelves: processed cheese, shelf-stable bakery products, dry yeast, cake and bread mixes, dehydrated milk, converted rice, freeze-dried foods, and the famous Tang. The latest in packaging comes complete with its own antioxidants, little aldehyde scavengers that keep the food from reacting with its container.

Besides thinking about combat cuisine of the future, the folks at the Combat Feeding Program spend much of their time and resources improving today's MREs (meals ready to eat). In recent years they've doubled the standard offering of twelve meals to a more varied twenty-four, produced the first pocket sandwich (field-tested in 2003 by soldiers fighting in Iraq), developed self-heated meals, and perfected nonthermal processing through the use of high pressure. They "squish the little buggers to death," explains Darsch, putting the rations into packages slim enough to fit into a pocket by using a technology developed following World War II. In the 1950s and 1960s government scientists developed a process that shrank food for easy carrying and made it possible to reverse the shrinkage, returning the food to its original proportions and elasticity.

Visitors to the Combat Feeding Program (generally members of the military) dine at the Temple of Food, the taste-testing center for the latest in field rations. Sampling the latest offerings, they are treated to a buffet of "huah" bars (high-energy bars in different flavors), vegetarian meals, ribs (strips of bland processed meat smothered in spicy barbecue sauce), a thick, sweet, supercharged green Kool-Ade, a limp, rubbery burrito, and shrimp jambalaya that one general swears is every bit as good as his wife's. Everything in this high-calorie meal is served at room temperature on special paper plates, a luxury reserved for visitors.

No matter how tasty a salisbury steak packaged in plastic might be, soldiers prefer hot meals prepared in a field kitchen. Anticipating soldiers' needs in future wars, engineers are developing pot surfaces that can be sanitized without water or fuel (substances often in short supply in combat). They've invented the pocket stove, niftier than any expensive backpacker's Sterno heater. Weighing a mere four ounces, it fits between a thumb and forefinger. The individual beverage heater, a small pouch, flamelessly heats a canteen of water to provide a hot cup of coffee or soup and thaws a frozen canteen in frigid climates. Its counterpart chills a canteen of water in hot climates. In recent years combat rations have gotten lighter (by 45 percent), tastier, and more durable, but the potable water required by a company in the field has been a constant, accounting for a good deal of the weight any foot soldier must carry.[19] Recent hydrotechnology, however, is addressing this problem. Future soldiers will be equipped with waferlike membranes that can be dropped into "the filthiest swamp you can imagine," according to Darsch, to produce drinkable water. Although field kitchens have changed little in the past fifty years, planners anticipate radical changes within the next twenty-five.[20] Budgets and technology willing, the old field kitchen and sanitation system manned by several cooks and dishwashers will give way to a camouflage-painted cargo container capable of producing individual hot meals on demand with no sweaty cooks, no pots to wash, and no diesel fuel to transport. Soldiers will simply insert their ID cards, which include their preprogrammed food preferences and provide up-to-the-minute vital statistics gathered from their high-tech uniforms, and the automated chuckwagon will instantly generate a hot meal.

Of course, a soldier is not simply the destination for a food delivery system. A soldier is a warrior who must target, engage, and destroy or disarm the enemy. But the conception of a warrior has been subjected to the same systems analysis that aims to produce revolutionary efficiencies in food delivery. As conceived at the U.S. Army Soldier Systems Center, an R&D center in Natick, the doughboy, GI, and grunt of past wars will be reborn as "Future Warrior 2025," "a tightly integrated system of systems, able to fight as effectively as a tank of 1995."[21] Much PR work has gone into promoting the "warrior platform," a spiffier name for uniform and gear.

Properly accoutered, the human becomes the machine, no longer a body but a technology. Although Natick staff members stress that Future Warrior 2025 is still a concept, it is a concept that they have aggressively promoted for the past four years. Not only has Natick featured images of Future Warrior prominently on its Web site, it pulled a handsome young sergeant from the ranks to serve as live model. Sergeant Patterson suited up for visiting dignitaries, the inquiring press, and toy company reps.[22] This sergeant-turned-cyborg went on the road, accompanied by a slide show and a mounted display, to promote this government lab's vision of tomorrow's ground soldier, with the goal of winning support for future research projects. In some quarters of the Army, rival military planners dismiss Future Warrior as more fantasy than fact, simply a slick promotion. Slick or not, it has caught the fancy of retired generals, whose influence on the Army's future should not be underestimated; and it has dazzled the toy industry.

So impressed were the Hasbro Toy reps with the trim Sergeant Patterson bedecked in his black spandex and black aerodynamic motorcycle helmet with its wrap-around smoke-colored vision panel (a far cry from the frumpy, lumpy, utilitarian combat soldier of today) that they vowed, according to Sergeant Patterson, to name their 2025 GI Joe doll after Natick's Future Warrior. Whether they do indeed issue a Sergeant Patterson doll, Hasbro will certainly introduce a sequel to its Land Warrior doll, which is complete with eye scope and computer, mimicking the Army's Land Warrior 2010. So not only will costumed sergeants at trade shows and impressive images of Hollywood-style soldiers on Web sites advertise Natick as a lab undertaking exciting futuristic work, but the toy industry's miniaturization of Future Warrior in doll form will promote the Army to a large group of future recruits. This is what the Hollywood promoters call "toyification"—assessing the value of ideas and innovations by their capacity to be turned into toys. It exploits the way in which a childlike wonder at technology binds all the participants in the process.

In fact, the original concept of Future Warrior 2025 was put together not by a young Tom Edison or Enrico Fermi but by Steve Smith, a graphic specialist from Geo Centers, Inc., working as a subcontractor at Natick. Smith was put on the spot to prepare something for a deadline. To bring some attention to the work of the Natick scientists and encouraged by trade show organizers to produce "anything futuristic," he dreamed up the display to draw convention-goers to the Natick booth. Smith incorporated ideas from a few technologies under development at Natick and from his reading of science fiction to produce a compelling image of a future warrior who could have walked off a Hollywood set. The response was overwhelming; so many important people were impressed that Natick representatives decided to refine the gimmick, which had been concocted simply as an eye-grabbing convention display, as their vision of the future. Since then, Future Warrior has made appearances throughout the United States and in other NATO countries, where it has encountered competition from England and Australia (the latter being hard at work on a "cyber digger").

Natick's ground soldier of 2025 will don a lightweight uniform complete with built-in body sensors that automatically adjust the uniform's microclimate delivery network by either heating or cooling. Equipped with a micro turbine engine, the suit will keep the wearer comfortable for six days without refueling. The uniform's fabric will feature "smart materials," which means that the new fabric will register environmental temperature and combine that data with the record of the soldier's heart rate and temperature to predict when he or she will need hydration. Presto! A small hose coming from the neck of the uniform will allow the soldier to take a gulp of cool water without stopping to unsnap and open a canteen. Sensors implanted in the outer layer of this waterproof, fireproof, bullet-proof, chemical-proof, and bioagent-proof second skin will also indicate whether toxic substances are an environmental threat. In the presence of such agents, the pH of the outer layer will instantly enhance its resistance to the toxin and warn the soldier of danger. But that's not all. Sensors at the wrist and neck will monitor blood pressure and heart rate. If the soldier is wounded, medics will use this crucial information to provide better triage. A minute transmitter in the dog tags of the wounded will store relevant medical history for an attending medic or field doctor.

The most dramatic aspect of the future uniform's multilayered fabric is an outer surface of pixels. As the soldier moves through a city, within a tropical forest, or across a snow-covered mountain, his helmet, complete with a 360-degree display, will record the environment and automatically project its image onto his uniform. The soldier-turned-computer-screen will be assured a complete disguise. This is a good concept for fields and streams, but no military analyst would rule out the possibility that the soldier of the future must be prepared for urban conflict. In congested cities, a digital camera will not only photograph concrete and brick, it will record people. It's one thing to wear the image of a brick wall; it's quite another to have the bodies of the enemy projected on a soldier's torso. Computer-generated mimesis promises a funhouse disorientation. In Somalia, more than one donkey lay dead on the streets, caught in the crossfire of the bloody confrontation between American and Somali fighters. Picture an Army Ranger, à la Shakespeare's Bottom, decked out with fur and hooves. A disguise, yes, but hardly the kind of camouflage that makes the soldier master of his surroundings.

Recent nanotechnology promises a uniform that will contain its own armor. According to Dutch DeGay of the Objective Force Warrior Program at the Natick labs, a thin gel sandwiched between the layers of a soldier's conventional camouflage battle dress uniform will become rigid like conventional armor the instant it senses a hit.[23] Unlike current body armor, which indents when hit, saving a life but maybe breaking a few ribs, the bulletproof hardened gel will distribute the impact throughout the uniform (or, in DOD lingo, throughout the soldier's "chassis"). Almost as quickly as the fabric changes from supple to steel, it reverts to its flexible state after absorbing the hit, allowing the soldier to hightail it out of harm's way. From a related technology the military hopes to perfect "fabric muscles" made from molecules that expand and contract with the application of energy: an upper sleeve that could tighten into a tourniquet for the injured soldier, or a pair of pants that could harden into a rigid exoskeleton capable of absorbing 40 to 50 percent of the weight an individual soldier must haul. For an illustration of the latter, DeGay suggested checking out Sigourney Weaver's clothes in *Alien*.[24] But in case these possibilities—a shirt that turns tank-hard and a pair of load-bearing muscle pants—don't pan out, the Army is developing a robotic "mule" that can travel over all terrain, relieving ground soldiers on the move of their heaviest gear.

PROBLEMS AND POSSIBILITIES

The soldier of tomorrow's wars will be required to manipulate sophisticated computer equipment. To create that kind of soldier in the numbers needed, basic training must expand from a protracted initiation rite in which the recruit acquires basic Boy Scout skills and facility with a bayonet into a computer literacy curriculum.[25] As if anticipating this, the Army in 2001 launched a new recruitment campaign to replace its twenty-year-old marketing effort. No longer does the Army encourage recruits to "be all that you can be"; instead, it promises that they will be outfitted with the latest technology to become solitary warriors. A real soldier in the commercials, Corporal Richard Lovell, aged twenty-two, says, "I am an army of one. Even though there are 1,045,690 soldiers just like me, I am my own force. With technology, with training, with support, who I am has become better than who I was. And I'll be the first to tell you, the might of the U.S. Army doesn't lie in numbers. It lies in me. I am An Army of One. And you can see my strength."

New technology will require a higher standard of recruitment and extended training time, both for individuals to master specialized skills and for units to practice their collaborative use. In the past, the Army has followed a model of interchangeable parts: one soldier within a specialty has been capable of replacing another. Frequent moves, the disbursement of group members, and the readjustment time each move requires have characterized Army life. Military readiness today means having healthy troops ready to deploy, equipment in good shape, and supplies accounted for and ready for transport, but it also presupposes that every soldier is fully trained to operate sophisticated digital equipment.

Future wars will probably entail highly visible missions in which traditional lines between civilian and military blur, as they certainly did in Somalia and Afghanistan, conflicts that occur in the populous streets of

major cities or in remote areas, and long-term commitments to the protracted task of nation-building. Twenty-first-century troops may find
themselves in what the former commandant of the Marine Corps General Chuck Krulak calls the "three-block war": "In one moment in time
our service members will be feeding and clothing displaced refugees—
providing humanitarian assistance. In the next moment, they will be
holding two warring tribes apart—conducting peacekeeping operations. And finally, they will be fighting a highly lethal mid-intensity
battle—all on the same day . . . all within three city blocks" (Donnelly,
1994: 10). Computers strapped to soldiers' backs may help identify the
location of members of their own unit as well as that of allies, but they
will do little to eliminate civilian casualties in a conflict in which hostile forces look like civilians.

In his book about the conflict in Somalia, *Black Hawk Down,* Mark
Bowden recreates in painful detail the chaos of multinational forces
who had never worked as a seamless single fighting force, of poor communication that inhibited providing aid to wounded American soldiers,
of sophisticated equipment rendered impotent by primitive weapons,
and of an enemy so fractured that there was no single entity to subdue
or persuade. Some groups wanted revenge against the foreigners and
took to the streets to achieve it; others simply captured GIs to ransom
for cash. Technologically advanced American troops trapped in a few
tight Mogadishu blocks were quickly rendered helpless by gun-toting
Somalis finding cover behind civilian women and children. Without a
multinational force willing and trained to act with one mind, without
interoperable communications systems between all branches of the U.S.
military and allies in joint engagements, and without a clear sense of the
enemy, military engagements are highly likely to spiral out of control.
Technological developments and training with computer games may in
fact foster a false sense of what to expect in real war. Few war games intentionally practice what to do when the computers go down.

On the digital battlefield, every land vehicle, every helicopter
and plane, even every individual soldier will be digitally visible. Some
within the military jokingly refer to the digital battlefield as "dial-a-
war," brought to you by the big DOD contractor Motorola, because it

presumes that the lines of communication will be abuzz between hot zones and cold, between the Army working the ground, the Air Force securing the skies, and the Navy ready to fire weapons offshore. There is a fundamental problem with this scenario. With so much communication, much of it using off-the-shelf technology, certainly eavesdropping or, worse, infection of the system will be attempted by any shrewd opponent. What if a hacker jiggered the system so that every X for enemy were replaced by an O for friendly? How long would it take to detect such an interloper? Bad or contaminated software immobilizes the most lethal hardware. Any enemy facing the daunting hardware of a superpower no longer needs to invest in a costly nuclear weapons system or in a messy and imprecise biological and chemical weapons program, or even in a generation of terrorists willing to commit suicide for the cause. Any enemy, rogue or legitimate, would be wise to pursue the less costly and potentially more debilitating counterforce: a crack unit of cyberwarriors skillful enough to disable any hardware behemoth. A "cyber Pearl Harbor," a preemptive strike that would disable U.S. banking, ground commercial flights, turn off hydroelectric plants, cut off phone conversations, turn off life-support systems, jam NATO Web sites, spam AOL, even darken traffic lights, would create a chaos far more impressive than an actual skirmish off in the global bush. This new form of war could render conventionally trained soldiers and supersophisticated weaponry obsolete. To maintain security, the United States must be able to both wage and defend against this kind of war.

As more and more of the military's weapons systems become equipped with technology linked digitally with headquarters, they become more vulnerable to cyberattack. In the past, a spy would have had to smuggle mountains of paper or photos of each page of relevant documents. Now an infiltrator has only to gain access to data sets. Although adversaries in any war seek to cut the lines of communication, when warfare becomes so digitally dependent that each soldier receives commands via a computer screen and fires on the enemy via computerized weapons, the need to keep the cyberwaves open increases. In a battle in which each ground soldier is equipped with a computer that records the exact positions of fellow soldiers, intercepting just one unit could reveal extremely important intelligence to the enemy. If a soldier equipped with the army's Land Warrior system were killed, wounded, or taken prisoner, "that soldier would be zeroized"—his PC turned off and his location digitally recorded by the person up the chain of command—according to the former project head Bruce Jette.[26] This presumes that the soldier would have the opportunity to relay a signal indicating the danger of enemy confiscation and voluntarily asking to have his lines of communication cut. Certainly the dead can't request such a blackout. Presumably many of the wounded would be unable to do so either, and capture may be too swift to permit such communication.

If the enemy manages to crash the communication system, the battle could conceivably end without a single casualty. To prevent enemies from infiltrating military communication systems, planners look to the National Security Administration to perfect a system that can't be cracked—a daunting task, considering the cleverness of would-be interlopers. When nuisances like the Love Bug of 2000 shut down businesses half a world away, how long can NSA keep the snoopers off the lines? How can we be sure that enemies won't jam our lines of communication with counterintelligence, the fakes and feints that can determine a battle's outcome? We must remember that any system can be cracked, and there will always be those dedicating a good deal of ingenuity to finding the combination. Furthermore, once a breach has occurred, it is very difficult to assign responsibility for electronic attacks and acts of cyberterrorism and determine whether they are acts of war or simply the work of precocious hackers showing off their adolescent computer skills for one another. As warfare grows more and more dependent on vast communication systems, it will become less geographically defined. Since communication will be digital, not oral or manual, members of the nine-person squad will no longer need to remain within sight. The advertising slogan is right; with the new technology, "An Army of One" is a real possibility. The conventional rear, where commanders plan and manage the war, will no longer be a place of relative security. When the target becomes not individual soldiers but their lines of communication, all ranks will be equally vulnerable.

Certainly such sweeping technological changes will produce new psychological pressures. In the past, even in the field there were periods when troops could rest and regroup and their commanders could take stock. Digital wars will eliminate these recuperative lulls. Army General Paul E. Funki has observed, "With the increased speed, range, lethality, and real-time communication capabilities of the modern battlefield comes a directly proportional increase in the chaos on the battlefield."[27] Increased communication may produce a babel of tongues that thickens rather than dissipates the fog of war. After twenty-eight years in Army Aviation, Colonel Howard Yellen of Special Forces fears that recent developments in technology have produced "data overload," simply too much information for an individual to process without delay—a delay that in the face of hostile forces could mean the difference between life and death. The digital advances may vastly increase the information available, but the individual pilot flying a supersonic aircraft, for example, worrying about hostile enemy in the air, antiaircraft weaponry on the ground, and the swift deployment of defensive weapons when attacked, may have difficulty processing all that information. It is true that senses are heightened in the presence of danger ("when passing through bad-guy territory," according to Yellen), but it may be just as true that bombardment by data distracts rather than guides the pilot.[28] The average digital cockpit displays over 100 screens of information; some recent aircraft display as many as 250.

Information saturation not only affects the work of pilots, it also promises to transform the job of ground troops. Instead of one small recon unit sending back details of the location and size of enemy troops, hundreds, maybe even thousands, of individual foot soldiers will automatically relay to the rear data that will have to be centrally processed, ordered, and acted upon. Having equipped individual soldiers with body sensors to capture heart rate and other physiological information, commanders will be able to assess the general fitness of a unit on a minute-by-minute basis. The challenge with all this information becomes, of course, how to decipher it. The fact that information is accurate doesn't mean it is useful. On the battlefield, do commanders abort a mission if they determine that a unit has slipped below a certain fitness standard? If individual sensors indicate that someone is at risk of hypothermia, commanders must determine whether to push forward or wait until the soldier can be removed to safety. Proponents of body sensors speculate that having data on the present fitness of a specific unit and processing it through a computer program, like the actuarial calculations of insurance companies, enables a commander to determine the wisdom of sending forces off to take the next hill. You can't dispute the benefit of a system of sensors to the medic, who must quickly diagnose and treat the wounded, but you have to question the role of up-to-the-minute fitness reports on each soldier in the thick of battle. The Army Research Institute for Environmental Medicine (ARIEM) is developing ways of collecting all of this physiological data without any consensus yet on what needs to be captured and what use such information will be put to. Data-gathering has no necessary connection to battlefield tactics. Planners are asking what physiological data to collect and how to collect it but not how it will assist commanders in war.

Those designing the wars of the future presume that technological advances will make war transparent, that delivering what all the eyes from the sky and ground see will turn tactical contingencies into strategic opportunities. In theory that makes sense; in practice, such an instant abundance of images may in fact confuse rather than clarify the picture of the whole. Intelligence runs uphill from platoon to company to battalion to brigade or regime and finally to division, a line of communication that in previous wars might have taken two hours or more.[29] With the new technology, that information becomes instantaneous, and with it comes the need for instant decision-making and less time to consult and second-guess. In digital war, human soldiers become not just those who deliver lethal force but individual intelligence-gatherers who, along with their counterparts in the air, generate minute-to-minute data on their own positions and the positions of any enemy forces, land vehicles, or aircraft. Surely such massive, rapid-fire transmissions of data will require sophisticated software to process. It follows that with proper modeling, such software could also analyze and prescribe courses of action—that it could run the war. The war room has become a computer lab.

Theoretically, computer modeling allows war fighters to run

through all the possibilities and, if not master all contingencies, at least to plan for those written into the program. War is various, however, and all the sophisticated planning models cannot anticipate every possibility. In the Kosovo conflict, for example, the planning model didn't take into account the fact that Serbia would refrain from using its antiaircraft weapons. Our planes, ready to take them out, couldn't act until the enemy turned on its radar control systems. Because the enemy did not use antiaircraft weapons, such systems remained hidden from U.S. detection and kept us from deploying a full contingent of Apache helicopters, designed to sweep into place after the antiaircraft weapons were cleaned out. The enemy destroyed the plan of battle by refusing to step on the escalator that American planners had so carefully designed. To lure them out of hiding, the United States deployed false targets so the Serbs' sensitive antiaircraft weapons would fire, but the effort failed to draw them out.[30] Neither computer-driven strategic planning nor computer-aided tactical adjustments were able to induce the enemy to play the game by which America insures technological superiority.

Although technology goes a long way toward determining how wars are fought and who will ultimately prevail, it provides no guarantees. Divided and rivaling command structures are capable of introducing enough noise into the system that no signals from the front can get through or no intelligence can be intelligently exploited. To fight future wars, the Pentagon must redesign itself so that the swift transfer of information produces swift decision-making and the consequent relocation of soldiers and weapons to needed areas before the enemy knows what is happening. This redesign must replace the *independence* historically apportioned to each branch of the military with a seamless *interdependence* of land, air, and sea forces. It must recruit and train military personnel to fight future, not past, wars, and it must fully utilize the talents of all military personnel, including women. It must face the likelihood of urban combat and cyberwar. Digital communication, the very technology that promises an advantage to the United States and its allies, opens a new and vast front of increased vulnerability. If the enemy's cyberwarriors can effectively turn off the power, they will have blinded the mighty Cyclops, castrating the superpower.

Whether the cumbersome Land Warrior system in its reconstituted version as Objective Force Warrior remains the model for the future or is eclipsed by the Army's sleeker Future Warrior, the armed services have set about the technological revolution as if their task were simply to develop new equipment that could substitute for old: a sophisticated computer for an old radio or a new rifle with a thermal sight. Military leaders, steadfastly committed to protecting their individual services, have done little to advance initiatives designed to restructure the military in light of a changing enemy, novel weapons, faster communication, and unprecedented wars. These leaders have offered general statements about the need to rethink the way things are done but have come up with little actual innovation.

Here's the promo: "Force XXI is America's Army for the 21st Century. Force XXI is the reconceptualization and redesign of the force at all echelons from the foxholes to the industrial base to meet the needs of the volatile and ever changing world. It will be a force organized around information and information technologies."[31] Information, according to Pentagon planners, is "the fifth dimension of war," the other four being land, sea, air, and space.[32] Impressive talk! But a sluggish bureaucracy, a rigid chain of command, and a conservative hostility to innovation stand in the way of any real reconceptualization and any fundamental redesign. Planners express no interest, for example, in considering the merits of any organizational structure other than the current one, which pits Army, Air Force, and Navy (and with it the Marine Corps), each with its independent interests, against one another in a fight for congressional funding. Although a merged two-force system achieved by combining sea and air forces on the one hand and all land forces (Army and Marine Corps) on the other might realize certain efficiencies and ease the transition to a single communication system, such proposals run head-on into a stone wall of tradition. Military planners so fundamentally define themselves first as Marine Corps, Army, Navy, and Air Force officers that few can look at the military and its future needs apart from that identity; they are "organization men" rather than warriors.

In Vietnam, famously, less than 10 percent of the military stationed in the war zone ever actually engaged with the enemy in battle. The rest made up the vast organization of logistical support and interference. The proportion of organization men to warriors is even higher today; regrettably, the military remains the last, best refuge for the organization man. Officers don't advance by questioning the structure of the military; they win their promotions by demonstrating that they can work well within the established structure. Tenured conservatives, they can't be expected to lead any move to reorganize.

In addition to the reluctance on the part of the Pentagon and Congress to undertake the reorganization necessary to fight the digital war, powerful retired generals and admirals still hold sway in all branches of the military, from their corner offices at Lockheed or in their new careers as defense industry operatives. Understandably, they hanker for the military they once commanded, one as strong as it was in its cold war days, and they promote the interests of their new employers with current military leaders who sometimes served as their subordinates. In many cases they have simply moved a few blocks from their cramped Pentagon offices to the corporate offices of defense contractors hovering in Crystal City, Virginia—as close as you can get to the Pentagon and not be on government land. They constitute a group with considerable influence but one that looks backward rather than forward. If the military were to reorganize in light of the future wars it will fight, these retirees would be out of work.

A notable exception to the backward-looking, inward-turning perspective is advanced by Retired Admiral Bill Owens. Owens realizes that having all the information in the world will do little to assist forces in war unless that information can be communicated quickly to those who need it. In his book, *Lifting the Fog of War*, he highlights a major weakness in our current defense system: the inability of one branch of the service to communicate swiftly and fluidly with another.

I can pinpoint the moment when I realized how dysfunctional and inefficient the U.S. military had become, and how sweeping was the need for a thorough reorganization of the armed forces to meet the challenges of the new century. It came midway through my tenure months after the end of the Gulf War in 1991. I decided to try an experiment in emergency communication. For this exercise I told each of my naval fleet units that I wanted it to demonstrate that it could communicate directly with a U.S. Army ground combat unit—any combat unit—somewhere in Europe. It is, of course, possible for U.S. ships to communicate with U.S. ground forces, and we do so all the time. But convoluted routings and different communication channels, switchboards, and operators are involved. For this experiment I wanted the Army unit ashore in Europe—not routed through a switch at some communications center or higher headquarters.

We tried to do it. We tried—*for six months*—to make the connection. And we never could link up with the Army. There was always something wrong. The Army and Navy units used different frequencies. The communications protocols employed by the Army and Navy were different. The communications personnel had never trained to do this. And so on ... What was it about our military services—and the Pentagon's leadership—that would allow such a serious problem to go on indefinitely? (Owens, 2000: 150–151)

Having new technology is one thing. Making it work is another. A communication system designed to connect military units deployed across the globe presupposes a command structure organized more efficiently, one that will allow an Army officer on the ground to call in air support from a carrier offshore and see it swiftly delivered. As long as the military rigidly maintains the separation of branches in vertical structures that must blaze convoluted trails to act in consort, they will be ill prepared for future military operations.

The current system of distinct and largely autonomous services notoriously generates duplication and competition instead of purposeful collaboration. Only cooperation within will insure competition without. Despite all the talk of "interoperability," technology is still typically "stovepiped" into each warfare community. As small, highly trained units practiced in securing sites in congested urban areas (like the cluttered streets of Mogadishu) and in remote rugged terrain (like the mountain caves of Afghanistan) are called to conduct missions against enemy nations and ill-defined terrorist cells, the smooth coordination of several branches of the military, as well as the Central Intelligence Agency, the FBI, the Border Patrol, the National Guard, and the newly constituted Department of Homeland Security, will be essential. To succeed, all agencies must operate with the same set of data. That way the CIA won't target a building it believes to be a munitions plant, which on somebody else's map is actually another nation's embassy. And the eagerness to go to war must not distort those intelligence data, as they did in Operation Iraqi Freedom. They must employ compatible communication systems that allow those in harm's way to communicate across the chain of command as well as up it, from one service to another and from one governmental agency to another.

If this had happened before September 11, 2001—if someone had connected the dots of all the known information regarding Al Qaeda terrorists and their likely targets—the tragic attacks of that day might have been prevented. Although the Pentagon has sponsored joint activities and the Department of Homeland Security has been assigned a coordinating role, traditional service rivalries and the historic autonomy of separate federal agencies threaten the necessary reorganization of the military, law enforcement agencies, and intelligence gatherers into a command structure that could imaginatively absorb and fully utilize technological advances in fighting wars and defending the United States—a command structure that could preserve and protect.

September 11 left all Americans with a sense of vulnerability, a sense that even a puny enemy operating from one of the most impoverished countries in the world could effectively execute ferocious attacks on our mainland. In response, President Bush announced a "war on terrorism" that would not only require the deployment of specially trained units to places like Afghanistan, the Philippines, and Indonesia to root out terrorists and of forces to topple old enemies like Saddam Hussein, but would also necessitate extensive efforts in disaster preparedness and civil defense. Armed guards were positioned at airports and government buildings across the country. The Pentagon formed a new Northern

Command to respond to terrorist threats to the United States, Mexico, and Canada. The Department of Homeland Security began preparing for future attacks. After September 11, Americans saw their country's margins—the long, sparsely guarded borders and shores—not as fronts on which to wage a war on drugs but as permeable membranes through which terrorists might smuggle biological, chemical, and nuclear weapons to be used on our soil. In response, some called for an expanded Coast Guard, Border Patrol, and National Guard and a new force of specially trained air marshals. Given the patriotic fervor in the months immediately following September 11 and the president's declaration of war against "the evil ones," many expected fresh recruits to flood military recruitment offices. Americans waved flags from front lawns, hung them on the sides of cars, draped them from office buildings and parking lots, even sported them on jacket lapels, but the anticipated new recruits failed to materialize.[33] The attacks of September 11, the promise of future attacks issuing from the White House (such as Vice President Dick Cheney's "not 'if' but 'when'" rhetoric), and President Bush's determination to finish the job his father started in Iraq have raised questions about our current defenses at home and our deployable force strength abroad—a strength in 2003 well below Desert Storm levels. In some circles this has rekindled a call for the reinstatement of a universal draft.

Ironically, those who advocate a universal draft also insist that women be excluded. Without the drafting of women and without the exemptions that freed most of the middle class to go about their civilian lives during much of the Vietnam War, proponents argue that a draft would restore a past era when young men served their nation as citizen soldiers and women maintained their place in the home. But history chronicles the service of women in all major conflicts: Revolutionary War, Civil War, Spanish-American War, World War I, World War II, Korea, Vietnam, Operation Just Cause in Panama, and the first and second Gulf wars, as well as the conflicts in Bosnia and Afghanistan. The Molly Pitchers, others who disguised their identity as women, those guarding strategic sites in Panama and Afghanistan, women who pilot and navigate fighter aircraft—all have engaged the enemy in combat. Simply being designated as noncombatants comes with no guarantee of safety.

Despite the regulations that prevent women from engaging in combat, many women have given their lives in the line of duty; many more have suffered wounds or endured the hardship of prison camps. The testimony of Rhonda Cornum, a flight surgeon and prisoner during the Gulf War, illustrates how the distinctions between such categories as offensive and defensive and combatant and noncombatant blur in times of war, especially when tactical mobility has dictated an increased integration of frontline and support troops. In such circumstances, battlefield necessity trumps institutional regulations. Cornum tells how the pilot of her Blackhawk rescue helicopter took the initiative to teach her as well as the male medics to fire the M-60 machine guns mounted in the side doors: "We flew over the desert and Godfrey called out targets for us to shoot: a wrecked car, a fence post, a fifty-five-gallon metal barrel. He flew us back and forth over the sand, and we became reasonably good at putting bullets on the targets. I thought it was a good idea for us to learn to shoot, and I never thought about asking one of my superiors for permission: it was smarter to just do it. I firmly believe in the theory that it's better to ask forgiveness than to ask permission. Especially when we were about to invade Iraq" (Cornum, 1992: 41).

Despite the widespread application of Cornum's theory, women must officially still seek a permission that has not been forthcoming. Women remain banned from serving in combat specialities in the infantry, cannon field artillery, several Special Operations positions, and the Navy Seals, purportedly to avoid direct contact with enemy ground forces. In May 2002, women who were trained to work alongside men in ground reconnaissance units were transferred to other units and their jobs restricted as male-only jobs because of pressure from conservatives to limit the role of women in the military.

Regardless of the political interference that compels the enforcement of anachronistic gender-based prohibitions in the regular military, the Air National Guard, a branch that prepares soldiers to protect air bases, has begun sending women through its sniper school. The innovation has met with considerable success. Reflecting on the difference between female and male trainees, Sergeant First Class Ben Dolan, the school's head of instruction and a former Marine sniper, states that "women can shoot better, by and large, and they're easier to train because they don't have the inflated egos that a lot of men bring to these programs. Women will ask for help if they need it, and they will tell you what they think" (Haskell, 2001).

Although Cornum's experience as a prisoner of the Iraqis in the Gulf War was a featured story, her short-term celebrity was modest compared to that of Jessica Lynch, who was featured in a made-for-television rescue that will likely prove to be the most memorable and controversial episode of Operation Iraqi Freedom. Lynch, an Army private, was injured in a truck accident near Nasiriya, Iraq, when her unit separated from the convoy of trucks they were traveling with. She was taken into enemy hands and held captive in two Iraqi medical facilities for a total of eight days, until she was rescued by a team of Special Forces soldiers. All wars produce focal anecdotes of bravery, grit, and sacrifice. Many of those stories emerge as the lore of the regiment, the battalion, and the service. At least since the emergence of battlefield journalism in the early nineteenth century, many such stories have been propagated, embellished, and even concocted by the press. The Lynch episode—both the rescue and the ensuing publicity—illustrates the way in which the electronic technology that developed to enhance mastery of the battlefield also confers on the contemporary military unprecedented mastery of the representation of the battle, by enabling it to construct stories designed to control public perception of and attitudes toward the conduct of a war.

In the modern era, strategic thinking in conventional war has responded to the metaphor of the theater of operations, a metaphor that implies the restriction of hostilities to a bounded space in which the relations between the backstage command and logistical support can be separated from the opposing forces on the stage, protagonists and antagonists who are oriented on axes of right and left, front and back. Strategy is the script that diagrams the movements of the actors in order to dictate the outcome of hostilities. In the conventional war of position, where lines are clear and sectors are defined, a soldier crosses into enemy territory only on a prescribed mission of reconnaissance or infiltration or as a captive. With the paradigmatic shift from the metaphor of the closed theater to that of the open field, and from the war of position to the war of maneuver, distinctions between friend and foe, soldier and civilian, the front and the rear blur and mutate. Conventional wars also tend to prescribe what is documented and reported about the war and who does that documentation and reporting. Military officials typically record the number of enemy and friendly deaths, report to headquarters acts worthy of distinction or rebuke, and log the specifics of every tactical encounter. Military personnel may employ photographs and video cameras, but those are typically intended for internal evaluation and instruction rather than for distribution to the larger civilian population. Occasionally, as in World War II, when notable Hollywood directors such as John Ford and William Wyler made features on assignment from Washington, adjuncts with special expertise have been recruited for propaganda purposes. Generally, however, the documentation of the day-to-day progress of the war as news for the audience back home has been the domain of the civilian press. Although the military deploys a large and sophisticated publicity apparatus that summarizes and spins objectives and achievements, advances and reverses for eager journalists at its official briefings, in past wars there was nonetheless a clear division of labor: the military plans and executes, journalists record and report, and stateside editors piece together the final story.

The Jessica Lynch story revives the figure of war as theater, although not in the conventional sense of spatial metaphor but as a characterization of the military's exploitation of an equivocal relationship between representation and reality. Here's what we know, as of September 2003: that Lynch was injured in a truck crash on March 23, 2003, in which others died; that she was taken to one medical facility, treated, and transferred to another; that civilian doctors and nurses did their best with the limited equipment and supplies at hand; that an ambulance commissioned by an Iraqi doctor to transport Lynch to the U.S. compound had to return to the hospital as a result of American fire; that a group of Special Forces soldiers took Lynch from the hospital; that the same soldiers filmed the incident as it occurred; that Lynch spent over seventy days in the hospital after her rescue. The operation played in the media as what Dennis Murphy of NBC's *Dateline* called "one of the most astonishing rescues in the annals of war" (Apr. 6, 2003). The report of her rescue on April 1 countered the gloomy news of effective Iraqi attacks on U.S. forces, even eclipsing the sad news of the corpses of U.S. soldiers discovered in shallow graves near the hospital when Lynch was removed. Although both the Army and Lynch claim that she has no recollection of the events she endured, she has signed a $1 million contract for the rights to her story.

We also know that the early reports that transmitted information from military officials were false. Lynch was reported to have sustained multiple stab and gunshot wounds. According to those who treated her, however, there were no such wounds. Lynch's injuries were consistent with the vehicular accident she suffered, although it is possible that assault with a rifle might have worsened her already severe injuries. Initial accounts of her abuse while in captivity include a particularly graphic description by Mohammad Odeh al-Rehaief, who claimed that he saw Lynch being slapped by an interrogating Iraqi officer. Because Lynch remembers nothing (as of this writing) and there has been no physical or testimonial corroboration of Rahaef's supposed eyewitness account, the entrepreneurial informant has played a central role in the ensuing drama, winning for himself a $500,000 book contract from HarperCollins and political asylum in the United States.

As with the war effort at large, initial euphoria at the ease with which operations were executed has given way to postmartial *tristesse* in the face of intractable facts that resist official spinmeisters and unofficial fabulators. Although the *Washington Post* reported a military official as saying that when captured "Lynch was fighting to the death," subsequent reports have cast doubt on whether Lynch managed to get off any rounds before her M-16 jammed.[34] Al-Rehaief's editor at HarperCollins, David Hirshey, who, in the course of an interview with National Public Radio's Michele Norris described the intense competition among publishers to acquire authentic narratives of Lynch's captivity and subsequent rescue, may have to shift al-Rehaief's story from the nonfiction to the fiction list. Follow-up stories by the BBC and the *Vancouver Sun*, which were based on extensive interviews with Iraqi civilians at the hospital where Lynch spent most of her eight days as a prisoner-patient, have challenged al-Rehaief's veracity and cast doubt on the necessity for Central Command to have staged a commando raid at all. There seems to have been no threat of Iraqi resistance. According to Iraqi hospital personnel, all enemy troops had pulled out before the Special Forces arrived with guns blazing. And it seems likely that there was no failure of intelligence, that the rescuers were prepared to meet no armed resistance, and that the effect of blazing, not the impact of bullets, was the point of the mission. Harith al-Houssona, an Iraqi doctor (so far without a book contract) who treated Lynch, described the actions of U.S. Special Forces to the BBC reporter John Kampfner: "Like a film of Hollywood, they cry 'Go, go, go' with guns and blanks without bullets . . . They make a show for the American attack at the hospital. Action movies like Sylvester Stallone or Jackie Chan, jumping, shouting, breaking the door."[35]

Dr. al-Houssona's account fairly reflects the video that was shot in real time by Special Forces personnel during the raid. Whether or not blanks or bullets were fired, assigning the role of videographer to a member of the commando unit speaks of either a remarkable tolerance of risk or a suspicious confidence that there would be little or none. Dr. al-Houssona's invocation of Hollywood was more appropriate than he could have known without access to the information that the Pentagon had indeed sought the advice of Jerry Bruckheimer, the impresario of *Top Gun* and *Armageddon*, on how to handle battlefield reporting. Unfortunately, although the Pentagon rushed out a high-impact action video that had the effect of galvanizing public support for the war effort, in the discouraging aftermath it has refused journalists' requests to release the unedited video footage that would corroborate or discredit the accuracy of its public relations blitz.

We may never know the reasoning of the military commanders who launched the rescue mission. Jessica Lynch may never recover the memory of her time in captivity. The staged event may never succeed to a definitive incident. History matters, of course, not only for the record but as a gauge both for future policymakers and for the congressional representatives who approve the military budgets. Yet, for the management of public opinion, more important than what *actually* took place in the hospital are the stories that give that theatrical operation meaning. They include the heroic narrative of the Pentagon video, the enthusiastic accounts of the U.S. media, the critical accounts of the foreign press, or the personal stories of Private Lynch or Mohammad Odeh Rehaef, which will no doubt appear in bookstore displays in the near future. The stories are important because they clarify, however partially or falsely, the obscurity of a war launched in an unprecedented climate of national emergency and in response to threats to national security conveyed by classified, if not contrived, intelligence reports filtered by politicians with their eyes on Field, Gallup, and whatever other polls claim authority on the mood of the electorate.

The Hollywood look, feel, and flow of the rescue did not go unnoticed by the American press, though they treated it as a reason for celebration rather than skepticism. Reporting for NBC, Dennis Murphy proclaimed the Lynch story as "right out of Hollywood." And for Murphy, the familiarity of the story invited a hackneyed reiteration of gender stereotypes. He evoked "the pretty teenager ambushed, held captive, and then rescued in a daring fashion"—the classic damsel in distress—and patronized her as a "a kind, spirited, itty-bitty country girl." When speaking to citizens of her hometown, Palestine, West Virginia, Murphy stated, "That little girl, you know, has become an American hero."[36] Numerous other articles cite Lynch's desire to become a kindergarten teacher and her title of Miss Congeniality at the Wirt County Fair—not attributes typically associated with soldiers. Indeed, as our investigation of the timeworn lore of the warrior would lead us to expect, the mainstream media relentlessly cast Lynch not as soldier but as civilian, not as an agent of liberation but as a surrogate for the women in the audience watching the evening news. Tucker Carlson, the cohost of CNN's *Crossfire*, characterized Lynch in the following way: "Private Jessica Lynch may be the most famous participant in the Iraq War. Her capture and rescue in Iraq have come to symbolize the qualities the U.S. military holds in highest regard: bravery, loyalty, endurance, and daring" (June 16, 2003).

Who is the subject here? Lynch displayed endurance, surely, but the other virtues adhere not to her but to the Special Forces soldiers—that is, if you buy the daring-rescue story. Famous by accident, a participant without volition or memory, Jessica Lynch offers only the blank slate of the mute female body on which a story of the war can be written and whose own (ghost)writing, when it appears, can contradict no eyewitness account, no canned action video, but only confirm the self-congratulatory stories of the men who saved her.

Both the civilian and the military powers that have conducted this war have needed that blank slate. Perhaps originally imagined as a ritualized undoing of the widely broadcast humiliation suffered by American prisoners dragged through mocking throngs on the streets of Mogadishu, as Carlson's hyperbole indicates, the Lynch tape has taken on ever greater symbolic freight. With the failure of the clandestine weapons of mass destruction to materialize as promised and thereby to confirm the trumpeted justification for invading Iraq in the first place, and with daily testimony that a substantial number of Iraqi citizens do not show the expected gratitude for their liberation, the videotape prepared by the Defense Department to document the first rescue of a prisoner of war since World War II remains the chief visual evidence of a threat undone and a mission successfully accomplished. Like the best stories, it is a simple one, a technological twist on the rescue fantasy that every child imbibes from nanny or Grimm or Disney and to which the child in the grownup still clings. No one, perhaps, clings to that rescue fantasy more than those nations and individuals who are challenged to be "an army of one"—the brave, courageous, and bold male liberator, but one who cannot suppress the unmanly feelings of isolation from the group and vulnerability to accident that shadow the ideal of omnicompetent autonomy. Jessica is another name for the unacknowledgeable fear of weakness within, which, when called "woman," can be neatly externalized and rendered harmless, whether as an object of pity or of scorn.

From a folkloric perspective, the Jessica Lynch narrative is just another variant on the stories that are the cherished lore of the military. But from a political perspective, it is an especially potent variant, for unlike the slanders of Hanoi Jane propagated on the Web or the doggerel chanted on the drill field, this variant has the imprimatur of the U.S. Department of Defense, which produced, edited, and distributed its videotape as irrefutable evidence that life imitates propaganda. When the military brings into its operations digital recording devices that enable it to script the scene, enact the prescribed roles, and perform the final cut, it makes war not on Iraqis but on reality, turning fantasy into fact and folklore into an instrument of policy.

Bibliography

Achtemeir, Paul, ed. 1985. *Harper's Bible Dictionary*. San Francisco: Harper's.

Alexander, Paul. 1996. "Brothers in Arms." *George*.

Adams, Abigail. 1993. "Dyke to Dyke: Ritual Reproduction at a U.S. Men's Military College." *Anthropology Today*, 9: 3–6.

Altemeyer, B. 1988. *Enemies of Freedom: Understanding of Right-wing Authoritarianism*. San Francisco: Jossey-Bass.

Alter, Jonathan. 1996. "Beneath the Ways." *Navy Times*. June 3.

Anderson, Christopher. *The Turbulent Life of Jane Fonda*. New York: Dell.

Bandura, Albert, Claudio Barbaranelli, Gian Vittorio Caprara, and Concetta Pastoreli. 1996. "Mechanisms of Moral Disengagement in the Exercise of Moral Agency," *Journal of Personality and Social Psychology*, 71, 2: 364–374.

Barthes, Roland. 1983. *The Fashion System*. Matthew Ward and Richard Howard, trans. New York: Hill and Wang.

Bateman, Robert III. 1999. *Digital War: A View from the Front Lines*. Novato, Calif.: Presidio.

Bettleheim, Bruno. 1971. *Symbolic Wounds: Puberty Rites and the Envious Male*. New York: Collier Books.

Biderman, Albert. 1963. *March to Calumny*. New York: Macmillan.

Birdwell, Russell. 1942. *Women in Battle Dress*. New York: Fine Editions.

Blakey, Scott. 1978. *Prisoner of War: The Survival of Commander Richard A. Stratton*. New York: Doubleday.

Blazer, Ernest, and Becky Garrison. 1995. *Navy Times*. Dec. 18, p. 6.

Boatner, Mark. 1954. *Army Lore*. Japan: Kyoya Co.

———. 1956. *Military Customs and Traditions*. New York: David McKay Co.

Boyer, Peter. 1996. *New Yorker*, Sept. 16.

Brownmiller, Susan. 1984. *Femininity*. New York: Simon & Schuster.

Burdick, Charles, Burton Moessner, and Ursula Moessner. 1984. *The German Prisoners of War in Japan, 1914–1920*. Lanham, N.H.: University Press of America.

Burke, Carol. 1989. "Marching to Vietnam," *Journal of American Folklore* 102 (406), pp. 424–441.

———. 1992. "Dames at Sea." *The New Republic,* Sept. 17 and 24: 16–20.

———. 1992. " 'If You're Nervous in the Service': Training Songs of Female Soldiers in the '40s," In *Visions of War: World War II in Popular Literature and Culture.* Paul Holsinger and Mary Ann Schofield, eds. Bowling Green, Ohio: Bowling Green State University Popular Press, pp. 127–135.

———. 1996. "Military Folklore." In *American Folklore: An Encyclopedia.* Jan Harold Brunvand. New York: Garland Publishing, pp. 484–485.

———. 1996. "The Naval Academy Brass Still Don't Get It," *Los Angeles Times,* May 6, p. B5.

———. 1996. "Pernicious Cohesion," *It's Our Military Too: Women and the U.S. Military.* Judith Stiehm, ed. Philadelphia: Temple University Press, pp. 205–219.

Bushnell, Amy. 1983. "Class, Caste and Gender in the Parallel Politics of Seventeenth-Century Florida." Unpublished paper presented at the Florida Historical Society, Deland, Florida.

Campbell, Rod. 1992. "Three ADFA Cadets Admit to Woofering." *Canberra Times*. Dec. 16, p. 1.

Carey, George. 1965. "A Collection of Airborne Cadence Chants." *Journal of American Folklore* 78: 52–61.

Castle, John. 1963. *The Password Is Courage.* New York: Simon & Schuster.

Charles, H. Robert. 1988. *Last Man Out.* Austin, Tex.: Eakin.

Charles, Roger. 1996. "It's a War for Soul of U.S. Military." *Baltimore Sun,* June 2, p. F1.

Clarke, Hugh, Colin Burgess, and Russell Braddon. 1988. *Prisoners of War.* Sydney: John Ferguson.

Colin, Helen. 1995. *Song of Survival: Women Interned.* Ashland, Ore.: White Cloud.

Cordwell, Justine. 1979. "The Very Human Act of Transformation." In *The Fabrics of Culture*, Justine Cordwell and Ronald Schwarz, eds. New York: Mouton.

Cornum, Rhonda. 1992. *She Went to War: The Rhonda Cornum Story.* Novato, Calif.: Presidio.

Coulthard-Clark. 1986. *Duntroon: The Royal Military College of Australia, 1911–1986.* Sydney: Allen & Unwin.

Cowham, Bill. 1987. "Lego Lingo," an unpublished glossary of cadet slang.

Crackel, Theodore. 1987. *My Jefferson's Army: Political and Social Reform of the Military Establishment, 1801–1809.* New York: New York University Press.

Cragg, Dan. 1980. "A Brief Survey of Some Unofficial Prosigns Used by the United States Armed Forces," *Maledicta: The International Journal of Verbal Aggression* 4 (2), 167–173.

David, Barbara. 1974. "So Proudly We Hail." *The Retired Officer.* March: 18–21.

Davis, Fred. 1992. *Fashion, Culture, and Identity.* Chicago: University of Chicago Press.

DeGrey, Slim. 1991. *Changi: The Funny Side.* Runaway Bay, Queensland: Self-published.

Derreth, J. Duncan. 1973. "Religious Hair." *Man: The Journal of the Royal Anthropological Institute* 8, 1: 100–103.

Diamond, George Arthur. "Prisoner of War." *New York Folklore Quarterly* 6: 177–196.

Donnelly, Elaine. 1994. "Opinion." *San Diego Union-Tribune.* May 29, p. G-1.

Durkheim, Emile. 1965. *The Elementary Form of the Religious Life.* J. W. Swain, trans. New York: Free Press.

Edney, Leon. Testimony before the House Judiciary Committee, Dec. 1, 1998.

Edwards, T. J. 1961. *Military Customs.* Aldershot, England: Gale and Polden.

Eisenhart, R. Wayne. 1975. "You Can't Hack It, Little Girl: A Discussion of the

Covert Psychological Agenda of Modern Combat Training." *Journal of Social Issues* 31, 4: 13–23.

Eliade, Mircea. 1994. *Rites and Symbols of Initiation.* W. R. Trask, trans. Dallas: Spring Publications.

Enloe, Cynthia. 1990. *Bananas, Beaches, and Bases.* Berkeley: University of California Press.

Ewing, Elizabeth. 1975. *Women in Uniform through the Centuries.* Totowa, N.J.: Rowman and Littlefield.

FitzGerald, Frances. 1994. *Fire in the Lake.* New York: Dell.

Fowler, William. 1993. *Military Insignia.* Secaucus, N.J.: Chartwell.

Fullinwider, Robert. 1983. *Conscripts and Volunteers: Military Requirements, Social Justice, and the All-Volunteer Force.* Totowa, N.J.: Rowman and Allanhead.

Gaddis, John Lewis. 1997. *We Now Know: Rethinking Cold War History.* Oxford: Oxford University Press.

Gibson, Janice. 1991. "Training People to Inflict Pain: State Terror and Social Learning." *Journal of Humanistic Psychology* 31, 2: 72–87.

Goffman, Erving. 1959. *The Presentation of Self in Everyday Life.* New York: Doubleday.

———. 1961. *Asylums: Essays on the Social Situation of Mental Patients and Other Inmates.* Garden City, N.Y.: Doubleday.

Greider, William. 1998. *Fortress America.* New York: Public Affairs.

Gruner, Elliot. 1993. *Prisons of Culture: Representing the Vietnam POW.* New Brunswick, N.J.: Rutgers University Press.

Harrell, Margaret, and Laura Miller. 1997. *New Opportunities for Military Women: Effects upon Readiness, Cohesion, and Morale.* Washington: Rand National Defense Research Institute.

Haskell, Bob. 2001. "First Woman Graduates from Sniper School." *The Beam,* April 27. http://dcmilitary.com/airforce/beam/6_17/national_news/6893-1.html.

Havard, Virginia, ed. 1991. *By Word of Mouth.* Lufkin, Tex.: Lufkin High School.

Havener, J. K. Undated. *Army Air Force Lyrics*. Fallbrook, Calif.: Aero.

Herdt, Gilbert. 1994. *Guardians of the Flutes, Vol. I.* Chicago: University of Chicago Press.

Hershman, P. 1974. "Hair, Sex, and Dirt." *Man* 9: 275–298.

Holm, Jeanne. 1992. *Women in the Military: An Unfinished Revolution*. Novato, Calif.: Presidio.

Howes, Craig. 1993. *Voices of the Vietnam POWs*. New York: Oxford University Press.

Hubbell, John. 1976. *P.O.W.: A Definitive History of the American Prisoner-of-War Experience in Vietnam, 1964–1973*. New York: McGraw Hill.

Hughes, Geoffrey. 1991. *Swearing: A Social History of Foul Language, Oaths and Profanity in English*. Oxford, U.K.: Blackwell.

Jackson, Bruce. 1967. "What Happened to Jody." *Journal of American Folklore* 80: 387–396.

Jacobs, Eugene. 1970. "Diary of a Hell-ship Journey." *Medical Opinion and Review* 6, 11: 66–79.

JHT. 1969. "The Duntroon Tradition." *Journal of the Royal Military College:* 50–51.

Johnson, Kathryn. 1983. "A Return Visit with POWs Ten Years Later." *U.S. News & World Report*. March 28.

Johnson, Sandee S., ed. 1983. *Cadences: The Jody Call Book, No. 1.* Canton, Ohio: Daring Press.

———. 1986. *Cadences: The Jody Call Book, No. 2.* Canton, Ohio: Daring Press.

Joseph, Nathan. 1986. *Uniforms and Nonuniforms: Communication Through Clothing*. New York: Greenwood.

Kelso, Frank. 1991. Defense Department Briefing. Oct. 17.

Kenny, Catherine. 1986. *Captives: Australian Army Nurses in Japanese Prison Camps*. St. Lucia, Queensland: University of Queensland Press.

Keough, David. 1981. *Vignettes of Military History, No. 191.* Carlisle, Penn.: U.S. Military History Institute.

Kinkead, Eugene. 1959. *In Every War But One*. New York: Norton.

Kotz, Nick. 1996. "Where Have All the Warriors Gone?" *Washingtonian*, July, pp. 95–103, 107–121.

Leach, E.R. 1958. "Magical Hair." *Journal of the Royal Anthropological Institute* 88: 147–167.

Lifton, Robert. 1973. *Home from the War*. New York: Basic Books.

Lurie, Alison. 1981. *The Language of Clothes*. New York: Random House.

Marlow, David. 1983. "The Manning of the Force and the Structure of Battle: Part 2—Men and Women." In *Conscripts and Volunteers: Military Requirements, Social Justice, and the All-Volunteer Force*, ed. Robert Fullinwider. Totowa, N.J.: Rowman and Allanheld, pp. 189–199.

McDuff, James. 1983. *U.S. Army Shoulder Sleeve Insignia of the Vietnam War*. Overland Park, Kan.: Shutt.

McMichael, William. 1997. *The Mother of All Hooks: The Story of the U.S. Navy's Tailhook Scandal*. New Brunswick, N.J.: Transaction.

McNeill, William H. 1982. *The Pursuit of Power*. Chicago: University of Chicago Press.

Milgram, Stanley. 1974. *Obedience to Authority: An Experimental View*. New York: HarperCollins.

Moore, Bruce. 1993. *A Lexicon of Cadet Language: Royal Military College, Duntroon, in the Period 1983–85*. Canberra, Australia: Australian National University Press.

Mead, Margaret; 1963. *Sex and Temperament in Three Primitive Societies*. New York: Dell.

Myers, James, ed. 1990. *A Treasury of Military Humor*. Springfield, Ill.: Lincoln-Herndon Press.

Neuman, Erich. 1994. *The Fear of the Feminine and Other Essays on Feminine Psychology*. Princeton: Princeton University Press.

O'Hanlon, Michael. 2000. *Technological Change and the Future of Warfare*. Washington, D.C.: Brookings Institution.

Owens, Bill. 2000. *Lifting the Fog of War*. New York: Farrar, Straus and Giroux.

Pratt, John Clark. 1988. *Vietnam Voices*. New York: Penguin.

Prentice-Dunn, Steven, and Ronald Rogers. 1981. "Deindividuation and Anger-Mediated Interracial Aggression: Unmasking Regressive Racism." *Journal of Personality and Social Psychology* 41: 63–73.

———.1982. "Effects of Public and Private Self-Awareness on Deindividuation and Aggression." *Journal of Personality and Social Psychology* 43: 503–513.

———.1989. "Deindividuation and Self–Regulation of Behavior." *Psychology of Group Influence*, 2d ed., ed. Paul Paulus. Hillsdale, N.J.: Lawrence Erlbaum, pp. 87–106.

Reed, Fred. 1994. *Navy Times*, August 29.

Reinberg, Linda. 1991. *In the Field: The Language of the Vietnam War*. New York: Facts on File.

Ricks, Thomas. 1997. *Making the Corps*. New York: Simon & Schuster.

Roush, Paul. 1999. "A Tangled Webb the Navy Can't Afford." In *Beyond Zero Tolerance: Discrimination in Military Culture,* ed. Mary Katzenstein and Judith Reppy. Oxford: Rowman and Littlefield, pp. 81–100.

Sanday, Peggy Reeves. 1990. *Fraternity Gang Rape: Sex, Brotherhood, and Privilege on Campus*. New York: New York University Press.

Sandler, Stanley. 1995. *The Korean War*. New York: Garland Press.

Scheol, Jonathan. 1967. "Report at Large." *New Yorker* 43: 28–40.

Schneider, Jeffrey. "The Pleasure of the Uniform: Masculinity, Transvestism, and Militarism in Heinrich Mann's *Der Untertan* and Magnus Hirschfeld's *Die Transvestiten*." Unpublished paper.

Schrader, Arthur. 1989. "Correspondence." *New York Folklore* 15, 1–2: 155–158.

Shatan, Chaim.1977. "Bogus Manhood, Bogus Honor: Surrender and Transfiguration in the United States Marine Corps." *Psychoanalytic Review* 64 (Winter): 4.

Shukman, David. 1996. *Tomorrow's War: The Threat of High-Technology Weapons*. New York: Harcourt Brace.

Smith, George. 1971. *P.O.W.: Two Years with the Vietcong*. Berkeley: Ramparts.

Stockdale, Jim, and Sybil Stockdale. 1984. *In Love and War: The Story of a Family's Ordeal and Sacrifice During the Vietnam Years*. New York: Harper and Row.

Strum, Philippa. 2002. *Women in the Barracks: The VMI Case and Equal Rights*. Lawrence: University of Kansas Press.

Sweetman, Jack. 1979. *The U.S. Naval Academy*. Annapolis: Naval Institute Press.

Synnott, Anthony. 1987. "Shame and Glory: A Sociology of Hair." *British Journal of Sociology* 28, 3: 381–413.

Thompson, Leroy. 1991. *Badges and Insignia of the Elite Forces*. London: Arms and Amour.

Timberg, Robert. 1995. *The Nightingale's Song*. New York: Simon and Schuster.

Todd, Frederick. 1940. "The Ins and Outs of Military Hair." *Infantry Journal* 47: 160–167.

———. 1955. *Cadet Gray*. New York: Sterling.

Tomes, C. T. 1924. "The Origin of Certain Military Expressions and Customs." *Army Quarterly* 8: 358–368.

Turner, Victor. 1969. *The Ritual Process*. Chicago: Aldine.

Underwood, Agnes. 1947. "Folklore from G.I. Joe." *New York Folklore Quarterly* 3: 287–288.

U.S. Department of Defense. 1993. *Tailhook 91, Parts 1 & 2*. Washington: U.S. Government Printing Office.

U.S. Department of Defense. 1998. *Representation of Minorities and Women in the Armed Forces, 1976–1997*. Patrick Air Force Base: DEOMI.

U.S. Navy. 1943. *Prisoner Sense*. Washington: United States Navy.

Van Gennep, Arnold. 1960. *The Rites of Passage*. M. B. Vizedom and G. L. Caffee. Chicago: University of Chicago Press.

Vietnam Veterans Against the War. 1972. *The Winter Soldier Investigation: An Inquiry into American War Crimes*. Boston: Beacon.

Vistica, Gregory. 1995. *Fall from Glory: The Men Who Sank the U.S. Navy.* New York: Simon & Schuster.

Wallrich, William. *Air Force Airs: Songs and Ballads of the United States Air Force, World War One through Korea.* New York: Duel, Sloan, and Pearce.

Webb, James. 1979. "Women Can't Fight." *Washingtonian.* November: 144–148, 273–282.

———. 1992. "Witch Hunt in the Navy," *New York Times.* Oct. 6, p. A23.

———. 1994. "Political Correctness Infects the Pentagon." *New York Times.* July 10, p. D19.

———. 1996. "The Navy Adrift." *Washington Post,* April 28, p. C7.

———. 1996. "Opinion." *New York Times.* Oct. 6, p. A23.

———. 1999. "Can He Come Home Again?" *Parade.* April 2, p. 4.

Weigl, Bruce. 1988. *Song of Napalm.* New York: Atlantic Monthly.

Weiner, Tim. 1996. "Harassment Inquiry Spreads to All Army Bases." *New York Times.* November 13, p. A1.

Westmoreland, William. 1980. *A Soldier Reports.* New York: Dell.

Will, George. 1988. "Opinion." *Washington Post.* Feb. 28, p. C7.

Williamson, Margaret Holmes. 1979. "Powhatan Hair." *Man* 14, 3: 392–414.

Zimmerman, Jean. 1995. *Tailspin: Women at War in the Wake of Tailhook.* New York: Doubleday.

Acknowledgments

Without the assistance of several institutions and many generous individuals within them, this book would not have been possible. The Yaddo Foundation awarded me a residency during which I spent several delightful weeks in Saratoga thinking and writing about military culture. The Council for the International Exchange of Scholars awarded me a Fulbright fellowship to conduct research at the Australian War Memorial, Duntroon, and the Australian Defense Force Academy. At the latter, scholars Graeme Cheeseman, C. D. Coulthard-Clark, Peter Dennis, and Gerald Walsh. Jeff Doyle and Susan Lever were especially helpful in directing me to the right individuals and collections. Bruce Moore's work on Australian cadet speech was particularly important. I have benefited as well from the special collections maintained by the Military History Institute at the Army War College, Fort Sam Huston, the WAC Museum, the United States Military Academy, and the United States Naval Academy. I am grateful to my former colleagues at Annapolis, especially Allyson Booth, Marlene Browne, Tom Cutler, Mary Howland, Rick Kuenning, and Mike Parks. Eileen Johnston, a gifted teacher who has dedicated her professional life to educating each cohort of midshipmen at USNA, volunteered to read and comment on a draft of this manuscript. She offered me, on the one hand, the perspective of one whose dedication to the institution she belongs to is unquestioned, and on the other, the shrewd insight of a critical reader.

The Peace Studies Program at Cornell University, with the assistance of the Ford Foundation, sponsored a series of annual meetings of scholars whose research engages military issues and forward-thinking members of the military who must translate theory into practice. These meetings were amazingly helpful, and I particularly profited from the useful suggestions and constructive criticism of Cynthia Enloe, Beth Hillman, Mary Katzenstein, Lawrence Korb, Barbara Lee, Judith Reppy, Georgia Sadler, David Segal, Mady Segal, and Judith Stiehm.

The Johns Hopkins University Women's Studies Forum and the Sociology Department provided me the opportunity to present and discuss work in progress. Colleagues at Hopkins and Vanderbilt whose support and advice I have welcomed include Jay Clayton, Carolyn Dever, Lynn Enterline, Teresa Goddu, Yoshi Igarashi, Leah Marcus, Mark Crispin Miller, Sid Mintz, John Plummer, Mark Schoenfeld, and Virginia Scott. I owe special thanks to Sam Girgus and Cecelia Tichi.

I have never taught at a university with other folklorists, so I have come to rely on the generosity of folklorists in the larger scholarly community. Three of these—Les Cleveland, Lydia Fish, and Bruce Jackson—whose work I admire and whose expertise I have relied on heavily, have kept me going during the life of this project. Thanks as well to my agent, Elaine Markson, my editor, Gayatri Patnaik, my research assistant, Tisha Kamlay, and my copyeditor, Liz Duvall. It was Michelle Maffett whose efficiency helped me find time for research.

Most important, I would like to thank my husband, Jerry Christensen, whose encouragement sustained me throughout the course of this project. This book is for him.

Notes

1. Camp All-American

1. After the sergeant passed on the information to me, I mentioned it to Mark Crispin Miller, who at the time was conducting research on CNN's coverage of the Gulf War. Miller filed a Freedom of Information Act request, to which the Army responded with uncharacteristic speed, denying that it had entered into any "contracts or formal arrangements with CNN."
2. From an e-mail correspondence in response to a request for her anecdote. Jan. 22, 2002.
3. K. Jean Cottam, in an e-mail message dated Aug. 25, 2000.

2. Military Culture

1. See Bruce Jackson's article on the fake vet, "The Perfect Informant," in *Journal of American Folklore* 103: 1990.
2. Soon after admitting men, for example, Goucher College noticed that its mascot, the gopher, had grown claws. A couple of years after men arrived, a male spring rite of passage, a cross-dressing beauty pageant, featured men vying for the title of Ms. Goucher.

3. Transformation

1. This verse from a bawdy old British song has made its way into cadence calls, as have verses from other songs, both ancient and contemporary.
2. An exercise in metaphor-making, this call typically continues for five or six more verses, comparing girls or ladies to holes in the road, telephone poles, bats in a steeple, hammers in a shed, bells in the tower, hoops in the gym, nails in a board, fish in the ocean, and clouds in the sky. Familiar to virtually all midshipmen at the Naval Academy in the 1980s, it is scarcely heard today.
3. The expression "high-and-tight" refers to a close-cropped haircut fashionable in the Marine Corps.
4. Drill instructors wear a hat that resembles the one worn by Smokey the Bear.
5. Collected from an enlisted Marine, Naval Systems, Annapolis, Maryland, 1988.
6. Contributed by a student from Virginia Military Institute, 1988.
7. Performed at the Naval Academy, Annapolis, Maryland, 1987.
8. Collected from an enlisted Marine attending the Naval Academy, 1987.
9. Performed at the Naval Academy, Annapolis, Maryland, 1987.

10. "Blood on the Risers" is a song and not a marching chant, yet soldiers occasionally march to it or sing it at an official Army function, one to which civilians are generally not invited. I have quoted only two verses of the ten-verse song, author unknown, contributed by Colonel John Calabro, United States Military Academy, West Point, N.Y., Feb. 14, 1989.

11. This chant and similar ones were performed at the Naval Academy from the early 1970s, but recent years have seen efforts to prohibit them. Although not as popular as they once were, they continue to be called in basic training programs.

12. Performed at the Naval Academy, Annapolis, Maryland, 1982–1986.

13. Collected from an enlisted Marine, Naval Systems, Annapolis, Maryland, 1988. In other versions, the children referred to as "fuckers" in the penultimate stanza are called "bastards" and "suckers."

14. In a conversation with Arthur Schrader on February 16, 1989, I asked him the meaning of these numbers. He claimed that their only significance to the men who shouted them was to keep the group together; they could, in fact, have been any three numbers, he claimed.

4. A Few Good Men

1. Shatan maintains that training insures not the recruit's manliness, which it in fact undermines, but the drill instructor's manliness. Basic training, according to Shatan, sets in motion "a profound psychological regression that makes boys out of men" (589). By surrendering his ego, the recruit is rewarded with a bogus manhood.

2. While these forms of address are no longer officially sanctioned, they continue to be used in all-male groups.

3. This story was related to me in 2003 by a recently released recruit.

4. See Prentice-Dunn and Rogers, 1981, 1982, and 1989, as well as the famous Milgram experiments.

5. See Bandura et al., 1996.

6. The quote is taken from a piece by Blair that appears on the Independent Women's Forum Web site, www.imf.org/pubs/twq/wi96e.shtml, downloaded July 4, 2003.

7. The quote appears in a transcript of "Think Tank/With Ben Wattenberg," on the PBS Web site, www.pbs.org/thinktank/bio_1382.html, downloaded June 30, 2003.

8. Harrell and Miller found that 66 percent of men in Army combat arms, 80 percent of men in Army noncombatant arms, 89 percent of Navy men, and 73 percent of Marine Corps men believed that women should be allowed to serve in their occupation or career field (1997: 48).

9. This and all further quotations from General Krulak come from an interview with Diane Rehm, broadcast on her National Public Radio program, *The Diane Rehm Show*, July 13, 1999.

5. Sex, GIs, and Videotape

1. See Van Gennep, Mead, Turner, and Bettleheim for discussion of initiation rites. Adams applies Van Gennep's three-stage process to an initiation that takes place at a U.S. military college.
2. The quotation is from a tape-recorded interview with Colonel Fred Fagan, U.S.M.C., Annapolis, Maryland, Feb. 1, 1989.
3. The anecdote was related to me by Peter Dennis, a military historian at the Australian Defense Force Academy, Canberra, Australia, Aug. 13, 1993.
4. Although the Duntroon initiations began in 1911 (Coulthard-Clark), they were little known outside the academy until 1913, when one cadet complained about his treatment in a letter home. His complaint became the subject of an article critical of the military academy that appeared in a Sydney newspaper. To present its own view of the proceedings, the *Journal of the Royal Military College* described the event in its inaugural issue:

   > At this time the arrival of the new fourth Class gave an added zest to college life. Many and deep were the schemes proposed for the initiation of the "freshers" into the mysteries beyond the threshold on which they stood. At last a scheme was evolved, which, though it proved successful enough in its intended purpose, as a piece of strategy pure and simple, paled into insignificance beside the corresponding arrangement of the previous year. In both cases, however, the secrecy observed and the clever duping of the adversary would have gladdened the heart of Stonewall Jackson himself. The newcomers, then, were duly initiated. At times they put up a very creditable resistance, but their efforts, though gallant, were spasmodic, and the superior discipline of those performing the ceremony was too much for them. Much vocal talent was discovered amongst the new cadets, and several were found to be very artistic dancers.

5. Margaret Easterbrook, *The Age*, May 4, 1991, p. 17; Rod Campbell, "Three ADFA Cadets Admit to Woofering," *Canberra Times*, Dec. 16, 1992, p 1.

6. Clothes Make the Soldier

1. According to Joe McDonald (of Country Joe and the Fish, 1990), Marines on shipboard used to wear big leather straps to protect their necks when dueling.
2. For more on the history of military uniforms, see Joseph, 1986.
3. For more discussion of the legends that follow, see Boatner, 1954.
4. Virgil Forbes, a retired master chief petty officer, was extremely helpful in providing information on changes to Navy uniforms during his extensive career, from the late 1960s through the 1970s and into the 1980s, in an interview with the author, Aug. 18, 1998.

5. From a memo sent to all midshipmen and faculty at the United States Naval Academy, Jan. 30, 1997.
6. The nineteenth-century similarity between male and female sporting fashion from the waist up contrasts nicely with the current fashion for young men and women to dress uniformly in jeans from the waist down but differentiate their upper bodies. For a more complete discussion of divergence of male and female fashion, see Joseph, 1986, p. 53.
7. For an impressive study of this, see Elizabeth Hilman's "Dressed to Kill?: The Paradox of Women in Military Uniforms," in *Beyond Zero Tolerance*, ed. Mary Fainsod Katzenstein and Judith Reppy (Lanham, Md.: Rowman and Littlefield, 1999).
8. Sometimes the uniform *does* make a man of even a woman soldier. Such was the case with Dr. James Barry, a successful soldier in the British army who rose to the rank equivalent to major general. When Dr. Barry died, fellow officers discovered that their companion was really a woman (Ewing, 1975: 35).
9. In a 1998 episode of the popular television series *JAG*, a female Marine Corps officer changes into the dress white uniform of a female naval officer. In reality, such a scene would be extremely unlikely. Although the Marine Corps is officially part of the Navy, no officer would ever swap her service uniform for a drier version, complete with insignia, worn by an officer in a sister service. The fact that the officer is a woman renders the change of uniform presumably more acceptable to the viewing public.
10. The women complain that whereas men can simply purchase fresh new parts to attach to the old hat frame when a part of the fabric becomes soiled or worn, they must purchase a completely new and costly hat.
11. See Crackel (1987: 116–121) for a more complete account of the Butler case.
12. Army Regulation 670-1, "Wear and Appearance of Army Uniforms and Insignia," Department of the Army, Sept. 1992.
13. Women can now have long hair but must wear it up while in uniform.
14. The term "sideburn" has a military origin. Ambrose Burnside, a Civil War general who led his Union troops to a dreadful defeat at Fredericksburg, had earlier been named by the West Point Board of Examiners as "the finest looking and most soldier-like [cadet] of the corps" (Keogh, 1981: 38.). See Army Regulation 670-1, "Wear and Appearance of Army Uniforms and Insignia," Department of the Army, Sept. 1992, for sideburn regulations.
15. According to Leach and Hershman, hair is to semen as the head is to the penis. Williamson's research identifies the Powhatan "werowances," chiefs who assume a state between shamans (the wild) and common people (the ordered). Typically, a chief would wear half his hair long in the fashion of women and half his hair shaved in the fashion of men. Williamson charts the relationships among members of Powhatan society on a scale from male to female, with the shaman on the extreme male side, the werowance or chief next in order of male, followed by common man and finally common

woman at the extreme female end of the scale; one end of the scale was associated with death and the other end with life (Williamson, 1979: 393).

16. See Leach for a more complete discussion of these cultural meanings of hair.

17. In the popular Hollywood film *G. I. Jane,* the first female elected to train for admission to the elite Navy Seals attempts to insure her integration by voluntarily shaving her hair. But only after a misogynistic beating by a superior does she become the androgynous figure required of her. With blood steaming from her face, she spits back at her attacker, "Suck my dick!"

18. In her book *Women in the Military,* Jeanna Holm documents extensive recruitment efforts aimed at attracting only good-looking women, including the use of photographic poses of applicants to insure a group of pretty women, or as the Marine Corps puts it, "the most attractive and useful women in the four line services" (Holm, 1992: 181).

7. Military Speech

1. Examples of military slang that have established their place in mainstream speech include "goldbrick," for shirker, and "snafu," from "situation normal, all fucked up."

2. Other acronyms and abbreviations include
   SAPFU: surpassing all previous fuck-ups
   FUBAR: fucked up beyond recognition
   NAAFI (Australian): not at all fucking interested; no aim, ambition, or fucking initiative
   BOHICA: bend over, here it comes again
   FIGMO: fuck it, I got my orders
   FTN: fuck the Navy (an FTN space is a small space in a ship where a sailor can hide from officers)
   PFC: proud fucking civilian (WWII)

3. Marines acquired the name "Leathernecks" because of the leather collar on their uniform, added to protect the soldier from sword swipes. More recently they have been called "grunts" and "mudpuppies."

4. The song "Boonie Rats" was composed in 1970 by John M. Del Vecchio. The folklorist Lydia Fish has dedicated her career to reclaiming and celebrating the soldier song tradition of the Vietnam War. Her notes, "In Country: Songs of Americans in the Vietnam War," which include the background on "Boonie Rats" as well as other soldier songs, are invaluable to any student of the period, as are recordings of the commemorative concerts she has organized.

5. The expression "Gomers" is a reference to the simpleminded hero of a popular television comedy, *Gomer Pyle, USMC.*

6. The term "doughnut dolly" first appeared during World War I to describe Red Cross volunteers who worked just behind the frontline, serving coffee

and doughnuts to the troops. "Jelly doughnuts" were overweight "doughnut dollies."

7. In *A Dictionary of Slang,* published in 1984 (New York: Prentice-Hall), Partridge claims that the term "gook" derived from the word *gugus,* from the Filipino insurrection in 1899.

8. Quoted in Frances FitzGerald, *Fire in the Lake,* from the Michigan Winter Soldier Investigation, 1971.

9. Many Vietnam vets brought back copies of this example, "What the Captain means is." John Clark Pratt quotes the popular satire in *Vietnam Voices.*

10. By contrast, a ditty that circulated among World War II troops appears quite tame on the subject of language. The following example of folk poetry circulated widely during World War II. A copy was given to me in 1989 by Arthur Schrader.

> Ode to the Four-Letter Words
> Banish the use of the four-letter words
> Whose meanings are never obscure;
> The Angles and Saxons, those bawdy old birds,
> Were vulgar, obscene, and impure.
> But cherish the use of the weaseling phrase
> That never quite says what you mean;
> You'd better be known for your hypocrite ways
> Than as vulgar, impure, or obscene.
>
> When Nature is calling, plain speaking is out,
> When ladies (God bless 'em) are smiling about,
> You may wee-wee, make water, or empty the glass;
> You can powder your nose——even "Johnny" may pass;
> Shake the dew off the lily, see the man about a dog,
> Or, when everyone's soused, it's condensing the fog,
> But be pleased to remember, if you would know bliss,
> That only in Shakespeare do characters piss.
>
> A woman has bosoms, a bust, or a breast,
> Those lily-white swellings that bulge 'neath her vest;
> They are towers of ivory, sheaves of new wheat;
> In moments of passion, ripe apples to eat.
> By the four-letter words all alone.
> Let your morals be loose as an alderman's vest
> If your language is always obscure.
> Today, not the act but the word is the test
> Of the vulgar, obscene, and impure.

11. I am indebted to Moore's excellent collection of cadet speech for many of the examples that follow. In 1993, during fieldwork in Australia's new tri-

service military academy, built near the site of Duntroon and incorporating officers-in-training from the Army, Navy, and Air Force, I found much of the speech Moore documented still in use. In addition, students provided me with copies of underground publications (*Pussy Ray, In the Book,* and *Bastian Bugle*) which included other terms.

Moore's lexicon is distinguished by his thorough effort to track down definitions and usages, but it is not the only attempt to collect military slang. Glossaries have floated among troops through all branches in both peacetime and wartime. The *Royal Military College Journal* alone records five glossaries of Duntroon slang. The primary collectors of such word lists are members of the military themselves, who collect words and their expressions not to instruct but to delight.

12. In his collection of midshipmen slang, *Good Gouge: An Investigation into the Origins of Naval Academy Slang* (Annapolis: U.S. Naval Academy, 1982), Michael Parker identifies the appearance of this term in 1897 and suggests that it derives from the nautical expression "to drag an anchor." If the expression were exclusive to students at naval academies, such an interpretation would be compelling, but since it has enjoyed a long history at both Australia's Royal Military Academy and at West Point, two army academies, the nautical derivation seems less persuasive.

13. See Neal Hertz's essay on Medusa as the "phallic woman" in *The End of the Line: Essays in Psychoanalysis and the Sublime* (New York: Columbia University Press, 1985).

14. The Virginia Military Institute and the Citadel are public military academies in which some, but not all, students prepare for military careers. Neither is under the direct control of any branch of the U.S. military, as are the academies of the Army, Navy, Air Force, and Coast Guard. These two institutions admitted women only in 1996, when the courts forced them to do so.

15. Since the names of actual cadets appear in these in-house publications, I have substituted pseudonyms.

8. Culture and Controversy

1. For further discussion of the rivalry between Larson and Boorda, see Kotz, 1996.

2. This incident is discussed more fully in Gregory Vistica's *Fall from Glory: The Men Who Sank the U.S. Navy.*

3. From an article prepared by the Center for Military Readiness in January 2002 for its Web site, www.crmlink.org/docowits.asp?docID=126.

4. Letter from Lawrence Garrett to Chief of Naval Operations Frank Kelso and Commandant of the Marine Corps Carl Mundy, June 2, 1992.

5. *Newsweek,* Aug. 10, 1992, p. 35.

6. Letter from Lawrence Garrett to Frank Kelso and Carl Mundy, June 2, 1992.

7. Eric Schmitt, "Now at Navy's Bridge, Engaging Sexism," *New York Times*, July 4, 1999, p. 8.
8. Bill McAllister and John Mintz, "Boorda May Have Worn Right Medals," *Washington Post*, May 18, 1996, p. A10.
9. McIntyre, Jamie. "Hackworth Says Error Doesn't Compare to Boorda Suicide Case," CNN, May 16, 1977. (www.cnn.com/us/9705/16/hackworth/)
10. A significant media partner in this reactionary movement has been the *Washington Times*. Paul Craig, a columnist for the *Washington Times*, argues similarly that "a warrior culture does not mean, as President Clinton's feminized Pentagon thinks, bloodlust and a desire to kill. It means a comradeship and esprit de corps that is the heart of an elite fighting unit" ("Cultural Demolition in the Military," Nov. 20, 1998). For Craig the two irreconcilables in his own statement are "feminized Pentagon" and "esprit de corps." Capable female officers who have made their way up through a military that has along the way questioned their right to be members have, of course, assumed positions in the Pentagon. Their feminizing presence for Craig, as for Webb, threatens segregated male esprit de corps.

    Consider an analogous situation involving race in the civilian workplace. Certainly it could be argued that an all-white construction crew might have a strong esprit de corps that might be challenged by the addition of a black or Hispanic coworker. But is the fear of that social adjustment reason to resist the integration of the crew? Of course not.
11. Entered on Hackworth's personal Web site on June 11, 1996.
12. Just a generation ago, two thirds of the members of Congress had prior military service; today it is only one third, and that figure will probably become even lower as older members retire.
13. From an editorial by George Will in the *Washington Post*, Feb. 28, 1998, p. C7.
14. From a March 21, 1996, news briefing.
15. When questioned about his participation in lewd behavior at a former Tailhook convention by a reporter from the *Charleston Gazette*, Lehman responded, "It's a perfect example of the depths that coverage of the Navy has fallen to. Every Navy leader of recent times and now every senior admiral has been subjected to this kind of gutter reporting" ("Lehman Dishes Out Blame for Navy's Problems," May 27, 1996, p. 3C).
16. Atkinson, Gerald. 1998. "PC Problems Plaguing the Navy," *Washington Times*, September 13, B6.

9. Prisoners of War

1. Although the deprivation British, American, and Australian soldiers faced was severe indeed, Germans reserved their harshest abuse for their Russian prisoners. One Australian prisoner recalled that "in less than three months

we buried more than 3,500 Russians." They died from starvation, cold, and untreated battle wounds (Clarke, Burgess, and Braddon, 1988: 39).

2. A total of seventy-seven American army nurses were interned in the Philippines; sixteen Navy nurses were imprisoned there.

3. A makeshift place of worship was erected by Australian prisoners in the Philippines. The Changi chapel was taken down at the end of the war by the Australian delegation sent to search for graves of fallen Australians, and its parts were transported to Australia. In 1988, the chapel was reassembled and dedicated on behalf of Australian prisoners in four wars. It stands today at the site of the Royal Military College, Duntroon, in the nation's capital.

4. From "A Santo Tomas Real Life Story," by Madeline Ullom, manuscript collection, Army Medical Museum, Fort Sam Houston, San Antonio, Texas.

5. "Prison Sense," p. 13.

6. From an interview with Allen Washington, conducted by Anthony Mack as part of an oral history project on prisoners of war, Houston, Texas, 1990 (Havard, 1991: 55).

7. Howes (1993: 96) documents the translation of Ho Chi Minh to "Horseshit Men," whereas Stockdale (1984: 245) recalls it simply as "President Horse-Shit Minh."

8. Clarke mentions several instances of this kind of desperate move on the part of imprisoned officers to preserve what was left of their military structure.

9. In its effort to celebrate the indisputable fortitude of the officer aviators who survived the horrendous conditions for so long in Hanoi, the film completely ignores the enlisted Americans imprisoned in jungle camps throughout North Vietnam and the civilian prisoners in Hanoi who opted for a less strict adherence to the chain of command. It also sidesteps the complicated issue of dissent voiced by Americans even from the prison camps of Vietnam.

10. See Biderman for a more complete discussion of the extent of prisoners' collaboration.

11. Although the United States had developed biological weapons for use in the Korean War, it is not clear whether epidemics in the North developed because of the deployment of such weapons or because the health system had collapsed during the war. In the face of the hard-driving propaganda campaign waged by the Communists, America demanded that charges of biological warfare be investigated by the International Red Cross.

12. Visions are a common part of incarceration. I have written elsewhere about the ways in which such visions give the prisoner a sense of eclipsing the power of the prison. See *Vision Narratives of Women in Prison* (Knoxville: University of Tennessee Press, 1992).

13. Not only did the Defense Department choreograph their return and control

their exposure to the press, but long before release, prisoners themselves, according to Craig Howes, had organized "toastmaster" clubs in prison to practice for the event. In addition, they discussed plans for book, speech, and endorsement requests and appointed camp historians, those who would serve as the group's "memory banks" (Howes, 1993: 9). They had had several years to contemplate the ways in which the enemy had exploited them through the media; it was their turn to exploit the media to tell their side of the story.

10. Jane Fonda, the Woman the Military Loves to Hate

1. The story of this goodnight ritual was related to me in 2001 by a faculty member at the Naval Academy who wished to remain anonymous.
2. Quote from www.rjgeib.com/thoughts/fonda/response3.html, July, 2001.
3. Quote from www.farfromglory.com/janefonda.htm, July 2001; second quote from www.gis.net/ffifm/not-fonda-jane.html, June 2001; *Steelyard Blues* anecdote from www.war-stories.com/fonda-3.htm.
4. First quote from Blake#1 on www.freerepublic.com, Sept. 20, 2000; second quote from www.freerepublic.com, Sept. 20, 2000.
5. From Comus on www.freerepublic.com, Sept. 20, 2000.
6. Quoted in "Oprah's Cut with Jane Fonda," *O, the Oprah Magazine,* July/August 2000.
7. Forwarded by Joshua Meisel, Nov. 10, 1999, 15:32 and downloaded from www.csf.colorado.edu/mail/socgrad/may99/msg00252.html on Feb. 29, 2001.
8. Ibid.
9. See *Houston Chronicle,* Nov. 6, 1999, p. A38, and *Omaha World-Herald,* Nov. 9, 1999, editorial, p. 17.
10. From wysiwyg://36http://wwww.rt66.com/ffikorteng/SmallArms/hanoi jan.htm, Feb. 29, 2001.
11. Fuck the Army was later named Free the Army, and a documentary film with that title was made.
12. "Blushing militia girls" is from Fonda's speech broadcast on Radio Hanoi, 1:00 GMT, Aug. 22, 1972.

11. Fighting the Digital War

1. Data provided by Retired Admiral Fred Lewis, director of the National Training Systems Association, in a phone interview, July 18, 2003. The operating costs quoted here do not include the cost of life cycle. If they did, according to Lewis, the savings would be even more dramatic. For example, a single F-16 costs approximately $30 million to manufacture.

2. Ibid.

3. Phone interview, July 7, 2003.

4. Phone interview with Colonel Howard Yellen, Special Forces, May 1, 2000.

5. Interview with Lieutenant Commander Pete Waters, Patuxent Naval Air Station, Patuxent, Md., Apr. 14, 2000.

6. Interview, Patuxent River Naval Air Station, Apr. 13, 2000.

7. Waters interview.

8. General William Hartzog, Commanding General, U.S. Army Training and Doctrine, *Army Times*, Mar. 4, 1996, p. 31.

9. Interview with David Silverberg, "Q&A," *Military Training and Technology*, 3, 6 (1999): 37.

10. Interview, May 15, 2000.

11. Phone interview, May 15, 2000.

12. The frequency-spreading described by Moore will replace the limited frequency-hopping which currently divides a message over only a few frequencies. Frequency-hopping offers less security and also calls attention to itself. Even though an enemy might not be able to decipher a message, it can often tell that one is being sent. Such detection is much harder with frequency-spreading.

   The major difference between communication between infantry regulars and between Special Forces is that the former communicates across a battlefield on an FM network. The latter must be able to communicate with a headquarters that is not yards away but 500 to 1500 miles away.

13. Interview, Fort Bragg, N.C., June 20, 2000.

14. This kind of weapon makes sense in a police action or if the war is decided in a single confrontation rather than a series of grisly encounters like those that defined the twentieth century's wars.

15. The quote is from the U.S. Army Soldier and Biological Chemical Command public relations Web site, www.sbccom.army.mil, Nov., 21, 2000.

16. Phone interview with Gerald Darsch, project director, DOD Combat Feeding Program, U.S. Army Soldier and Biological Chemical Command, Natick, Mass., July 23, 2003.

17. Phone interview with Gerald Darsch, May 4, 2000.

18. Ibid.

19. Phone interview with Gerald Darsch, July 23, 2003.

20. Clearly, the Department of Defense has invested its technology dollar in perfecting individual food that can be taken into the harshest of conditions rather than in modernizing the field kitchens, which look very much like they did thirty years ago. In fact, most field kitchens still employ a standard range designed in 1959 to feed between two hundred and three hundred people. Kitchens were designed to last seven years; now many in use have met their twenty-year commitment and then some. Understandably, the DOD has mandated a single fuel for kitchen ranges, planes, trucks, and Humvees; all must be converted to diesel by 2010. Natick has a new, more

portable kitchen ready to be field-tested, with a heater employing more efficient oil rather than water and a fridge that employs ammonia so that frozen meat can be thawed safely.

21. "Army After Next Clothing and Individual Equipment Concepts," issued by U.S. Army Soldier and Biological Chemical Command, July 18, 1999.

22. Phone interview, July 7, 2003.

23. After his assignment at Natick, Sergeant Patterson went on to become part of the Army's "Army of One" recruitment campaign.

24. Interview with Dutch DeGay, July 7, 2003.

25. As more and more recruits come to the military with poor high school training and with English as their second language, training must also incorporate basic reading, writing, and math skills.

26. Interview, May 15, 2000.

27. "Monitoring Emerging Military Technologies," 48, 1 (Jan.–Feb. 1995).

28. Interview, June 21, 2000.

29. According to Scott Davis of the Navy's manned flight simulator, communication from the battlefield in World War I took place at an estimated 10 words per minute, in World War II at 40, in Vietnam at 100, and in the first Gulf War 100,000. By 2010, military planners estimate that 1 trillion words per minute will flow in the heat of battle.

30. Charles Sinex, in a discussion held at the School of Arts and Sciences, Johns Hopkins University, Baltimore, Md., Jan. 15, 2000.

31. U.S. Army Pamphlet 350-70-xx, June 3, 1996.

32. General Ronald Fogleman.

33. Despite the disappointing show at military recruitment offices across the country, the armed forces did realize an increase in reenlistments, in part because of the handsome reenlistment bonuses the Pentagon authorized.

34. Schmidt, Susan, and Vernon Loeb, 2003. "'She Was Fighting to the Death': Details Emerging of West Virginia Soldier's Capture and Rescue" *Washington Post,* April 13, p. A01.

35. From a BBC broadcast on May 15, 2003 at 8:50 GMT by John Kampfner, "Saving Private Lynch story 'flawed.'" See http://news.bbc.co.uk/2/hi/programmes/correspondent/3028585.stm.

36. From a transcript of NBC's *Dateline,* April 16, 2003.

Index